W9-BNO-090

Big Praise for
Wake Up, I'm Fat!

"A liberated, humorous, triumphant story . . . the writing is as fresh and as friendly as the Emmy winner's speech . . . You'll want the author to come over to your house to gab . . . Anyone could benefit from her lessons in living large."

—*Entertainment Weekly* ("A-" review)

"*Wake Up, I'm Fat!* is the heartfelt and ballsy story of how [Manheim] learned to be comfortable in her own skin . . . Inspiring without being soap Oprah-ish, Manheim is a natural writer; she has fine powers of description (her chapter on Emmy night is at once dishy and spellbinding) . . . her dignity and self-reliance are downright refreshing." —*Salon*

"A funny, wickedly candid book." —*Good Housekeeping*

"Manheim's wit runs from impish to slashing; this may be the funniest book about fat acceptance ever written."

—*Dallas Morning News*

"A jubilant autobiography." —*In Style*

"An open and unabashed look at being fat that's crammed with funny, poignant and painful insights." —*Parade*

"[A] hilariously fascinating and truly inspiring personal story."

—*Glamour*

"A stand-up story of being fat in a thin-is-in culture . . . Amusing, gossipy, frank [and] filled with stories of the psychic nicks and scrapes that fat people face every day." —*Kirkus Reviews*

"Both moving and entertaining, *Wake Up, I'm Fat!* can evoke both tears and laughter simultaneously . . . a must-read for anyone on the journey of self-acceptance." —*Big Beautiful Women*

"Manheim's passion and honesty are evident throughout . . . [her] story holds appeal for everyone who has ever let insecurity hold them back from realizing their dreams." —*Publishers Weekly*

"Manheim is opinionated and raucous, charismatic and convincing . . . she gets her point across in anecdotes that are alternately hilarious and harrowing." —*Library Journal*

Wake Up, I'm Fat!

Camryn Manheim

Broadway Books ■ New York

BROADWAY

A hardcover edition of this book was published in 1999 by Broadway Books.

WAKE UP, I'M FAT! Copyright © 1999 by Camryn Manheim, Inc. All rights reserved. Printed in the United States of America. No part of this book may be reproduced or transmitted in any form or by any means, electronic or mechanical, including photocopying, recording, or by any information storage and retrieval system, without written permission from the publisher. For information, address Broadway Books, a division of Random House, Inc., 1540 Broadway, New York, NY 10036.

Broadway Books titles may be purchased for business or promotional use or for special sales. For information, please write to: Special Markets Department, Random House, Inc., 1540 Broadway, New York, NY 10036.

BROADWAY BOOKS and its logo, a letter B bisected on the diagonal, are trademarks of Broadway Books, a division of Random House, Inc.

Visit our website at www.broadwaybooks.com

First trade paperback edition published 2000.

The Library of Congress has cataloged the hardcover edition as:
Manheim, Camryn.
Wake up, I'm fat! / by Camryn Manheim.
p.   cm.
1. Manheim, Camryn.   2. Actors—United States—Biography.
PN2287.M284A3   1999
792′.028′092—dc21
[b]   99—10954
CIP

Book design by Brian Mulligan

Photos on pages 176 and 241 © 1999 by Gerhard Yurkovic.

ISBN 0-7679-0363-3

00   01   02   03   04   10   9   8   7   6   5   4   3   2   1

For Sylvia, Jerry, Lisa, and Karl

Who each in their own way taught me not to go quietly

Special Acknowledgment

One of the best things about writing this book was the time I spent with Kevin Hench. My writing mentor, my confidant, my friend. He listened to my stories with patience and compassion. As I unraveled my life, layer upon layer, he witnessed the accumulated residue of joy and pain. He loved when I loved, and felt anger when I hurt. He stood watch over me as I traveled through these rough waters. For that I am eternally grateful. It was through him that I came to understand my own voice.

Acknowledgments

(In order of appearance)

With thanks to Lynn Perlman, Ingrid Aall, Laura Vural, Wilma Marcus Chandler, Tony Kushner, Marcia Gay Harden, Alan Parker, Adele Agin, Wendy Pankin, Nancy Quinn, Cindy Tolan, Linda Hill, Lisa Iacucci, Mark Brokaw, Randy Rollison, Barbara Busackino, Derick Stenborg, Jason Boyd, John Augustine, Chris Durang, Lucy Iacucci, David Esbjornson and the Classic Stage Company, Erin Sanders, Carol Fishman, Carole Rothman, John Mackessy, Rosemarie Tichler, Morgan Jenness, George C. Wolfe, The Public Theater, Michael Ritchie, Alan Moyer, Kenny Posner, the Great Rabbi Agin, Kevin Geer, Maryellen Mulcahy, Peg Donegan, Randy Stone, Gregory Hines, Kevin Pusateri, Annie Fort, Kim Sandifer, Michele Weston, Deborah Feingold, Dov, Linda Masson, Julie Nathanson, Ann Mathews, the 1987 graduate acting class of NYU, David Kelley and all the folks at *The Practice*, and Diane Holm for putting up with me as I typed into the wee hours.

My gratitude to David Vigliano and Alex Smithline for finding me, and to my editor Lauren Marino, Marc Glick, Michael Mayer, and Marlene Hoffman for all their invaluable red marks on my manuscript. And to Bob Kirsh who has been there every step of the way.

A very special thank you to Rosie O'Donnell for showing us how to do it right, with strength, conviction, and without apology.

I am indebted to all my friends, family, and life teachers who have offered their encouragement, patience, and support over the years.

I have an army of unnamed helpers, whose names are not included because they all should go first.

Contents

Foreword

by Rosie O'Donnell

Tucking.

There. I said it. Does anyone know what I'm talking about? I tucked once. I'll never forget it. It was 1982, "An Evening at the Improv" hosted by Cicely Tyson, and there, on national television, you could see it. The unmistakable line of the top of my pants as my shirt discreetly disappeared below. I had tucked. Not only had I tucked, I garnished the entire experience with a belt. Shocking, but true.

For most people, tucking is a nonevent. But for those of us who tend to the round, it isn't so simple. To tuck or not to tuck? That is the question. It comes loaded with issues of self-perception and self-acceptance.

Camryn Manheim is a tucker—a proud and consistent tucker. To me, her tucking is emblematic of her journey to be defined and, most important, to define herself on her own terms. In her hands, tucking is a celebration.

Wake Up, I'm Fat! is the work of a loud and independent spirit that ultimately refused to be constrained by shame. The push-pull of weight as an armor or albatross, the internal deals and monologues, the yearning to be on the inside while eternally feeling on the outside are explored with a courageous honesty. We see her struggle to shed the layers of self-loathing and replace them with a sense of her own value. We see her slowly accept herself. The story here is of a heart, mind, and soul that learned they deserved to be held in equal measure to their external package — no matter who or what said otherwise. The achievement of that exquisite balance is exhilarating and inspiring. In short, a great read.

I watched Camryn win her first Emmy Award and, along with millions of women, cheered as she dedicated it to "all the fat girls" out there. When she asked me to write the foreword to this book, there was no way I could refuse. Camryn Manheim is a compassionate maverick. She built the bandwagon and she is pulling it. I, for one, am jumping on.

Author's Note

For most of my life I was waiting for my life to begin. When I was ten, all I wanted was to be thirteen . . . so I could finally be a teenager. When I was thirteen, I was just waiting to be sixteen . . . so I could drive. Then I was waiting to be eighteen . . . so I could vote. Then I had to wait three more years to be twenty-one . . . so I could drink. When I was twenty-one, I was waiting for college to be over, so my life could finally start. And then there was graduate school, and life certainly couldn't start there. And then I was twenty-eight, thinking now my life can finally start. But then another year passed and I was twenty-nine, waiting for a great apartment, then I was thirty and waiting for a great job, and then I was thirty-one and waiting for a great boyfriend so my life could finally start.

Waiting, waiting, waiting, waiting. All my life I was waiting for my life to begin, as if my life were somehow way up ahead of me, and one day I would just arrive there. I've wanted to write a book for ten years now, but I was waiting. Waiting to be thin, so I could write about what it was like to be fat and how I emerged the righteous champion: the conqueror of my fat!

But a few years ago I finally realized something. My life was not way up ahead of me. I was standing smack dab in the middle of it. In fact, I was standing on the corner of "Life" and "You better get going, Camryn," and the way I saw it, I had two choices: I could either cross that street or just keep waiting for a few more years of green lights to go by.

I no longer wanted to be a bystander, a spectator watching my life unfold. I wanted to be the writer, director, and star of my story. And so, in August 1993, I began work on my one-woman show, *Wake Up, I'm Fat!* Despite that chronic, nagging feeling that I had nothing particularly special to offer, I realized that there was one area in which I *was* an expert. I knew every nook and cranny of what it was like to grow up fat in America. And guess what, it's no fucking picnic. To make matters worse, I was cursed with a singular passion for acting. Not astronomy. Not veterinary medicine. Not haberdashery. No, I was in love with acting, a profession that is all too often based on how you look. It didn't matter what an agent or a casting director actually said when they rejected me, all I heard was "You're too fat."

This book, however, is not the whiny lamentation of a girl who was never asked to dance (well, maybe occasionally whiny). It is a celebration of ass-kicking. It is my enthusiastic rejection of the beauty myth and a call to arms in the fight for self-acceptance. This is my journey, from victim to victor.

The following anecdotes are true. I think. Over the years, after-dinner stories tend to bend and twist and become more colorful and dazzling than they originally may have been. A flourish here, a double entendre there, a wee embellishment for emphasis. Sometimes the truth is drab, redundant, and ludicrous and needs a little decoration or refinement. This has been my greatest challenge: to be precise without boring you to tears, to be honest without making enemies, and to be candid without getting sued. Wish me luck.

Levi's, Lesbians, Sex, Drugs, and Rock and Roll

(not necessarily in that order)

Ah, coming of age, that perilous time that shapes the rest of our lives. We all have to go through it, hoping we don't get too damaged along the way. Growing up is so damned hard. I can't believe so many of us make it. We should all be given medals.

I spent most of my childhood in Peoria, Illinois. Peoria is a little left of Chicago, which is fitting, since everything about my family is a little left of something. You may have heard the saying "It'll play in Peoria." Translation: It won't offend anyone. Ah, yes, safe, safe Peoria. Picket fences, general stores, the whole nine. Peoria was also the home of Caterpillar tractors. And it was those ugly yellow monstrosities that put Peoria on the map.

So it was no wonder that, year after year, when I was a kid in the late 1960s, my family went on constant road trips in search of culture.

Nothing could stop us from traveling to see relatives, historic sites, or points of so-called interest. Sometimes it just seemed like we were on a quest to see every museum in the United States, desperately trying to connect the dots on the map in hopes of creating the picture of a well-rounded, well-adjusted, well-educated family. It was as if we'd win some big prize if we hit all the museums *and* national monuments before the decade ran out. By the time I was ten, I had an aversion to all art galleries, military forts, and especially to Niagara Falls and the Grand Canyon. Maybe that's why I love the theater so much. It's the only cultural experience that wasn't shoved down my throat. Even now, though it's hard to admit, because I want you all to think I'm a cosmopolitan New York gal, my teeth clench at the suggestion of visiting a museum.

When I was nine, my folks' old Plymouth Fury III broke down. I was so happy because we were finally going to spend a summer at home. But my joy was short-lived. My older brother, Karl, who was away at grad school, had left his dilapidated, taxi-yellow Studebaker on the front lawn of my parents' house. My mom was constantly complaining about what an eyesore it was (I think my brother bought the paint for the Studebaker from the Cat plant), so imagine my surprise when I saw my mom and dad loading it up for another endless field trip. My annual begging and pleading fell on deaf ears, and we were on the road again.

I remember the fabric on the ceiling of that old jalopy drooping down over my father's head, obscuring his view of the road. So my older sister, Lisa, and I were on drooping patrol. Our arms were killing us from holding up that torn and frayed upholstery all the way from Peoria to Southern California. Why we didn't just rip out the material is beyond me. Was it Mr. Studebaker's bright idea to put a rug on the *ceiling* of a car?

The part of traveling I actually did enjoy, though, was singing songs in the backseat with Lisa. But older siblings have a way of including you and excluding you at the same time, and Lisa was a master of this (she could give you a crumb and convince you that you had a whole piece of cake), so even this bit of fun had a downside. While she got to sing each new verse, I was forced to hold the last note of the chorus to provide what she called a "harmonious counterpoint." My protests were met with music theory and high-handed explanations about how my nine-year-old voice could sustain the higher notes more organically than her age-worn fourteen-year-old voice. So while she was singing:

It was sad, so sad
It was sad, so sad
It was sad when the old ship went down
To the bottom of the . . .
Husbands and wives
Little children lost their lives
It was sad when the old ship went down.

I was singing:

. . . SEA . . . EEEEEEEEEEEEEEEEEEEEEEEE

But I was happy to sing my little part, because at least we were to-gether in the backseat of the car and she couldn't tell me to get out of her room.

Unfortunately, my brief moments of happiness were often in-terrupted by regular I-don't-feel-so-good pit stops. So while the rest of the family was seeing the country, I was seeing the gas sta-tion toilets of America. My dad told me that he used to get carsick a lot, and the only way he could take long trips was if he were dri-ving. So in the interest of arriving at our destinations on time, my father put me in his lap and let me steer.

Never had nausea been so handsomely rewarded. I was perched on my daddy's lap with the steering wheel in hand. There was no way you could have convinced me that I wasn't dri-ving that car. Then, by some amazing coincidence, my otherwise stomach-like-a-rock sister started complaining about an upset stomach. But she was too late to usurp my throne. Not only did I get to drive, but she had to sing all the songs by herself. She'd beg, "C'mon, do your part." And I'd say emphatically, "You can't sing when you're driving!"

When I got bored of driving, the only other respite I could find from the constant nausea was hanging my head out the window and daydreaming.

This was in the late '60s, early '70s, and I remember seeing lots of VW vans with peace signs and Day-Glo flowers painted all over them. Usually some long-bearded man was driving the bus, and a beautiful woman in tapestry skirts would have her bare feet up on the dashboard. I could hear wafts of music billowing out of their love bus. Later I would recognize some of the songs; Joni Mitchell, Joan Baez, Pete Seeger, all blowing in the wind.

I remember feeling a deep sense of jealousy at the freedom they had, the wings they spread, the peaceful easy feeling they embodied. At ten years old I felt embarrassed to be singing songs with my family and sitting on my father's lap. I wanted to be the girl in the front seat, weaving a wreath of garlands to put in my hair.

I was shaped by the '60s scene, the peace movement, flower power, and free love. I had always felt I was born ten years too late. I would have been a good hippie. I always envied that generation. They had been galvanized by Martin Luther King Jr., Vietnam, Kent State, and the Grateful Dead. At age ten, I couldn't have articulated why I envied these people, but I was already feeling alienated from my own generation. While those groovy folks were giving us Angela Davis, Allen Ginsberg, and Bob Dylan, my generation would one day embrace the likes of Anita Bryant, Danielle Steel, and David Cassidy. To me, my generation has always seemed adrift in a sea of banal mediocrity and shallow disco music.

The '60s were the battleground for affirmative action, women's liberation, and peace over war. The '70s paved the way for eight years of Ronald Reagan. Of course I know all that now; however, as a young girl with my head out the window, all I really wanted was a tapestry skirt, flowers in my hair, and a long-bearded boyfriend singing "The Times They Are a-Changin'."

And I would dream about adding some years to my age, so I could ride with the hippies from Haight-Ashbury to Woodstock. Though I never made it to Yasgur's farm, Joe Cocker, Richie Havens, and Jimi Hendrix came to me via my sister's record collection. I would defy the KEEP OUT sign on her door, skulk into her room, and "borrow" her albums.

When I was twelve I taught myself to play the guitar. I learned every Neil Young song ever written, which really isn't that hard. Just different variations on the same theme: A-C-D-E, D-C-A-E,

A-E-D-C, and maybe he'd toss an F in there just to throw you off. That's everything from "Cowgirl in the Sand" to "Sugar Mountain." I wanted to have some kind of offering for the long-bearded man who would later pick me up hitchhiking.

*   *   *

While I had never been too excited about our never-ending field trips, I was thrilled when I heard the news we were moving. Not just driving around in circles but actually moving from A to B. My dad was leaving Bradley University to become the Dean of Letters and Science at Cal State Long Beach. California, here I come!

As a child I was thin. Though many of my immediate and extended family struggled with their weight, I was spared the cruel jabs and muffled giggles from those informative playground years. I often wonder if it was during those eleven years that I unknowingly defined my self-esteem and built up a cache of confidence that I would later use to survive. But in the Midwest, we didn't really think about our bodies. We never showed them, we never talked about them, and we certainly never celebrated them. So you can imagine what a shock it was when I got off the boat in Southern California.

Southern California, where people shop for groceries in bikinis. That's right, the two most terrifying things in the world—shopping for food and being practically naked—these sun-soaked creatures do simultaneously. For me, picking up a box of Double Stuff Oreos in a bikini is a no-no. Soon after I moved to California, perhaps as an allergic reaction to all that proudly exposed skin, I panicked and became fat, thereby avoiding the mandatory requirement of wearing a bikini in public.

Conversations with My Fat: Part One

Have you ever had a best friend who was also your biggest rival and, at times, your worst enemy? The girl or boy who would be the first invited to your birthday party but the one who made you cry. The friend who one week you couldn't live without and the next week you wished were dead. The friend who listened sympathetically to all your deepest secrets, then turned around and used them against you. The friend you loved and hated, needed and needed to get away from.

When I was eleven years old, I met this "friend." His arrival was altogether unwelcome, but I soon found that I leaned on him for protection. It wasn't Billy Fallon or David Rosenthal. It was my fat. I know it says something about me that I consider the personification of my fat to be male, but over the years I've realized that its tyranny is quintessentially masculine. Which isn't to say that I blame men for my fat. No, rather I just view my fat as Mussolini. It is a terrible oppressor that makes the shame run on time.

Like all dysfunctional relationships, my partnership with my fat is quite complicated. It has caused me great sorrow but also saved me from heartbreak. It has made me timid and given me courage. My fat became my teacher. It taught me not to be average, not to conform, not to go quietly. It made me a fighter. I had to equip myself with a vast arsenal to defend against my fat and was later able to use these weapons against everything else the world threw at me.

But when my fat arrived in 1972, I had no idea that I was entering into a long-term relationship. And that was the year that my lifelong dialogue with my fat began.

He showed up without any warning.

FAT: *Hey! I'm here! How ya doin'?*

ME: *Who are you?*

FAT: *I'm your fat. Who did you think I was?*

ME: *My what?*

FAT: *Your fat! You've been asking for me for about a year now and here I am.*

ME: *I think you've got the wrong house.*

FAT: *Is this 41 Neapolitan Lane?*

ME: *Uh, yeah, but . . .*

FAT: *Well, my records say that you requested me. So here I am.*

ME: *Requested you? Are you crazy? Nobody requests fat!*

FAT: *Well, judging by your wastepaper basket with the Snickers wrapper and the Almond Roca foil, I'd say you sent for me ASAP.*

ME: *Those aren't mine. Those are, uh . . . my sister's. Oh, right, you've probably come back for her.*

FAT: *Nope. We're done with her. It's you that needs me now.*

ME: *Uh, no, this is a really bad time. I'm eleven and very self-conscious. Maybe you could just come back in like fifty years.*

FAT: *Nah, I think I'll settle in, make myself at home.*

ME: *No, really, you gotta go. I just moved here to sunny Southern California from the Midwest and I'm trying to make friends and I don't think they'd like you very much. So, seriously, just get out.*

FAT: *You don't need those friends. I'll be your friend. I'll go everywhere with you, you can always count on me.*

ME: *That's a nice offer, but no thanks. I'd really prefer to make friends on my own.*

FAT: *You made this one all on your own.*

ME: *Look, I don't think it's very nice for you to come here uninvited. And I'd really appreciate it if you'd just leave.*

FAT: *I'm not going anywhere without you. I go everywhere you go.*

ME: *Everywhere?*

FAT: *Yep. School, birthday parties . . . I even follow you into the shower.*

ME: *You can't follow me into the shower. I'm only eleven.*

FAT: *The shower, the mirror, the beach . . . you name it, I'll be there for you.*

ME: *This is ridiculous. Look, Kevin Hutchinson's mom is picking me up in fifteen minutes, and Kevin and I are going together to a birthday party and you can't come.*

FAT: *C'mon, it'll be the three of us, you, me, and Kevin. It'll be fun.*

ME: *You don't understand. I really like Kevin and want him to like me back. But he won't if you're there. So please go away. Please, pretty please.*

FAT: *Will there be cake at this party?*

ME: *Of course. It's a birthday party, but you can't come.*

FAT: *I do like birthday cake.*

ME: *Listen, there won't be enough room for you in the car.*

FAT: *If there's enough room for you, there's enough room for me.*

ME: *I'll make you a deal . . . I'll go to the party, you wait right here, and we'll talk about it when I get back.*

FAT: *What do you think this is, some kind of negotiation? I'm your fat. You want me here. You need me here. Besides, you don't want to go to that party, they'll make fun of us. Why don't we just stay home, make some buttered popcorn, and watch a movie?*

ME: I can't stay home! I'm the new kid. I have to make friends or I'll never be popular.

FAT: There's some cookie dough in the fridge. We don't even have to bake 'em, we can just eat it right out of the mixing bowl.

ME: Well . . . that does sound pretty good, but I already told Kevin . . .

FAT: And if we go to the party, we won't even be able to eat the cake because everyone will be watching us and you know how much better cake tastes when we're sitting home alone.

ME: Well, that's true . . .

FAT: And what about that box of See's candy your mom has all wrapped up for that dinner party she's going to tomorrow night?

ME: See's candy? Where'd she hide it?

FAT: If you promise to stay home with me, I'll help you find it.

ME: Okay, I'll call Kevin and tell him we're not going.

And thus began the endless conversations with my fat. It was often adversarial but also at times comforting. I didn't really understand my relationship with my fat. I was never able to articulate it, but, at some level, my fat made me feel both inadequate and secure.

*   *   *

Shame arrived right on schedule with the onset of puberty, and I began covering up my body at all costs. We lived in Long Beach, a beach community with "beach" right in the name no less, and still I hardly ever went to that dreaded sandy, skinny-folk Mecca. The whole time I was in Long Beach, I remained vigilant about never, ever letting people see my body. I'd wear the heaviest jeans and the baggiest shirts I could find. This was my uniform, my armor. My mother would try to bribe me into wearing the dresses she had bought for me against my will, but I would rather have gone naked and heard gasps than wear one of those dresses and heard whispers.

But Mom, too, was determined. My commitment to wearing jeans was matched by her commitment to getting me into a dress, and she actually began hiding my Levi's. When I begrudgingly put them in the hamper (every couple of months), they would mysteriously disappear. I don't know what she was thinking. Like I was going to look for my jeans, not be able to find them, and then say, "Hey, Mom, you got one of those great sundresses you bought for me?" So to foil her sinister scheme I began sleeping in my Levi's. My idea of washing them was to wear them into the shower. (Note to wide-eyed reader: I am not kidding.) I wore those jeans twenty-four hours a day. I'd fall asleep listening to Peter Frampton, dreaming that my jeans were Roger Daltrey.

I was the unofficial poster child for Levi Strauss. It was all part of my monumental effort to never reveal my body. To anyone. I didn't even want to know I had a body. Because knowing led to crisis: "Oh my God, I have a body. What am I going to do with it? Oh, shit."

Then came the day of David Rosenthal's bar mitzvah. My mother stalked me carrying matching mother-daughter sundresses. It might as well have been Anthony Perkins following me into the shower with a knife. That's how terrified I was of those damned dresses. But Mom persisted.

MOM: You are not going to David Rosenthal's bar mitzvah wearing Levi's. Put this dress on. You look like a truck driver!

ME: A what? Some good socialist you are, Mom! Truck drivers are the basis on which your bourgeois existence is founded. They bring you produce, they bring you lumber, they bring you steel . . .

MOM: **YOU ARE NOT GOING TO DAVID ROSENTHAL'S BAR MITZVAH WEARING LEVI'S!**

ME: **FINE. I WON'T GO!**

And that's why I missed out on almost all the *baruch atah adonai*'s of my thirteen-year-old friends.

Around the time my mother dubbed me "truck driver," my sister had her own set of lovely little nicknames for me, and among my favorites was "You're going to grow up to be a lesbian!"

"No, I'm not," I shot back. "I'm gonna be a truck driver, stupid. Mom even said so!"

She laughed and said, "See what I mean."

And then I said what I always said when backed into a corner: "Shut up!" Clever, eh?

I was thirteen. What the hell was a lesbian? I wasn't sure, but when someone is really mad at you and they say in a threatening voice "You're going to grow up to be a lesbian," it's just, oh, I don't know, an intuitive thing, but you get the feeling it's not a compliment. I mean, people just don't scream at you when they're saying something nice. I would have been totally confused if she had yelled "You're going to grow up to be an architect some day!" I knew it had to be bad. So whatever it was, I didn't want to be a lesbian when I grew up. If I were smart I would have just said "So, what's so wrong with being a lesbian?" That would have shut her up, but I didn't learn those tactics till I was much older.

I should have just asked her what it meant, but I couldn't. She had said it in that tone that meant I was supposed to know the word, and the worst thing a thirteen-year-old can do is ask her older sister what the definition of something is, because then you not only *are* that thing, but you're a *stupid* one at that.

So I waited patiently, wondering what the hell it was I was going to grow up to be.

When I was finally alone in the house, I went to the Great Wall of Books to look it up. I took down L-M-N-O of the *Encyclopaedia Britannica* and began flipping through it madly. LAB, LAZ, LED, LEP . . . flip, flip, flip . . . Leprechaun, leprosy . . . LESBIAN! Yea! I was so excited I could barely focus on the words. I was about to learn my fate.

lesbian\\'lez-bē-ən*n.*, *often cap* an inhabitant of Lesbos, an island off the coast of Greece.

Huh? Why did she make it sound so horrid if all it was was a great vacation spot?

In a way though, Lisa was partly right. Soon I began showing the signs of being a young lesbian. I bought cowboy boots, a leather jacket, and was saving up to buy a motorcycle. I was on my way. Just one problem. I still had that image in my head of the long-bearded man. And I had more than ever to offer him. I had become a fairly accomplished guitarist and had everything in my repertoire from Led Zeppelin to Creedence Clearwater Revival.

In the intervening years my brother had traded the ugly, old Studebaker for a beautiful Gibson LG-1 acoustic guitar. The guy who received the droopy-roofed yellow submarine in trade got taken to the cleaners, if you ask me. I had spent enough time down at McCabe's guitar shop to know that that Gibson was special. I started visiting my brother more often, especially when he wasn't there. I'd grab the key under the mat and make a beeline for the hall closet. Karl must have known how much that guitar meant to me. On my sixteenth birthday he bought me a red plastic toy guitar, and on the card he gave me he wrote: "For your birthday I give you two guitars . . . this is one of them." The other one remains the greatest gift I have ever received.

As I grew older and got the wanderlust spirit in me, I would hitchhike around the country with my backpack, my sleeping bag, and my faithful Gibson guitar. I sang for my supper and riffed for a ride. That guitar would be my ticket out of Long Beach, the wasteland of Southern California. Pot, sex, stealing . . . it's a miracle I got out of there alive. On the surface Long Beach in the 1970s was a clean, prosperous beach community. We all smiled for our family portraits, unaware that this town would swallow up so many of us. A lot of my friends didn't make it, lost to drugs or just to indifference. On their parts and their parents'. Every spring, as a member of the Woodrow Wilson High School yearbook staff, I would help compile the memorial page of kids killed by ennui.

The summers were the worst. Most of my friends were completely disconnected from their parents, and we ended up playing Spin the Bottle and Truth or Dare in the back alleys of our middle-class neighborhoods.

To be in the jock crowd or the cheerleader clique, you had to be good at sports or be pretty, respectively. To be in the nerd gang, you had to be smart. To hang with the low riders, you had to have a Camaro. But to join the drug culture, all you had to do . . . was do drugs. I had sought and been denied membership in all the other cliques, but I met the requirements to join the druggies. The entrance exam went something like this:

"Hey, you want a hit?"

"Uh, okay."

"You're in."

Just as ninth grade gave way to tenth grade, which gave way to eleventh grade, we graduated from pot to acid to cocaine and some, sadly, went on to heroin. By taking a hit every time a joint was passed around, I fulfilled my duty as a bored, middle-class Southern California beach kid. But I never liked it. I didn't like the taste, I didn't like the burn in my throat, and most of all I hated the way it made me feel. But there was no quicker way to be ostracized then by declining the offer. And no force on earth is as powerful as a teenager's urgent need to belong. So I smoked.

But then came acid. Somewhere in my travels and travails, I heard that acid stayed in your system for seven years. Like many delusional teenage girls, I thought I'd have 2.5 kids by the time I was twenty-two. And there was no way I was going to poison my babies with traces of LSD. Still, I wasn't ready to be an outcast. I bought my $2.00 tabs of four-way windowpane just like everybody else. The only difference was, I would slip an uncoated piece of paper under my tongue and throw the psychedelic square away. So while all my friends were tripping the light fantastic, I was pretending to be Lucy in the Sky with Diamonds. Nobody ever realized that I was faking it. Ironically, because I wasn't actually taking the acid, I quickly gained a reputation as someone who could really handle her drugs. Everyone wanted to take it with me because I was so "cool" and could "maintain" so masterfully. I babysat many a newcomer through their first acid experience and held many a hand on the way to the emergency room during a bad trip. As long as I kept up the ruse of being the Grande Dame of lysergic acid, my social status remained unquestioned. Now I could say "no" to pot and still be cool. When I turned my nose up at a joint, people would whisper, "Don't you know, man, she's the acid queen." Never has a reputation been so undeserved. But somehow I pulled it off. I was popular and I wasn't doing drugs. Cocaine and heroin, however, were waiting just around the corner. And snorting a line and piercing a vein would be a lot harder to fake.

My parents, of all people, provided me with an out. They were still trying to get me involved in art and educational events. Even though, at the time, I couldn't bear the thought of one more cultural adventure. They asked me if I wanted to go up to the hills above Los Angeles to the Renaissance Faire. I didn't, of course. I was fifteen! Who wants to go anywhere with their parents when they are fifteen? Frankly, I don't know how they got me in the car. Whenever I drove anywhere with them, we'd be on the road for about ten minutes when the quiz would start.

"How many senators to a state?"

"What is the electoral college?"

"What state has the most representatives?"

When most families play Twenty Questions, it's fun. But when we played it, we got grades. It was worse than school. Imagine a class in which you're called on every time. I'm sure being a professor's daughter has its benefits, but trapped in the back of the Plymouth Fury III on the 405 Freeway, I couldn't think of any.

As we drove over the Agoura Hills into the parking lot of what otherwise was the old Paramount ranch, we were greeted by young nymphs and merry men. All fabulously garbed and having the time of their lives. None of them looked any older than me. But all of them looked happier.

As we entered the Renaissance Faire, my eyes feasted on a kaleidoscope of colors and sounds. Fat women with their breasts bowing to the sun, women of all shapes and sizes kissing men and singing harmonies. Wenches and princes and strolling minstrels. Children and lovers frolicking in the streets. There were banners and processions and horses and thieves. Jugglers and fire-eaters and beggars and knaves. It was heaven. Heaven as I dreamed it, and the only thing that ruined it was my mom and dad, chirping away "Oh, honey, look at the juggler, look at the acrobat" as if my eyes were voice-activated and had they not pointed them out I would have missed them. (When you're fifteen, everything your parents do is annoying.)

I felt so excited and so miserable all at the same time. I knew in my gut that I belonged there. That I should be frolicking in the grass, drinking make-believe ale, and singing madrigals. I wanted to have flowers in my hair and bells on my toes. Much to my surprise I wanted to shed my Levi's and don long colorful skirts and bodices that celebrated breasts. I wanted all those gorgeous young men to be shouting out my name and running after me in the dusty streets. I wanted to say "Make way for the queen." And "Dost thou know what time it be?" I wanted to finally be in a world that devoured curvy women and honored them with due respect.

But at the same time, I felt sick to my stomach. Have you ever wanted something so badly that to have just a little bit of it made you want to have none of it at all? I asked my parents if we could meet up in an hour or so, and I walked around the fair with such longing, such desperation to be a part of this magical event. I looked up and saw a group of young girls, singing a soft, sweet ballad, and I nearly cried. I needed so desperately to be a part of this universe. A place where I could embrace myself and be adored by others.

All I wanted to do was get the hell out of there. It was too painful to see the life I wanted just out of my grasp. Agoura Hills was over an hour from my home. I didn't have my driver's license yet, and I didn't know a single soul there. I saw no chance of making my way back there anytime soon. On my way out I took a flyer.

I was quiet on the ride home. I felt I had just missed my one opportunity to learn to fly. Instead of reveling in its glory, I hated knowing what I was missing. That ride home seemed endless. Back to Long Beach, the wasteland of dreams.

I quickly forgot about the Renaissance Faire. Well . . . I successfully blocked it out anyway. School started up again, and I dragged my feet through tenth grade. The routine was becoming mind-numbing. Get up, go to school, explain why you're late, sleep through geometry, dream about my guitar, pretend to do drugs, take friend to emergency room, go home, argue with parents, go to sleep. Get up, go to school, explain why you're late, sleep through geometry, dream about my guitar, pretend to do drugs, take friend to emergency room, go home, argue with parents, go to sleep. Day after day.

And like most—well, probably all—teenagers, I felt totally trapped by my transportation limitations. When I finally did get my driver's license, I still had to beg my mom for the car keys or solve a math problem for my dad before he'd hand over the keys to the old Plymouth Fury III. And the alternative was even more humiliating. Is there anything more embarrassing for a high school junior than being dropped off at a party by her folks? So I instituted the block-away ritual.

"Yeah, Mom, right here's fine."

"This doesn't look like a party, honey."

"Uh, it's around back. Don't wait up. Bye."

And then I'd walk the rest of the way as if I had just parked my sweet ride down the street.

The flip side to that misery is the ultra-cool arrival. And there is nothing cooler than pulling up to a party on your motorcycle. So in one shrewd transaction, I made the leap from mega-dork to motorcycle mama.

When I was sixteen, I saved up $200 from working at Lynn Perry's Pizza and bought myself a cherry red Suzuki 185 two-stroke. My life would never be the same. Thankfully, both my brother and my sister had owned motorcycles before me, so my parents were already broken in. Now *I* needed to be broken in. I had ridden on the back of my brother's bike a couple of times, but that was pretty much the extent of my cycling experience. Karl was up in Los Angeles, so he couldn't take me out for a lesson. But he did the next best thing, he taught me Motorcycle Riding for Dummies over the phone.

"One down, four up . . . neutral is between first and second. Left hand clutch, right hand accelerator. Right foot brake. Right hand brake. Use them both at the same time. Watch out for oil. Assume nobody can see you. Good luck."

I was off. I rode around the block for three hours, attaining that sense of invincibility that only sixteen-year-olds have, and proceeded to the DMV to get my license. Let me tell ya, that written test was pretty rough with questions like:

You should wear bright colors because:

A. They match your motorcycle.
B. They help you blend in with other vehicles.
C. They make you easier to see.

So I passed the written test with bright, flying colors. The road test was actually quite difficult, staying between the lines, doing figure eights at very low speed without stalling. I'm gonna let you in on a little secret about the Darwinian evolution of fat girls. If you have no stamina and can't run up and down the basketball court, you'd better have a pretty accurate shot. I was forced to develop my eye-hand coordination so that I wouldn't always be picked last for hoops. (Being 5′10″ didn't hurt either.) So I negotiated the cones without a single deduction and earned my new California driver's license, with "Class M" stamped on the front.

Once I had that bike, there was no more begging, no more borrowing, and no more of my dad's annoying word problems. Instead, I'd just say to him on the way out the door, "If a girl leaves her house on a motorbike averaging 60 mph, how far away from home will she be in two hours? See ya."

But if you think showing up at a party on a motorcycle is cool, wait till you show up at a rock-and-roll concert. If Long Beach had a hall of fame for cool people, I would have been inducted.

Enter Wolf and Rissmiller, rock promoters. You couldn't get me out of bed on time for a biology midterm, but when Wolf and Rissmiller began giving away free tickets every Tuesday morning to fill the Long Beach Arena every Saturday night for a televised rock concert, my alarm was set. Emerson, Lake and Palmer; Allman Brothers; Steely Dan; REO Speedwagon; Steppenwolf; ZZ

Top; Dave Mason. These concerts gave me something to look forward to, an oasis in the dusty desert. I quickly became concert savvy and, like the rest of my fellow druggies, was looked up to by the jocks and cheerleaders and nerds and low riders, all of whom envied the ease with which we maneuvered through the halls of rock and roll. By the time I was sixteen, I was a concert connoisseur and it was time to move beyond Wolf, Rissmiller, and the Long Beach Arena.

My favorites—Crosby, Stills, Nash and Young—were coming to the Los Angeles Forum, and I was determined to be there. Unlike the Wolf-Rissmiller shows, I had to buy tickets to that concert, and all I could afford were the cheapest seats.

Getting there was another problem. My girlfriend Phyllis's mother wouldn't let her ride on the back of my motorcycle, so we had to try to borrow my father's car. Sometimes my father would hand over the keys without protest, but other times he'd decide that if I wanted to use the car, I would have to jump through mental mind hoops to get the keys. "So you want to borrow the car," he'd say, dangling the keys in front of me. "How much does it cost to drive a mile?" That was easy. Thirty-five cents a gallon, thirty miles to the gallon . . . "1.1666 cents a mile!" My father would just smile at me and say, "You have to figure in wear and tear on the car, insurance costs, depreciation, and of course my emotional stress." I wanted to say "Fuck that, I'll walk!" But Los Angeles isn't exactly hoofing distance from Long Beach, so I told him—loud enough so my mom could hear—I would just take my motorcycle, which, of course, made my mom force him to hand over the keys.

The Los Angeles Forum was a lot bigger than the Long Beach Arena, and I needed to draw on all my concert savvy to look cool and unimpressed. When we found our seats, I couldn't mask my disappointment. Neil Young would look like a shaggy ant from our nosebleed seats. This was pre-Jumbotron, and we couldn't see a damn thing. After two songs I got that I'd-rather-have-none-than-this-little-crumb feeling and I told Phyllis I wanted to go home. It was too depressing.

We were headed for the exit when Phyllis spotted David Weinstein, an older boy we had known from the Long Beach Jewish Community Center. We had never paid him much mind, but that usher's vest he was wearing sure made him look more attractive. We were prepared to grovel to get closer to the stage, but it wasn't necessary. David pulled back the velvet rope and "ushered" us right on to the floor.

I just wanted to get as close to Neil Young as I could before they checked our tickets and kicked us out. When we were five rows from the stage, close enough to see his sweat, I noticed four seats folded up in the center of the row. Just in case any ushers were within earshot, I shouted, "Oh, look, there are our seats." I grabbed Phyllis and we sat down.

I sat in the fifth row while Neil Young, Stephen Stills, Graham Nash, and David Crosby sang "Helpless" and "The Needle and the Damage Done." I had played those songs so many times before. I felt like a disciple at a religious gathering. My chest felt too small for my heart.

Just as they were starting to play "Carry On," I saw two girls wearing backstage passes making their way toward us, and I feared that my rock-and-roll fantasy was about to end. But instead, it was just beginning. One of the girls yelled out my name, and said, "Oh my God, it's so good to see you. I can't believe your seats are right next to ours. Just hang out for a second and I'll go get you a backstage pass." And as she walked away I turned to Phyllis in shock. I had no idea who she was. But if she came back with passes, she was my new best friend. Even if I never saw her again I'd be happy as long as we got to stay in those seats.

But when she returned bearing "all access passes," my hands were trembling. It was like holding the Holy Grail. Now I was less interested in Neil Young and more interested in making sure everyone knew I had a backstage pass. We went backstage after the show. Me, Phyllis, and my new best friend, What's-her-face. On the way she kept asking me how I'd been, what I'd been up to, where I'd been hanging out. Still I could not figure out where I knew her from. When What's-her-face was talking to somebody else, I told Phyllis that I was going to go to the bathroom (wink, wink) and that she should introduce herself to the mystery girl so she could get her name. With that information I would be able to deduce who the hell this girl was. Phyllis did her job and upon my return whispered, "Diane." Which was no help. I was looking at this girl, I now knew her name, and I still couldn't place her. I was starting to worry that maybe I had dropped all that acid after all. But at that moment, who cared? I was fifteen feet from Neil Young. I considered approaching him to tell him about my classic Gibson LG-1, but my legs wouldn't move. I was paralyzed by awe.

Before we left the Forum, I thanked Diane for the most amazing experience and she assured me that we'd do it again real soon. We exchanged numbers and I floated out of there, singing "Suite: Judy Blue Eyes."

True to her word, Diane called me and invited me to the Emerson, Lake and Palmer concert. I didn't even know any of their songs, but of course I said yes. A backstage pass is a backstage pass. I sure wished I could have remembered who she was, because she was the coolest person I had ever met. How could I forget somebody so cool? She took me to a different concert every weekend and got backstage passes to them all. If only I would have admitted at the CSN&Y concert that I couldn't remember her, it probably would have been fine. But with each incredible concert, Heart–Genesis–Queen–Aerosmith–Eric Clapton, it became more and more impossible to 'fess up. For some reason, Diane never spoke about the days when we were supposedly good friends. But thanks to her, my Gibson guitar case was covered with coveted backstage passes.

For the longest time I was afraid to ask her how she got passes to every concert in Southern California, because I thought it would reveal that I had forgotten some conversation we had when we were best friends about how her dad was the president of Ticketmaster. But when we were air-lifted with Ted Nugent in his private helicopter to the California Jam, I had to know. At the festival I confessed.

"Diane, I have tried and tried for the past year to remember how you and I first met, but I've been too embarrassed to admit that I forgot." She explained that when we were in junior high, she was a fat, unpopular kid and I had sat with her at lunch every Friday, and this was her way of repaying me. Oh my God, Diane Dellassandro, now I remembered. Still, looking at that sexy, confident, sassy spitfire, it was clear that the Diane I first met had long ago disappeared. It occurred to me that the junior high Diane had never mentioned her father, the ticket master, which prompted me to ask how she got all those backstage passes. I must have seemed like the most naive sixteen-year-old in the world. She gave me a look and said, "I've got friends backstage" in a tone that meant, you don't want to know. Even then I still didn't get it, but she sensed my sexual inexperience and said no more. I was glad that we had that little heart to heart, but she was embarrassed. She had assumed that I knew all along what she was doing, but the revelation that I was completely unaware created a division between us. That was the last concert we went to together.

* * *

Spring turned to summer and I was facing another wasted season working at the pizza place. I was moping in my bedroom, switching backpacks from my old dorky one to a new one, when I came across the flyer for the Renaissance Faire. Every image came flooding back to me. And I sat in my room and dreamed of the day I could escape this desert of dreariness and reinvent myself.

I don't know what possessed me, but for the first time in my life, I made a move that would alter the course of my destiny. I called the number on the flyer. And from that moment on, I never looked back.

The lady on the other end of the phone sounded like an angel sent from heaven. "What's your name?" "Uhm . . . uhm . . . Debi." (Not to worry, I'll explain the whole name mystery in the chapter after next.) "Hey, Debi, so glad you called. We're having a meeting for new employees next month. I'll put your name down on the list, and I look forward to meeting you. By the way, you need to think of another name. Everyone at the fair picks a different name. Think about it. Be creative!"

That's when I became Chloe Blue. The brown-haired, blue-eyed girl with beads and bells and flowers in my hair.

I waited three weeks for that meeting. Which in teenage-girl-years is about a year and a half. I thought if I brought my guitar it would help my chances of getting in. Since there was no way to carry my Gibson on my Suzuki, I was forced to go through the mental gymnastics and quantum ridiculousness to get those car keys from my dad. When I entered that meeting all of my hopeful expectations were confirmed. I belonged. You didn't have to be skinny, you didn't have to be a jock, you didn't even have to take drugs, all you had to do was want to be there.

I worked at the Renaissance Faire for four summers. First as a court jester and then as a wench. It was my personal revolution. Sexual, emotional, and spiritual. I learned pretty much everything I'd ever need to know in the rolling hills of Agoura.

By that time I didn't even need my dad's car. I would just grab my backpack and my guitar and hitchhike there. I preferred it, really. Part of the whole peace-love-hippie picture. When I arrived, I'd bid good day to Dimitry the juggler and Sebastian the shoemaker and then head to the part of the fair where the actors camped out.

In the evening when the fair had closed, all the actors and dancers and singers and members of the court would entertain each other. The Flying Karamazov Brothers would do an X-rated version of their hilarious juggling show, astrologists would do free Tarot and palm readings, and the court jesters would tell dirty jokes. Then someone would request a song and I'd get out my guitar and we'd sing until dawn. As I sat there strumming my Gibson I felt like my life had just begun. I was doing something I loved to do and being loved for it. My popularity wasn't the result of some artifice, it was earned. I was the girl with the sweet voice and warm laugh who people wanted to be near. How strange. Men were being so kind and affectionate that I felt I needed to remind them that I was fat and that they really weren't attracted to me. But I had slipped into a parallel universe and here women like me were worshipped.

When I first arrived backstage at the actors' camp, I was mortified by the open showers, no doors, no walls, no nuthin'. And the countless naked bodies strolling about all day and night. But it was more conspicuous to be wearing clothes than to be nude. So I threw my skirts off and let the sun kiss my naked body. I had cast off the shackles of self-consciousness and self-loathing. I was embracing my newfound freedom and was yearning to be embraced.

* * *

Adam was a juggler. He was long and lean, kind and gentle, and he had great hands.

* * *

I was born in the summer of my sixteenth year. That summer and the three that followed, I celebrated my body. And Adam had an open invitation to the celebration.

In the four summers I worked at the Renaissance Faire, I learned how to walk around naked. I learned to love my body, and I learned to love that others loved my body. Who knew that what I had accomplished at age sixteen would be systematically taken away from me until I learned to hate myself? But over those four glorious summers I did learn to fly.

To this day, if you ask about Chloe Blue, I'm sure there would be some tales lurking in the rolling hills of Agoura.

Myth America

It was during those glorious summers at the Renaissance Faire that I learned about Santa Cruz from the Flying Karamazov Brothers. They had told me what a cool, hippie-dippy place it was and how I would fit in perfectly. They clearly dug their hometown. I couldn't imagine gushing about Peoria or Long Beach like that. So when it came time to choose a college, I followed my heart and the advice of a bunch of crazy jugglers.

By the time I arrived at UC Santa Cruz, I had a pretty complete understanding of what a lesbian was. Which was good because Santa Cruz has the largest per-capita lesbian population in the country. Santa Cruz is Santa Claus for lesbians.

The Birkenstock-wearin' girls saw me as one of their own. And in many ways I was. When in Rome, or rather when in Lesbos . . . well, the point is the Karamazovs were right. I felt so accepted, like I belonged. Santa Cruz, where the ocean meets the redwood forest, and the '60s never ended. It was paradise, so I wasn't going to sweat the details.

Santa Cruz was tofu, crystals, sensory deprivation tanks, and the MISS CALIFORNIA PAGEANT! Talk about incongruity. Right through Hippie Town, USA, came an annual parade celebrating the objectification of women and the glorification of the beauty myth. Each year, in a town dedicated to naturalness, anti-materialism, feminism, liberalism, and earthy values arrived a procession of capped teeth, long blond hair, and plastic surgery.

Now, protesting the evils of a beauty pageant is just the kind of meaty issue a radical feminist, vegetarian, undecided lesbian like me likes to sink her teeth into. Bring it on, Barbie!

I had lent my support to a radical feminist group called the Praying Mantis Brigade. You know, the praying mantis, the large winged insect, where the female *eats* the male after mating. That should give you an idea of the political slant of this organization. It was such a comfort being with those women. I never felt judged by how I looked.

Every year the Praying Mantis Brigade had a little pageant of its own in protest of the Miss California Pageant called the "Myth California Pageant." Women would come wearing gowns made entirely of meat, wearing sashes that said "Miss Used," "Miss Treated," "Miss Understood." At the end of the parade was a Cadillac convertible with a 500-pound woman sitting on the back, wearing a bikini and a tiara, with her fat flowing over the sides of the car. She looked absolutely regal, doing the obligatory elbow, elbow, wrist, wrist; elbow, elbow, wrist, wrist wave.

One year the Praying Mantis Brigade asked women who had at one time been raped to donate blood to be used in a protest against the pageant. And on the night of the Miss California Pageant, the Praying Mantis Brigade took raped women's blood, went up to the Civic Auditorium where the pageant was being held, and threw the blood on the stairs so all the gowns and tuxedo pants would have to drag through it.

It was just like *Carrie*, only, y'know, more political.

The following year the pageant was moved to Pasadena.

Well, there I was, a confirmed Praying Mantis. But was I a confirmed lesbian? The entire lesbian community certainly thought I was. Don't you just hate that? That patronizing "Well, you just don't know it yet, but you're one of us." That's as annoying as a guy telling a lesbian "Just give me one night with you, and I'll convert you."

Like any minute now I was going to break out into that Holly Near tune "Imagine My Surprise."

Echoes of my sister's taunts came back to haunt me.

My family was beginning to suspect and certainly all my friends thought I was headed down that Lesbianic Trail. But motorcycle and all, I was still not convinced. I felt guilty, hanging out with all these really cool women, but at the same time missing those dexterous hands of Adam the Juggler.

Amid all those wonderful dykes, I had had a revelation. I was not a lesbian. I wanted to be a lesbian. I tried to be a lesbian, and God knows I would have been a great fucking lesbian. I mean, after all, I lived in Santa Cruz, I had a motorcycle, I was an activist, a liberal, an artist, a feminist. I love women, they love me, fat and all, and my sister always said I would be one. I even gave it the good old college try. Not once, but twice.

It would have been so easy if I could have been a lesbian. But no, I had to settle for heterosexuality, which, as some of you know, is no day at the beach.

Being exposed to those beauty queens and Praying Mantises at the same time made me ask myself some hard questions. Would I have been so radical had I not been so fat? Could I have been one of the women on the other side parading my beauty of which I was so proud? As I stood there holding my JUDGE MEAT NOT WOMEN picket sign, I recalled all the people who had said to me throughout my life, "You've got such a pretty face." But they never finished the thought. The whole phrase is "You've got such a pretty face, too bad you're fat." But what if I weren't fat? Would I still have attacked this "Meat Parade" so fiercely? The truth is, my fat has informed my politics. And while I'd like to think I would have been just as ardent in my opposition to the objectification of women had I been thin, I'll never know for sure.

But at the time, standing there with my picket sign, I was guilty of that little-girl fantasy. I imagined hearing my name called. Lowering my head to receive the tiara. Roses landing at my feet. Adjusting my tiara. My mascara tears leaving streaks on my face. The flashbulbs popping. Adjusting my tiara. The other girls so gracious and genuine in their congratulations. Adjusting my tiara.

Had they known what I was thinking the Praying Mantises would have taken away my bullhorn.

But even if I had been thin enough, I never would have entered a pageant. Or would I?

No! For Christ's sake, this is the most politically offensive dream sequence I ever had. I can't believe I was actually on the front lines of feminism falling prey to the beauty myth. And yet you never know. If I were 5´6˝ and weighed a 105 pounds—

slipping back into a dream—I would kneel down gracefully and tentatively pick up my flowers. I would twirl my baton and wave to my boyfriend, who would say "Hey, you look great in that tiara."

You know, it's hard to say what your life would be like given a whole new set of circumstances. C'mon, there are a lot of benefits to being in a beauty pageant.

For example, I'd do it for the scholarship. I'd travel the world and meet interesting people, and I would tell them that their language was wrong and they should learn English. Because English is the best! I'd go into the ghettos and impoverished countries, but never spend the night. Never, never, never, never, not even if they promised me a grant, because my boyfriend would tell me not to. And my boyfriend would do *this* for me, and my boyfriend would do *that* for me, and my boyfriend would name a boat after me, and my boyfriend, my boyfriend, my boyfriend, my boyfriend, my boyfriend, my boyfriend . . . blech.

CUT TO REALITY:

Man, that is a lame fantasy and one I wish all little girls could steer clear of. I mean, even if you're pretty and thin enough to be crowned Miss California, forty-nine of fifty women go home losers on Miss America night. And if I ever get to host the Miss America pageant, I'll end the show by saying "Some people might think there were forty-nine losers up here tonight. But really there were fifty. Because everybody who enters a beauty pageant is a big loser. Good night!"

*   *   *

During my four years in Santa Cruz, the Praying Mantis Brigade had won me over politically, if not sexually, and it was tough leaving those women . . . and those crazy jugglers. But I had fallen in love with the theater, and there was no doubt what I wanted to do with the rest of my life. And there was only one place to do it. New York City! (Sadly, there would be far too many times when acting would also seem just like an elaborate beauty pageant.)

The Artist Formerly Known as Debi

Let's clear this up once and for all. I'm sure there have been a couple of confusing moments for you regarding my name. For many actors, taking on a stage name is a way to distinguish themselves. I never took a stage name; I just changed my name altogether every few years until I got it right. Though I don't think they were smoking angel dust at the time, for some reason my parents decided to name me Debra. (To all Debs, Deborahs, Debbies, and Debras, please do not take offense, but this name sucks!) The hilarious part is that my parents agree that this is an awful name, which begs the question: "Well, then, what the hell were you thinking?"

They always apologized to me by saying "We were going to name you Erica Francesca." It's as if they were telling me "You see, we had a good idea for a name, but something went horribly wrong at the hospital and you ended up with Debi." I would have been fine with Erica Francesca, but I got Debra Frances. And so I went through life with this albatross around my neck, a name with no character, no euphony, no style. Then, lucky me, they made a whole porn series called *Debbie Does Dallas*. That really helped me through high school.

So it should come as no surprise that, at an early age, each time I went away to summer camp, I would adopt a new name. The first year at Camp Kamoroff I was Chloe. It was sexy, irreverent, the kind of name they use for perfumes. Can you imagine dabbing on a little Debra before a date? The second year at camp, before I was dismissed for bad behavior, I insisted on being called Dusty. It was rugged, the kind of name that says "Don't mess with me, or I'll saddle up, hunt you down, and hog-tie you." Well, that's what it said to me anyway. My parents would send me letters addressed to Debi Manheim and I'd look at the counselor and say, "Never heard of her."

After being wrongfully expelled from one of the summer camps—well, the punishment didn't fit the crime—I was shipped off to Idyllwild School of Music and the Arts.

There I was Blue, and I don't mean sad, that was my name. Blue. (I didn't learn until much later that one of the Manson Family girls was named Blue.) When you're at an art school, you want people to say "Ooooh, her name's Blue. She must be cool." Never in the history of names has someone said "Oooh, her name's Debi. She must be cool." However, I'm sure things like *this* have been said. "Debi? What were her parents thinking?" Later I would combine Chloe and Blue to come up with the ultra-cool Chloe Blue, whom you've already heard about:

I lived through countless temporary name changes, trying to find the right fit. And the problem was, until I came up with a name I could really commit to, I couldn't get anybody to stop calling me Debi. My parents laughed at all my halfhearted attempts to lose the offending moniker.

But when I graduated from college, about to embark on my new life, I knew this was my one and only chance to reinvent myself for good. As a graduation present, my folks sent my sister and me to Israel. Which didn't make a whole lot of sense since it was *my* graduation. What I failed to remember was that my sis was never that thrilled with the name Lisa Jan, so she understood my desperate need for a new name and enthusiastically agreed to help. So I was glad she was coming. Like everyone else in my family, including aunts, uncles, and cousins, she thought Debi sucked too.

After a thorough examination of the options, I had whittled it down to three finalists: Sam (short for Sammy Frances, not Samantha), Sydney, and Camryn. I just always loved boys' names. I wanted a good, strong, don't-fuck-with-me name.

I flew to England, which is where Lisa was living at the time, and spent two weeks there before we flew to Tel Aviv. Now, Lisa is just about the coolest person to see the world with. She is an amazing artist who was able to help me divine the deeper social meanings in art from the Victoria and Albert Museum in London to Yad Va-Shem in Jerusalem. It's still hard to get me into the museums, but when I go with Lisa, I actually enjoy them.

While in London, the first name I tried on was Sam. Lisa really made an effort, but it was hard. She'd call out, "Debi . . . I mean, Sam, pass the Vegemite." Then she'd get crossed up and say, "Sam, I mean, Debi, I mean, Sam . . . whatever! There's

Piccadilly Circus." Just when she had it figured out, I decided Sam just wasn't quite right. Sam I am? No, Sam I'm not.

Next up: Sydney. Now, I really liked Sydney and this name had a good shot of sticking. Lisa kept trying. "Sam, Debi . . . Sydney . . . oh, for chrissakes, you!" Then one night we were in a pub and Lisa had it down. She was calling me Sydney on the first try every time, and I was really feeling like a Sydney. Sydney, Syd, Sydney Manheim . . . yes, you can tap your toe to it. It was all set.

Then Lisa skipped to the loo and I was approached by a handsome bloke drinking a pint of stout. He came up to me and said, "My name's Simon, what's yours?"

I was practically bursting at the opportunity to run my new name up the flagpole. "Hi, Simon, my name's Sydney."

And without so much as a nanosecond's pause, he said, "No, it's not." Instead of fighting for my new name, I caved immediately. "You're right, it's Debi."

Lisa returned from the bathroom and said loud enough for the guy to hear, "Hey, Sydney."

I snapped at her, trying to prevent any further embarrassment. "My name's not Sydney, it's Debi."

To which she said, "You sure it's not Sybil?"

If it was so obvious that I wasn't a Sydney, then I would just have to scrap the name.

I had one chance left. We arrived in the "Promised Land" and I had all my hopes riding on Camryn.

Okay, now, we all know that some pretty heavy stuff has happened in the Holy Land—you know, signs from God and all. Some people get to the Wailing Wall and have a vision; I heard a voice.

"Camryn . . . Camryn . . . Camryn." Somebody—a benevolent

spirit perhaps—was whispering my new name to me. Lisa thought I was out of my mind. *I* thought I was out of my mind, but never has anyone been so happily out of their mind. Camryn it was.

Now, for those of you who doubt that some divine intervention was at work here—and how could anyone really doubt it?—listen to this little postscript. I had worn tank tops all over the Holy City and was, in fact, asked to leave the Wailing Wall before a woman loaned me her shawl. I was unaware of the no-bare-shoulders commandment and was determined to get a golden bronze tan, which, you should know, makes you look thinner.

When I was done wailing, I gave the shawl back. I was still hearing the voice. And every time, it was as if someone were following right behind me and whispering over my left shoulder "Camryn, Camryn," then disappearing when I spun around to see who it was. The voice always came over my left shoulder and into my left ear. Big deal, right? Get this.

The following week at our hotel in Tel Aviv, I was brushing my hair in the mirror when my sister came up behind me and shouted, "Oh my God, look at your arm!" I figured there was a tarantula on it or something from her tone of voice and began asking frantically "What, what, what is it?"

She said, "Look at your left shoulder—the one you always said someone was standing behind! You're tan all over except for that one area!" Oooooh . . . creepy.

"See, I told you somebody *was* standing behind me the whole time."

"Yeah, either that, or maybe you were just carrying your purse there."

Who cares? I got my sign and that night, my sister, the fabulous artist, sat on the bed, teaching me my new autograph.

Cameron Frances Manheim

Camren F. Manheim

Camron Manheim

Kamryn F. Manheim

Camryn Frances Manheim

✦ Camryn Manheim *for autographs*

✦ Cam Manh *for checks*

When I later arrived at New York University for graduate school, I told all my new friends and classmates that my name was Camryn. They seemed to believe me, but for months, every time I introduced myself, I looked into their eyes, half expecting them to say "No, it's not." The hard part was convincing myself. I'd hear somebody yelling "Camryn! Camryn! Camryn!" And I'd wonder who the poor sap was looking for. It took me a full calendar year before I really owned Camryn. But once I did, I knew I'd never let it go.

As for Debi . . . see ya, didn't want to be ya.

If I Can
Make It There . . .

By the time I graduated from the University of California at Santa Cruz, I had run a theater company, bought a house, and taught a class at the university. To say I was a big fish in a small pond would be an understatement. I was twenty-two going on forty. I knew I could have anything I wanted in Santa Cruz, but I had bigger dreams. It was time to move on. To the big pond.

I applied to the elite eleven drama schools for my Master's of Fine Arts. But really, I was interested in only two—Juilliard and NYU (though I would have gone to Yale just so I could wear the sweatshirt). I wanted, no *needed*, to be in New York City, the theater capital of the world, and therefore the center of the universe.

So a few things had to happen: I had to fill out eleven applications, write eleven checks for $60, make eleven copies of my statement of purpose (whatever that was), and prepare for eleven auditions.

Filling out the applications was a lot easier than wringing the $660 out of my dad, but he was so happy that I might actually get into Yale that he forked it over. And the thought that I would be able to put some letters after my name—M.F.A., T.G.I.F., I.U.D.—anything but I.O.U.—excited him greatly.

Applications, no problem. The auditions I was actually excited about. But the statement of purpose? What the hell was that? Create world peace? Be a good citizen? Christ, I just wanted to act and hear some nice applause, and they wanted me to have a purpose. I went to a guidance counselor at UCSC and learned that "statement of purpose" was really just code for "why you should pick me." So in less than 500 words I set about explaining exactly why these schools couldn't do without me. Now I could have dressed this up and edited it and made it look pretty, but this book is about honesty—no matter how much it hurts—so here it is, my statement of purpose (complete with confusing title):

The Confessions of a Would-Be Mathematician

I was supposed to be a mathematician but then there was The Lion, the Witch and the Wardrobe, *and believe it or not, Lucy was much more exciting than polynomials. You see, I come from a family where everyone holds a Ph.D. in some absolutely academic subject, so you can imagine their surprise when they found that I was leaving Descartes for Artaud. Art was definitely "appreciated" in our family (I've been to over 500 museums); however, it was something to be looked at and not done.*

The notion of being a professional actor was regarded as a non sequitur and was sure to offend their Jewish tradition of success.

I recall as a child being very interested in the theater. Then I was regarded as cultured and cute. However, when I entered college as a Theater Arts major, it suddenly became decadent and, how shall I say, no longer "cute." Over time it became obvious that I was never going to become a lawyer, or a doctor, or a . . . mathematician, and dismay gave way to tolerance, which in turn yielded to enthusiastic support. (The kind that, try as they might, parents can never seem to resist.) Although I am still the youngest one at the Seder, it is my mother who asks each year, "Why is my daughter different than all other daughters?" "Different" is an abbreviated and possibly euphemistic summation of my character. I was always told to start with my best foot forward. However, it is tactically important that by the end of this essay, you have forgotten all of those things about me that are probably better left unsaid in the first place and only remember those things that would be appropriately mentioned in my eulogy. Accordingly I will begin with the less desirable aspects of myself: I am blunt—never afraid to ask questions others only wonder about. Nosy—and I ask them even if they're none of my business. Demanding—I expect a lot from people. Intimidating, aggressive, anxious, and not alive in the A.M. Therefore it is reasonable to expect: I will be in the office three times a week asking many unrelated questions in a generally complaining tone of voice, and if asked to rehearse too early in the morning I will be wearing two different colored leg warmers.

Well, I only have one hundred and twenty-three words left to show you my brighter side. So here goes. Do you know those who jump on the bandwagon? Well, I'm usually the one who builds it. And if I can't find someone to pull it, I'll pull it myself. I am known for giving free motivational therapy, because nothing excites me more than working with a group of people who have a passion for their work. I am warm, always good for a big hug. And I am very conscious of the people and things that surround me. I am open, eccentric, SpoNTaNeoUs, social, bouncy, motivated, yet rational, logical, just, prompt, and hopelessly dedicated. In addition to mismatched leg warmers and the like, you can also expect: my enthusiasm for pounding nails at 2 o'clock in the morning or painting sets on the weekends. Being five minutes early, even when half asleep. Doing anything that is required or finding someone else who will. Offering my services at any time to better the quality of a project. A cheerful disregard for "I don't do that, I'm an actor." A desire to learn and a devotion to my art.

I have always believed there are two kinds of actors, those who want to act and those who must. In the face of all the above, it should be obvious that had I merely wanted to act, I would have been a mathematician.

Debi F. Manheim
Jan. 10, 1984

*   *   *

So that was my statement of purpose or, more accurately, my statement of purposefulness. Dog-ear this page. I'll need you to refer back to it later.

And now on to the audition. Here's how it worked. The top eleven dramatic art schools in the country formed an organization called the League of Professional Theater Training

Programs. They were looked upon by the industry as the schools that groomed the best talent in the nation, so any serious actor would want to attend one of these schools. No pressure.

The auditions took place in New York, Chicago, and San Francisco. Santa Cruz is just over the hill from the Bay Area, so it was obvious which audition I'd be attending. I'll bet I was the only aspirant among the thousands who showed up on a motorcycle. Hey, that helmet is a great ice-breaker.

Each of the schools' top brass was there: Yale's Lloyd Richards, Juilliard's Michael Langham, NYU's Zelda Fichandler.

I wheeled my red Suzuki 185 into the parking lot, wedging it carefully between two cars. I could just imagine scratching Mr. Langham's rental and being sent home. The chin guard on my helmet was wet from the forty times I had recited my two monologues on the ninety-minute ride from Santa Cruz to San Francisco. With drool dripping from my helmet and my hair matted from the ride, I prayed I wouldn't encounter anyone important before I was able to get to the bathroom and transform into "the only actor who mattered."

Upon arrival, I was confronted by a wall of lists—pages and pages of names and schools and times. And from these I had to divine when and where I was supposed to be to present my two monologues and a song. The disturbing matrix of names and times seemed like something out of Orwell. Imagine a tidal wave of lists, thousands upon thousands of applicants. I felt instantly insignificant, just another name in a sea of names. How was I going to stand out? I was clearly no longer the big fish in a small pond.

The first day of the two-day inquisition was spent auditioning for all eleven schools. Day 2 was reserved for any callbacks you might have earned. After each gut-wrenching offering of my talents, I'd run back and consult the Wall of Lists. "Who's next? Uh-oh. Yale. This one's for you, Dad." I was halfway through my Chris Durang piece when I could have sworn I heard ol' Langham order a turkey on rye. So it wasn't a big surprise after my first monologue when one of his cronies looked up and said, "Thank you, that was great. I think we've seen enough." Really? Did I mention in my statement of purpose that I was blunt, intimidating, and aggressive? I think I did. So I said, "Well, I paid my sixty bucks to do two monologues and a song and I'm not leaving until I've done them." Gulp. They hadn't heard that before. But they realized it was best just to let me finish.

The fantasy version of this story is that I so blew them away with my second monologue and my singing that they handed me a first-class ticket to New Haven, Connecticut, and gave me a 100 percent cotton sweatshirt. The reality? "Next." Sorry, Dad.

Day 2: Callbacks. I dreaded the long approach back to the Wall of Lists, fearing my name wouldn't appear on any of them. But deep down, I sensed they'd be fighting over me. That's how deluded and invincible I felt back then. Of course that naive innocence would soon be crushed, but not on this day. Six schools, including NYU, had asked to see me again.

CUT TO:

Dear Debi,
New York University's Tisch School of the Arts is privileged to welcome you . . .

Oh . . . my . . . God! New York City, here I come.

How can I describe that feeling of anticipation? From over 1,200 applicants, I had been selected with 28 others to pursue a master's degree at New York University's Tisch School of the Arts. I was cruising at 30,000 feet on a plane to New York, the City, the only city that mattered. If I could make it there, I could make it anywhere. Broadway. Shakespeare in the Park. Radio City. The in-flight magazine held very little allure for me. The in-flight movie? C'mon! I was on my way to the stage of all stages: the Big Apple!

In retrospect, it was like whistling on my way to the gallows, but I had no idea what was coming.

As I look back on those Halcyon days—capital H because they required prescription medication—it seems entirely appropriate that I entered New York City via that Gateway to the Grand Guig-nol, John F. Kennedy Airport.

I was a hippie-dippy, Birkenstock-shod Southern Californian with my head on a swivel, looking left and right for any kind of as-sistance. It never came, which is just JFK's way of preparing you for life in New York City. You are on your own, baby. Good luck finding a cab.

Somehow I made my way to Greenwich Village and the beau-tiful edifices of New York University, established 1831. I'd like to tell you that I melted effortlessly into the unique rhythms of NYC, but the truth is I didn't see the city for the next three years. Pretty much all I saw was the fifth floor of 721 Broadway, Tisch School of the Arts, twelve hours a day, actors' boot camp.

Day 1: The chairperson starts by giving us an introduction to the program. It went something like this: "You are all magicians. You are the vessels through which great minds will speak. You take noth-ing and you transform it into something special. A bare stage be-comes a castle, a labyrinth, a battlefield. You have the power to take people on great journeys. You will make people think and feel. You will inspire and enrage. You will teach people to build bandwagons, to be leaders. Your body is your instrument and you will play upon the souls of the people! You can and will change the world!"

In that instant I had found my Mecca. I was taken in. Hook. Line. Sinker. She was selling and I was buying. I wish that I had taken notes or taped her message to the class. Because I knew if my parents could hear her lecture, they would not be so freaked out at spending $15,000 a year, if they knew their youngest child would eventually become a world leader. And, as if that weren't enough—or, as the Jews say, *Dayenu*—just before we took our break she recited the most inspiring quote I had ever heard. It was from the British poet Christopher Hogue, and it went something like this:

> *"Come to the edge"*
> *"It's too high"*
> *"Come to the edge"*
> *"We might fall"*
> *"Come to the edge"*
> *And they came*
> *And he pushed them*
> *And they flew!*

I couldn't move. I was transfixed by her power, mesmerized by her passion. In that wide-eyed, awe-inducing moment, I loved her.

Finally my head cleared and I thought, "Wow! Here I can take risks, here I will be nurtured, here I will become an actor, with a master's degree, which will really please my parents, because if I don't get acting work, and I don't become a world leader . . . I can always teach."

After the break, she came back and launched into the second

half of what we could expect from the graduate acting program at NYU. More inspiring words were tossed around, pumping our egos and feeding our dreams. Then, out of nowhere—well, from Hell perhaps—our chairperson delivered the most horrifying announcement. Although I don't know what it's like to have testicles, at that moment I sensed what it must feel like to be kicked in them.

The NYU Masters of Fine Arts Program had cuts.

Not all of the twenty-nine chosen ones would make it through the three years. We were told, "There is no magic number of how many students will be cut. You will know before we do if this program isn't right for you." As it turned out, nearly one quarter of the class (seven of the twenty-nine) would be cut. Cut as in "See you later, bye, thanks for the thirty grand, love to get that extra fifteen grand from you, but you suck. Oh, and by the way, you won't be getting your master's degree." Who gets "cut" as an adult? That should have been my first clue that the faculty had no intention of treating us like grown-ups during our course of study. Sadly, nobody had bothered to tell me that there would be "cuts" before I packed up everything I owned and moved halfway around the hemisphere. I'm sure nothing brings out quality acting work quite like the fear of being tossed out into the street. Whatever happened to "you are entering a place of white light and acceptance"? Oh, yeah. She came to the edge . . . and he pushed her . . . and she plummeted to a fiery death.

If anyone was going to get cut, it was going to be me. I was kicked out of summer camp (on trumped-up charges), I was suspended several times in junior high and high school, and I almost didn't graduate from UC Santa Cruz: all for rebelling against the system. Given my history, you can imagine I was none too happy to hear the news about these cuts. Well, I could kiss that master's degree good-bye. Guess I won't be teaching.

And on that first day, as the chairperson was describing the program and how wonderful it was, I was concocting a lawsuit against them in my head. If they cut me, I would sue them.

I'd save all my pennies so I could retain a lawyer, because deep down—in that well from which great acting is supposed to spring—I knew I was going to be cut.

Okay, confession time: You may find this hard to believe, but I've been known to have a little deficiency in the attitude department. My behavior can, at times, be confrontational, cynical, antagonistic. I have a bad attitude and I'm fat, a volatile combo to say the least. Two . . . two . . . two deficiencies in one. I never start trouble, but if someone fucks with me, you better believe I will fuck with them back. NYU drama teachers included.

Oh, those pernicious pedagogues. And Man-oh-Manischewitz did they fuck with me. Now, I am sorely tempted to use my teacher Richard's last name because I hated him with such a passion that my one and only recourse would be to trample on his name. But I'm more mature now, and I forgive. So let's just call poor Richard . . . Dick. Okay, I have a lot of displaced anger. Dick taught a class called "Styles." Don't worry, we didn't know what the hell it was either, but since there was no homework and we didn't have to memorize scenes, we thought it would be a nice, relaxing respite from our real classes.

One day Dick came into class with a sense of purpose. "All right, class, it's time to work! Today our exercise is about power. You will come to the center of the stage. You will claim your space, find your strength, own your power! Be sure to plant yourself firmly and find your light. The text is '*C'est moi!*' You are in Firenze, and the style, commedia dell'arte." You know, maybe it's just me, but if I'm supposed to be in Florence, why am I speaking French? Shouldn't I be saying "*Sono io*"? I'm just saying . . . when in Rome, speak Italian. But I digress. Dick asked for volunteers. A few of my classmates' hands shot up in the air, but Dick seemed to overlook their eager faces and said, "Camryn, why don't you give it a go?" Why me? Why of all people did he have to pick me? Oh, for God's sake. Now I had to get up, which right there was more than I'd ever intended to do in this class, and "find my pool of light."

I got up and found the damned center of the stage and my stupid pool of light. And with all the commedia dell'arte in me, I took a bow and proclaimed, "*C'est' moi*." I nailed it. Part of what gave it that magical touch was that I was secretly pretending to be in Versailles. Yet I had them all believing I was speaking French in Firenze. Now that's acting. Also it helps to have cleavage when you're bowing. The guys in the class like that.

Then Dick started talking and in his most patronizing tone offered, "Now, aren't you glad you went first?" And as I returned to my seat, I thought, "Not really." He clapped his hands and invited the rest of the class to do the same. "Support your peers, class, support your peers. Now, Camryn, I have a question for you."

"Yes?"

"What are you doing about your body?"

I don't know what sounds make you sick to your stomach, but his lilting, squeaky voice talking about my body gave me instant nausea. So with all the commedia dell'arte taken out of me, I stammered, "Uh—uh—well, Dick—I bathe." Nervous, uh-oh-a-confrontation laughter filtered across the room. Later my classmates would become quite comfortable and quite accustomed to these scrapes, but in the beginning, they would seek refuge behind chairs and scripts and each other. My hope was that Dick would sense the tension in the room and politely end this line of interrogation. But, after all, he's a Dick and he persisted. My classmates, for whom questioning authority was simply anathema, continued to cower as teacher and student squared off. They knew as well as I did that a teacher had to earn the right to ask such intimate and controversial questions. And as far as I was concerned, Dick had forfeited that right when he humiliated me in front of the class. But he proceeded as if he had every right to ask the impertinent question.

"No, I'm serious, what are you doing about your weight?" In front of my whole class, mind you. Now, traditionally, this would be where I would say "Fuck you, asshole, you're about to get hurt!" But with the evil, daunting prospect of being "cut" hanging over me like the Sword of Damocles, I said, "You know, I don't think this is an appropriate place to discuss this issue. Why don't we talk about this after class?" Which I have to admit was handled pretty damn well on my part. I could even see my classmates peeking their heads out from their shelters. But my newfound maturity went unrewarded and Dick kept right at it.

"Well, Camryn, if we can't talk about our shortcomings with our peers, how can we be expected to grow?"

"Listen, Dick, I'm with you on that one but . . ." And just then I caught a glimpse of Marissa, the cute little ingenue in the class, and said, "But why can't we talk about her shortcomings, for example?"

And then he said, without a trace of irony, "Camryn, if you can't trust me, who can you trust?" Ah, every bit as comforting as Uncle Claudius putting his arm around poor nephew Hamlet.

"Yes, trust is very important," I began. "I've been working on that, really I have. But I prefer not to discuss things that humiliate me in front of a large group of people. I prefer to be humiliated in front of smaller groups of people or, perhaps, plant forms. I'm particularly sensitive in front of those with whom I am highly competitive and have to spend the next three years convincing I'm a team player. So we can talk about this *after class*, privately, or you can continue to discuss it *here*, and I'll see you tomorrow. Your life, your choice!"

So Dick's mind began racing, his beady little eyes rolling back in his head. And then he tried a little sleight-of-hand by taking the focus off me, turning to the class and suggesting "It's time that we *all* thought about our bodies as our instruments." Oh, that made me feel better, trying to include the nine skinny girls in our little dilemma. Sensing my imminent volcanic eruption, my brave friend Shannon firmly took my hand, squeezing mightily trying to prevent the malice that must have been registering on my face.

As I strode to the door, Dick said, "Camryn, I hate to say it, but you have a bad attitude!"

"Did you say I have a fat attitude?"

"No, I said you have a bad attitude!"

"I heard you! I'm too fat for styles class!" And I slammed the door behind me.

Now, I don't recall reading in the *recruitment* brochure that NYU only accepted thin actors. Oh, that's right, page 12: "The Tisch School is proud of its commitment to producing only the finest and *thinnest* actors in the world."

Remember Cat Stevens? He wrote "Peace Train," and then he changed his name to something like Yusef Salami and said Salman Rushdie must die. I could relate. That whole peace-loving pacifist turned vengeful psychotic thing. I wanted the whole staff dead! By the end of the first year, I was possessed.

It's all I ever thought about. I'm too fat, I've got to lose some weight, I'll never get a professional acting job if I'm that fat.

And even though there were times when they'd actually say nice things about my acting, like: "Camryn, that was great, really nice job."

I of course interpreted it as "Camryn, your acting in that scene was much less fat, that's the kind of slender acting we like to see."

That was my goal. To be a fat-free actor.

Enter teacher number two, Patrice. Patrice taught a class called "Masks." I loved this class. We would pick a mask, stare at it, touch it, live with it for a few days, and then create a character based on our interpretation of it.

Now, one fine and lovely day, I walked into masks class, eager to discover the hidden agenda of my mask, when my teacher Patrice made her first mistake. "Class, I think it is interesting to point out that Camryn is wearing a natural mask today, for she has chosen to wear her hair down, to try to cover herself up."

To which I responded, "Class, I guess it wouldn't be quite as interesting to point out that Camryn is wearing her hair down because she doesn't have a hair tie."

But Patrice wouldn't leave it at that. "Well, that would be the obvious answer, Camryn, but I think natural masks go far beneath the obvious. They are a way of suppressing our subconscious feelings."

Not wanting to suppress my subconscious feelings, I quickly tied my hair in a knot and stuck a pencil through it, unshrouding the labyrinthine mystery that Patrice was projecting onto me. To sum up: Hair down, mask on, hair up, mask off.

But apparently you can't undo a natural mask quite so simply. Because despite the fact that I took my hair and tied it in a knot, Patrice held to her Psych 101 hard line and said, "Camryn, you go right ahead and believe what you will, but I maintain that there is something very painful that you are hiding from us today." What the fuck, why is it always me they seem to enjoy making a fool of?

At this point, my patience and politesse wore off and I said, "I hate this shit, please don't use me for your stupid illustrations to demonstrate your idea of a natural mask." I guess I wasn't much of a diplomat. My classmates began their customary search for cover as the patronizing lecture began.

"Camryn, I know two ways of teaching. I lead people to the water, and I ask them to drink. And if they don't drink, I pick up a stone, and I beat them over the head with it until they do drink. I have tried both these methods with you, and you are not responding. Perhaps this program isn't right for you."

I thought about that for a minute—okay, a second maybe—and since we had already entered the realm of condescension and disdain I simply said, "Oh really, that's interesting. I've been doing some thinking on my own. I pay $15,000 a year to go to what some consider the best school in the country. If you only know two ways of teaching, maybe this school isn't right for you," and she literally pointed her finger at me and said, "You, Camryn Manheim, have a very bad attitude!"

"I have a fat attitude?"

"I said you have a *bad* attitude."

And because I do have a bad attitude, I was blocking out all verbal cues from her and was convinced she said I was too fat for masks class. "Well, you Miss Natural Mask Woman . . ." I began, but then quickly softened my tone. "You are in luck because they are announcing cuts next week and my master's degree is worth a whole hell of a lot more than winning this argument with you."

God, these cuts were like having a gag order.

As awful as Dick and Patrice were, they were trumped by Susan. (All names have been changed to protect the guilty, except for Dick, whose real name is Dick.)

When I was at NYU, I was a pretty heavy smoker. I'm happy to say I've quit since then, and June 10, 1999, will be my twelve-year anniversary. Anyway, one morning I was in my speech class when around nine-thirty I had to go to the bathroom. So I stood up to leave when my teacher asked me where I was going. I said, "I'm going to the bathroom," and she said "Oh, no you're not," probably thinking I was going outside to have a cigarette (which is something I might have done). I obeyed and sat down. A few seconds later I thought, "My God, I'm twenty-four years old, I have to go to the bathroom, this is ridiculous, I'm going." And off I went. That afternoon I was called into the chairperson's office and asked to have a seat. "So, Camryn, you went to the bathroom at nine-thirty, after your teacher asked you not to?" "Yes, that is correct, I did indeed go to the bathroom at nine-thirty after my teacher told me not to." "Why did you do that?" "Well, ummm, I had to pee." "Why didn't you go at nine before your class started?" "I didn't have to go at nine." "Well, perhaps you should go anyway before class, so this wouldn't happen." This shocked me. "Is there a problem leaving the class for a few minutes to use the bathroom?" "Well, it's very disruptive to your fellow classmates to have people walking in and out when they're trying to concentrate." "Well, I don't know what to tell you here, because I tend to use the bathroom fairly often." "Do you have a medical problem?" "As a matter of fact, I am currently going through a series of tests for this very reason." "Well, then, I suggest that you write a little note to all of your teachers, explaining that you have a medical problem and that they can expect that you will need to be excused from class frequently. This will avoid any further misunderstandings."

What's so hard to understand about "I have to pee!"

So in my brief time at NYU I had been told that I was too fat, that wearing my hair down was a self-conscious natural mask, and that, no, I couldn't pee just because I had to. What fun. It was like EST, only more expensive. Still, I was desperately afraid of being cut.

Ah, cuts, the grist for my nightmares.

You see, their theory was that after the first year you need to take the summer off to digest everything you've learned, and then you come back to school and apply all that wonderful knowledge. So they give you the first part of the second year to show them just how much you've learned. But if you didn't get it, didn't digest it well enough to apply it, then in the middle of December, right before Christmas, in the dead of winter . . . the guillotine falls and they announce who will not be returning.

The day before Christmas break, letters that held our fates were placed at the drama school's reception desk. One by one we each picked up our envelopes and retreated to a room that had been reserved for us, so that we could open our letters in private. And we read them. It was horrible.

I love this "cut" system; it really encourages people to take risks and be bold with their choices. All the while they're watching to see if you're talented or not. And on that dismal mid-December day, as the hours crept closer to doom, I took a look around, and I knew I'd miss the stupid place. I took my letter, went into my room, and read it. This is what it said.

Dear Camryn:

At the last faculty meeting there was a careful evaluation of each second year student with regard not only to their talent and potential for professional achievement but also for their citizenship, attitude towards the group, capacity to be a member of an ensemble, and the ability to take responsibility for one's own behavior.

The faculty consensus was that you had considerable talent and were growing in your acting skills, but that there were significant deficiencies, shown in a number of your classes, in being sensitive to the needs of others and responsive to as well as respectful of your teachers. It was also noted by some that you brought negative attitudes to class, that you left classes at miscellaneous times to attend to personal needs that should have been anticipated, and that you were not always accurate in assessing which skills you still really need to investigate and master.

You will recall that I brought these matters to your attention at the last "Fair." Evidently, some improvement has been noted in certain classes, but not enough to set our minds at rest that you can serve the theatrical community with social awareness and a mature sense of responsibility.

We ask you to ask yourself honestly if you can meet the standards we are trying to set and, indeed, are insisting upon, or whether at this time in your life they are eluding you and should be reexamined at some future point.

We also want to say that should you decide to give it a real try, we'll go along with that in good faith; but if problems of attitude don't dissipate over the next semester, we will have to, reluctantly, ask you to leave school in May. We are all on your team, rooting for you, but a number of the faculty members are quite restive about the matters I raise here.

Do please come in to talk with Paul and me in my office on January 23 at 2:00 P.M. The rest of the faculty will be available to meet with you on that day as well.

Sincerely,
The Chairperson

*   *   *

You're kidding. Can you imagine someone at the Wharton School of Business or Stanford Medical School being upbraided for "leaving class to attend to personal needs that should have been anticipated"? As both a student and teacher I can tell you that it just isn't that disruptive for someone to slip out for whatever reason. It is, however, terribly disruptive for the teacher to stop class to scold someone or for a student to pee on the floor.

As for my bad attitude, I ask you to refer to that dog-eared page containing my statement of purpose. Now, when I dug that up from the cobwebbed archives I couldn't believe how honest I had been, or how NYU had completely ignored the warning signs. I think if you write in your statement of purpose that you have an attitude problem and then exhibit an attitude problem at the school that accepts you, you should be extolled for your honesty, not chastised for your impudence. I mean, I told them what they had in store and they accepted me. And now they were pissed because I was following through on my statement of purpose.

Christ! I was *STILL* on probation! The only one. I mean, the ones who got cut got cut. That was it. They could move on with their lives without living in fear. And of the twenty-two who survived, only one—*c'est moi*—was still in that nebulous purgatory under constant threat of termination. I could *still* get cut. Fuck!

So for the next excruciating four months, I bit my tongue, clenched my teeth, and held my temper. I smiled when I wanted to scream. I laughed when I wanted to kill. I deferred when I wanted to destroy. All for those three little letters, M.F.A. In retrospect, B.F.D.

Well, May came along and I was called into the chairperson's office for a little tête-à-tête. Had my attitude improved? Was I a better citizen? Would I be asked back next year? Would I be kicked out? Would I be put on probation again? Who fucking knew? We talked about my work, we talked about my bad attitude, and we talked about my weight. It was short and not so sweet. "Camryn, we think that you should consider losing some weight this summer. There would be so many more opportunities afforded to you if you were thinner." I almost expected her to say "We hope to see a lot less of you in the fall."

I couldn't believe it, I had successfully gotten myself put on probation for the entire three years I was at NYU. And because I see the world through fat-colored glasses, in my demented little mind I heard "either lose weight or get kicked out."

That's when I discovered crystal meth. *SPEED!*

Imagine dumping some Ajax kitchen cleanser onto a mirror, cutting it into two narrow lines, grabbing an ordinary straw, and snorting with all your might. It felt like shards of glass, tearing at my septum. Ouch. But, hey, gotta lose weight, gotta get that master's degree.

As you know, I had never been into drugs. All the mystery and allure had been kind of ruined for me when I smoked my first joint with a friend of mine's mom. That'll take the fun out of being a degenerate right away. It's only worth it if you feel like you're getting away with something. I didn't like pot, I don't drink alcohol, I've never done a hallucinogenic, no downers, uppers, poppers, pills. I just never was interested in drugs. But I had heard about speed. I even knew someone who dealt speed. And I paid that friend a visit. The scary thing about speed is it works. Sure it may kill you, but you'll look great in that coffin.

I was doing speed in the morning to get through the day and Valium at night to get to sleep. Speed in the morning to get through the day and Valium at night to get to sleep. Speed in the morning. Valium at night. Speed in the morning. Valium at night. Speed. Valium. Speed. Valium. Speed. Valium. *(Pant, pant)* Speed and Valium . . . it's got a certain rhythm, but you can't dance to it. Life was going by at a hundred miles a minute. I wasn't eating a thing and I was exercising more than ever. I was playing tennis, racquetball, swimming. I was really improving my cardiovascular system and destroying it at the very same time. By the end of the summer, I had lost about thirty-five pounds, and when I returned to NYU I was celebrated by my peers. My teachers took a brand-new interest in me and I felt like a star. I was afraid if I stopped taking the speed I would gain all thirty-five pounds back, so I decided to keep taking it during my last year at NYU. I was a wreck but a trimmed-down wreck, and that kept NYU happy. By spring I was the thinnest I had ever been in my adult life, about eighty pounds less than I am now. I don't think anyone ever noticed I was on speed, but then, ya know, I could have been in denial.

I don't get it. I just don't get it. If Art is supposed to imitate Life, why do they want all the actors to be thin? There are fat people in the world. Shouldn't there be a few of us actors to represent them?

Maybe I shouldn't complain. When I was at NYU, I got to play some of the best roles in theater history. The only drawback was that they were all parts over fifty.

I played Arkadina in *The Seagull*, Mrs. Peachum in *Three-penny Opera*, the Mother in *Curse of the Starving Class*, the Nurse in *Romeo and Juliet*, Rebecca Nurse in *The Crucible*—she's at least eighty. Queen Margaret in *Richard III*—she's not just old, she's dead. She just comes back as a ghost and haunts everybody.

I wanted to play Nina, Pirate Jenny, Elizabeth Proctor, Queen Ann. I wanted to play Juliet, for God's sake. By the time I was in my third year of NYU, I had never played anyone my own age. And with just one production remaining, it looked like I would never have to, oops, I mean *get to* act my age.

Conversations with My Fat: Part Two

By this time, I was having so many conversations about my fat with other people that it made him feel very important and he became even more impertinent.

FAT: *Hey, I heard the faculty is talking about us.*
CAM: *No, they're talking about you. They think I should get rid of you.*
FAT: *Why?*
CAM: *Because they think I'll have more opportunities, working without you.*
FAT: *But you don't want more opportunities.*
CAM: *Of course I do. I want all the opportunities I can get.*

FAT: *Really? Are you saying you want to be successful?*
CAM: *Duh! Who doesn't?*
FAT: *I don't know . . . I just have a hard time believing that someone who really wants to be successful would work so hard to keep me around.*
CAM: *Are you suggesting that I keep you around because I have a fear of success?*
FAT: *Man, took you long enough.*
CAM: *Well, I do want to be successful and I'm sick of playing characters over fifty years old. I'm never going to get to play an ingenue as long as you're around.*
FAT: *You mean you'll never <u>have</u> to play an ingenue as long as I'm around.*
CAM: *But I want to play an ingenue.*
FAT: *No, you don't. Admit it, you're terrified of being the object of someone's desire and that's why you keep me here.*
CAM: *Fuck you!*

He had a point. I was terrified of intimacy, and the last place I wanted it to rear its ugly head was in NYU's hallowed halls of white light and acceptance. And the thing about success is you have to work for it, and I wasn't sure I had what it took. But as long as I was fat, I wouldn't have to question my talent and my commitment because I could chalk up every rejection to my weight.

*   *   *

There was no denying the anticipation of that grand finale, the "Big Production." The class was divided into three casts. One cast would be performing the lavish costume drama *A Month in the Country*. The second would be performing Chekhov's elegant *Uncle Vanya*. And the third cast would be slogging around in a muddy potato field in Caryl Churchill's dark drama *Fen*. Now, some of my classmates had to consult the posted lists to find out which play they'd be in. Me, I kind of had it figured out on my own. You see, there are a few things I know for certain: I gotta pay my taxes, some day I'm gonna die, and if there's a muddy potato field, I'm gonna be in it. Just for fun I checked the list. Not so much to see if I was on it, but to see what other unlucky bastards would be slogging around in the spuds.

Also on the list was the name of the director: David Chambers. Even I knew who that was. He was an up-and-coming big shot on the regional theater scene. We were all so excited to work with him, partly because if he liked us, he'd be able to employ us down the line.

A day before rehearsals began, we got the news. David Chambers had received a better offer. What? A better offer than potatoes at NYU? With such short notice, the only director they could get was some guy named Tony. Typical. We were all so pissed off. Our last show and we get some nobody named Tony.

Enter Tony. Tony Kushner. Had we known he'd go on to win a Pulitzer Prize and an armful of Tony Awards for his play *Angels in America*, maybe we wouldn't have been so snotty.

Tony was given the six actors in my class that the administration never knew what to do with. The two black women. The quirky ingenue, the recluse, the homosexual, and the fat girl. *C'est moi*.

The first day of rehearsal, Tony said, "I don't know who any of you are. So let's just go down the list of characters. You take the first one, the second, third, fourth, and so on until they're all gone." Now, I was sitting directly to his right so I took the first listed character, the ingenue, the girl who kisses the boy (ha, ha, ha, ha, ha). And Marissa, the real ingenue in our class, had to play the grandmother, which I kinda got a kick out of. I'm thinking "Come on, Marissa, show me you can *age*." And so we read the play. It was fine. It's a great play. It didn't matter who read what, it was always going to work.

After that first reading, Tony said, "Okay, we're going to read it again and this time you tell me who *you* want to play." Almost before Tony had finished, Marissa said, "I'll play the ingenue." And the other parts were quickly snatched up, and then I said, "I'll play the grandmother. It's mine!"

We read the play again, and it was great. This, I figured, was the way it would be cast. And then Tony said, "Y'know, fate is wise. I think the first way we read it is the way it should be cast."

CAM: Um . . . excuse me, Tony. I think you've made a mistake. I played the ingenue the first time through.

TONY: I know, I think that's how it should be done.

CAM: That's very funny. Really, but I think you should let Marissa play the ingenue, and I'll play the grandmother—that would be best.

TONY: Camryn, why wouldn't you want to play the lead?

CAM: Cuz I play grandmas, that's what I do. I've never played anyone my own age. I really don't want to rock the boat. I'll play the grandmother.

TONY: I'm sorry you feel that way, Camryn. But I've made up my mind. You will play the ingenue.

I was going to have to kiss a boy onstage. In the seven years that I went to college to study acting, I had never kissed a boy onstage. During rehearsals for our play I would tell my stage lover, "Okay, here is where we kiss," and I'd kiss the air pretending to kiss him before adding "We'll do it for real during the performance."

And thus I tried to avoid it for as long as possible. Finally Tony said, "You *have* to do this." He pushed all the other actors out of the room, put a dim light on us, and said, "Go ahead, be brave."

I did it. I kissed a man onstage. I played a woman my own age, and in my final year at NYU I became an actor. But not just any actor . . . an actor with a master's degree. Tony Kushner was sent to me from on high. He is truly an angel in America.

Well, I hung my master's degree on my wall, looked at it from time to time, and asked myself that same question that all young actors out of conservatory programs ask themselves: "What the fuck do I do now?"

While that insidious question will invade the psyche of every performer at some time or another, at NYU it was momentarily answered for me. You see, another one of the perks of going to one of the League schools is that you get to attend what they call the League Presentations, a very high-powered audition, at Juilliard. Producers, agents, casting agents, directors, all came to prey on the new talent that was soon to flood the market. We all got one shot, three minutes to display our wares, to impress them, to convince them that we were the artist of the moment, the star of the future. My scene partner and I did a scene from the play *Children of a Lesser God*. We both knew sign language and we wanted to do something that would stand out. It was also a good ploy on my part, I thought, because the director of the presentation thought that I should have a small part in another scene just to make sure everyone knew I could talk and that I wasn't really deaf. So, I was pretty excited to finally be able to strut my stuff for all of these people who could change my life.

Here's how it worked. Each agent, director, casting director, producer, etc. was given a work sheet with their company's name on the top. While they watched each school's presentation, they would write down the names of the students they were interested in meeting and possibly signing. At the end of each presentation, the industry folks would hand their work sheet to a monitor. No one told us how this information would be distributed. We had no idea how we'd learn about our fate. But I should have been able to guess that if there was an extra-painful, extra-humiliating way to break the news, they'd think of it. After our class did our one-hour presentation, we took a break, enjoyed some snacks and beverages, and were told that in a few minutes we'd be invited to a room where all the lists would be posted for us to peruse. Ah, back to the Great Wall of Lists.

Let me just make this clear: We were about to be confronted with dozens upon dozens of lists. Everyone was excited to get into that room. There was a palpable ache in the air. The wildest fantasies collided with the worst nightmares. What if everyone wanted me? What if no one wanted me? Rationality didn't stand a chance. Everything was so heightened. All serious actors have at least a hundred occasions when they wrongly convince themselves that this is the most important moment in their career, the defining moment in their lives. I didn't need much convincing.

We were finally allowed to enter the hall, pen and paper at the ready to take down the names of all the agencies and producers and casting people who'd want to meet us. It was like scanning a list of survivors from a war or natural disaster, only we were looking for our own names, hoping we had survived.

Every wall had rows of sheets with the agent's name on top, a contact number, and then a list of the actors they were interested in seeing. My classmates were walking around the room, eyeing the lists closely. Some people were writing feverishly: ICM, William Morris, J. Michael Bloom, Rosemarie Tichler, Meg Simon. Some were not. *I* was not. I felt so ashamed. No one wanted to meet me, not one. No agents, no directors, nothing. And I walked away from Juilliard wondering if I could ever face my classmates again, knowing they also knew that no one wanted to meet me.

We still had a few more weeks of classes left, but I couldn't go. At school my classmates were buzzing. "I met with Gersh and William Morris yesterday." "Yeah, I think I'm going to sign with ICM." Not me. I felt stupid, ugly, fat, untalented, and pathetic. I dropped out of sight.

At the time I was up against a wall of blinding pain. I had been rejected in the one arena where I thought I had some talent. My acting was the one thing I had to offer, and no one wanted it. And if no one wanted me, how could I even consider teaching others? Even my fallback plan had been ruined. And at this point, world leader was pretty much out of the question.

I spent eight months in solitude. Lots of therapy, lots of weeping, lots of feeling sorry for myself.

It didn't take me long to put the weight back on, and I can't remember a time when I felt more miserable. People always say that those college days are the best years of your life. I left NYU thinking "God, I hope not."

Parents Know How to Push Your Buttons

(because, hey, they sewed them on)

I had hit rock bottom.

During my three years at NYU I had developed elaborate defense mechanisms and an ordered system of self-reliance. Much of this, of course, was a facade. I was honing my lying skills as I perfected my acting skills. I was putting forth the image of the jolly fat girl to cover up a morass of self-hatred, despair, and deceit. Nobody knew any of my secrets or anything substantial about me. I was defending the inner sanctum like a lion defends her cubs. Only I was a cub. I was told and I believed that it was my fault for being fat and that if I wanted to change it I could. Not only did I suffer the slings and arrows of being a fat girl in this soci-ety, but I suffered the shame and humiliation of knowing it was all at my hand, and that is why I built up the armor and the weapons to keep anyone from discovering it. But the system was built on a precarious foundation; lies and amphetamines do not a sturdy base make.

I was sliding down the slippery slope. After fighting and strug-gling and kicking and screaming for that fucking master's degree, I skipped my graduation ceremony. I couldn't face anybody. Ob-viously people were going to ask about the Leagues, and I would have had to say "Nobody wants me." My parents asked about graduation and were looking forward to hopping on a plane. But with my well-crafted lies I was able to convince them that we weren't having a ceremony. And in reality, marching at gradua-tion is really an afterthought. The truth is, the League Presenta-tions are the de facto graduation at NYU. Either the agents, pro-ducers, and casting directors want you or they don't. You are either ushered into the business with fanfare and congratulations or you are ignored and dismissed. Leagues provide the equivalent moment of throwing our mortarboards skyward in celebration. But for me there was no celebration, only embarrassment. I couldn't have imagined walking up to the stage, accepting my diploma, moving my tassel from right to left, and returning to my seat with all my classmates watching and whispering and my par-ents sitting there, wondering "What the hell is she going to do now?" Or worse: "Well, there was forty-five grand down the drain."

All that time I was fighting for that degree to please my parents, to have that teaching career path open to me, but that's not what I wanted. Nobody goes to NYU to get a master's to teach drama.

We all wanted to act. For a living. We wanted to be good, the best. And everybody who was anybody had just told me that I wasn't, so that piece of paper didn't mean anything to me anymore.

I was still doing speed because, sad as this sounds, it was the only thing that was bringing me any acceptance. Men paid more attention to me, I was less self-conscious, but I was also numb with despair. I was less self-conscious because I just didn't give a shit anymore. I was bartending four nights a week at a sleazy neighborhood bar on the Upper East Side, as far from the downtown epicenter of disappointment as I could be. As a bartender, if you remember a guy's name and what he drinks, you are the equivalent of, well, a god. I was Bacchus. Every night I would set my sights on a different guy and systematically reel him in. There's nothing quite like gratuitous, semianonymous sex to make you feel really good about yourself. Just some more self-flagellation. I began to wonder if I *were* a lesbian because I hated being with these men. I always thought that if I were thin, men would be attracted to me and that would make everything all right. But it doesn't matter if *they* like you if you hate yourself. I hated myself on so many levels. I was lying, doing drugs, being promiscuous, I thought I couldn't act. The only redeeming feature of my downward spiral was that I wasn't hurting anybody else and I vowed not to take anybody else with me.

I had cut myself off from everybody who cared about me. I only wanted to be with people who didn't care about me because they wouldn't challenge me. They wouldn't insist that I get my shit together.

So there I was, at some guy's house doing speed and philosophizing about anything at all as long as we didn't have to talk about ourselves, when my chest began to tighten. I was short of breath. I lost my bearings. Waves of fear and paranoia swept over me. I thought I was dying.

I asked this guy to call an ambulance but he refused because he said he had so much stuff lying around the house that he was afraid he'd get busted. So I sat on his bathroom floor until morning. When he went to work, I called two friends to come over and watch me sleep, so they could wake me up if I stopped breathing. My heart just couldn't take any more, and I mean that in every sense.

After that near-fatal overdose, I had two choices. I could continue down this path of self-destruction or I could grow up. But, as we all know, growing up is rough.

In the next few months, I quit smoking, quit speed, quit having gratuitous sex, quit lying (except to my parents), and I went into a period of major withdrawal. I was regaining control of my life, but at a price. I was also gaining all the weight back. What had taken me a year and a hundred grams of speed to lose, I put back on in four months. But I had decided that it was better to go into a bathroom, get on a scale, and be disappointed by the readout than to be lying on a cold bathroom floor wondering if I was going to die. All my defenses were being stripped away and I was bare. My illusory armor had protected me from the stinging bite of truth. And now I had to face the rest of my life.

Change can be exhilarating, but it takes a toll. I was feeling stronger and more fragile at the same time. I had never reached out before because I was too busy erecting walls to keep everybody away. But in my efforts to face the truth about myself I began reaching out. For the first time I allowed myself to need somebody. I must have been out of my mind because I looked to my parents for comfort.

I got on a plane and flew to Los Angeles. The city where what you look like is the most important thing. I felt fatter, stupider, uglier, more pathetic than I ever had. Welcome to L.A.

Before I go into all the hurtful stuff I went through with my parents, I want to tell you what makes them so special.

They are fearless when it comes to defending the weak and attacking immorality. Like a lot of lefties, they were galvanized and motivated by McCarthyism, the civil rights movement, and Vietnam. Everyone was picketing, protesting, and sitting-in back then, but they *still* fight the good fight. Whether it's bringing medical supplies to Cuba or hopping on a bus full of senior citizens to protest nuclear sites, they are still invested in creating a brighter future, not for themselves but for the rest of humanity.

Protesting injustice is a way of life in my family. One summer in Santa Cruz I was arrested and thrown in jail for participating in a pro-choice rally. So I called my parents to get me out.

CAM: Mom, Mom, I'm in jail.

MOM: You're what?

CAM: I'm in jail, Mom.

MOM: Oh my God, what for?

CAM: Mom, I was arrested for participating in a pro-choice rally.

MOM: Oh, honey, that's wonderful. *Mazeltov!* Jerry, Camryn got arrested for civil disobedience.

DAD: That's great honey, Go Go Go! Fight fight fight.

MOM: Stop it, Jerry. It's long distance prime time, for God's sake.

CAM: *(screaming)* Mom? Get me out of jail!

MOM: No, honey, you stay in there and make your point. *Click.*

On my table in my living room is a photograph of my father standing in front of a segregated restaurant, holding a picket sign. It says DON'T DISCRIMINATE! My mother took that photograph fifty years ago. That is my legacy, that is what I am most proud of.

But parents know how to push your buttons, because, hey, they sewed them on.

Now, my parents have always been offended by my weight, embarrassed maybe. They had hounded me throughout my childhood about my weight. And they did what any good parent in Southern California would do: They sent me to psychiatrists, to hypnotists; they bribed me. When I was eleven, I signed my first contract: "If you lose 15 pounds by March we'll buy you a brand-new bike." And I signed it. "If you lose 30 pounds by September we'll buy you an 8-track player." And I signed it. I always got the feeling my parents would have sold their souls if it would've made me thin.

My parents had been so happy when I had lost all that weight. I should have known that when I told them that I had quit smoking I wasn't going to get any Mazeltovs from them. No, they were afraid I would put the weight back on. My dad would ask me on the phone if I had gained any weight since I had quit, and I'd say "A little. You know, it's to be expected."

I couldn't bear the thought of another lecture on "the importance of being thin" by Sylvia and Jerry Manheim. So I didn't tell them the truth. I thought I'd just surprise them when I got off the plane.

I tried to hide behind the other passengers as we disembarked, just to delay the inevitable frowns of disappointment. But there was no getting around it. I was there. They were there. At some point, we were going to see each other.

When they saw me, they didn't even try to mask their obvious disappointment. Neither of my parents share my acting skills, so their tight-lipped disapproval registered as plain as day. I could sense that all the plans my mother had made to show me off to her friends were now being reorganized in her brain.

My father was just plain quiet. The usual family conversations about politics and the national *zeitgeist* were replaced by a brittle silence. The whole point of my trip home at this fragile time in my life was for support, caring, you know, good old-fashioned we-love-you-just-the-way-you-are sentiments. But instead we moved past each other in the kitchen and the hallways with barely a word exchanged. When I needed to be feeling warmth, all I got was the cold stare of judgment. My father is not one to bite his lip and edit himself. (I guess I got that from him.) I knew he would eventually confront me, so it shouldn't have been a surprise when he blurted out, "You told me on the phone that you had only gained a little bit of weight. Why did you lie to me?"

I was stunned. "I don't know, Dad, I guess I didn't want to disappoint you."

And I had a minifantasy that he would put his arms around me and say "Don't be ridiculous, we wouldn't be disappointed in you. We love you. We just wanted to know how you were doing."

But instead I got: "Well, maybe you should start smoking again until you can successfully keep the weight off, then you can think about quitting." Yes, my father, one of my primary caregivers, looked me in the eye and suggested I start smoking again! I don't remember how I responded at that moment, but the next day I packed my bags and left. I didn't speak to my father for close to a year.

My mom would call and beg me to talk to him. She would

plead with me to attend family gatherings, but I refused as long as I knew he'd be there. My father wrote me letters, trying to explain how being fat was virtually a crime against humanity. He would couch it in I'm-saying-all-this-for-you terms, about how I'd have better success with men and acting jobs if I lost weight. After a particularly painful acting rejection, he wrote this in a letter:

> . . . *heard also that you came in second on two auditions. I'm sorry about that—but I must say—I'm not surprised* . . .

That's when I started sending his letters back unopened. My father has always been a vicious letter writer. I'd watched him fight many battles with his mighty pen. But now he was turning its poison on me. He wanted to fight but I wasn't taking the bait. And it made him powerless. He couldn't win if I didn't engage him. I knew I could never win a war of words or ideas with him because he is a logician who can distort reality to suit the needs of his position. He is a fierce competitor. And nothing pisses off a fighter more than an opponent who refuses to fight. I would get reports from my mom that it was driving him mad, which gave me great comfort.

My mom was always trying to be the peacemaker between my dad and me. It was easy to resent my father because his transgressions were so obvious. My mother's attempts to control my weight were more subtle but no less destructive.

Do you remember the go-with-the-parents rule?

We all know this rule. Go with the folks they pay, go alone, they don't. When I was a kid and I'd go to the movies with my parents, they'd always buy my ticket. But if I asked for five dollars to go with a friend, they'd say, "If you want to go to the movies and you want us to pay, then you go with us, and you suffer!" When I was a kid I had no money, so I took advantage of this rule. Now I'm no longer a kid and make my own living, but I still take advantage of this rule. Let's face it, you want your parents to buy you things. It's a law of nature.

Several years after my fallout with my dad, my mother and I set out on our obligatory shopping spree. Oh, joy. I was shopping for, a drum roll please . . . a dress for my ten-year high-school reunion. *If* I decided to go.

I didn't want to shop at the fat-girls' stores, because it embarrassed my mother, which in turn embarrassed me.

So I always contemplated saying "Mom, why don't you give me a couple hundred bucks, I'll go shopping by myself, and I'll spare us both the agony." But then the *Go-with-the-Parents Rule* wouldn't have applied, so we were off. Martyrs walking into the arena to be crucified would have been more optimistic.

I remembered that Bloomingdale's had a large women's section, but it didn't have an obvious fat-girl name to it, like Big and Beautiful, so we could shop there and my mother would never know that we were in a (whispering) "fat-girls' store."

As I was trying on clothes, my mom wanted to get into the dressing room with me; I don't know why—maybe to marvel at my fat. Next stop, Judgment City. Now, there are two main reasons why I don't want my mom in there. One, it makes me feel very uncomfortable. And two, because I am so fat, there's no goddamn room for her. So I always send her out to get me things. "Can you get me this in blue? Can you get me shoes that match the dress? Can you go down to housewares and look around for an hour?" So I'm trying on this dress, which I liked but was a little too small, and I asked my mother if she would get me the next size up—a 22. While my mom disappeared for the next five minutes, I stood there amazed that I was actually considering wearing a dress to this reunion. The last time I had worn a dress was that awful pink floral number that my mom had strong-armed me into wearing to David Rosenthal's bar mitzvah. (Yes, she made me go.) She returned with the dress, tossed it over the door, and waited patiently for me to model it. I tried it on, and it didn't fit. Shit. I couldn't believe I didn't even fit into a 22 anymore. I was devastated. My mom called out, "How does it look? Is that the one?" There I was in a cell of despair, not even close to fitting into this fucking dress. I was trapped in this tiny cubicle, four feet by four feet, filled with mirrors. It wasn't so much a prison cell; that would actually have been an improvement. It was more like a cell in a madhouse, where all of your nightmares were crashing in around you. It's the fat-girls' section, for God's sake. Couldn't they give us a bigger dressing room? So let's sum up: tiny cell, ill-fitting dress, mirrors on every wall, revealing all my inadequacies, a thin unlockable door, barely protecting me from my overly enthusiastic mother, and no emergency exit, no fire escape, no secret trapdoor, no way out.

And again: "Honey, do you like it? Come on out and let me see it."

Oh my God, panic mode. There was no way in hell I was going to model a size 22 that was way too small. "Uh, it's not really . . . uh . . . me. It's too . . . uh . . . blue."

I started beating myself up and, defeated, I took the dress off and hung it back up. And then I noticed the tag. My mother had not brought me a size 22, she had brought me a size 16.

Now, my mother is a teacher. I did not ask her to bring me a whole new selection, I did not ask her to bring me a new color. I simply asked for the next size up, a 22. Same fucking digits, Mom!

But no. My mother thought that if she brought me a smaller size, she'd throw it over the door, I wouldn't notice the size, I'd put it on, it wouldn't fit, I'd be so frustrated that I'd beat myself up, and that would be the day I would miraculously decide to lose all the weight. But what really happened is my mother threw the dress over the door, I didn't notice the size, I put it on, it didn't fit, I got so frustrated that I did indeed beat myself up, and I wanted to go home and eat a single-serving pint of Häagen-Dazs!

It wasn't the first time she had used subtle sleight-of-hand to trick me. But this time I'd had enough. I checked the dress tag again to be sure, swung open the door, and in the middle of the fat-girls' section of Bloomingdale's I screamed, "Mom, WAKE UP . . . I'M FAT!"

P.S. There is no such thing as a free dress.

*   *   *

Right about now you might be rolling your eyes and worrying that this is the it's-all-my-parents'-fault chapter. Well, it's not. That's the next chapter. Just kidding. I'm not blaming my parents for my being fat. I'm simply acknowledging the truth. It's not my interpretation, not my revisionism, it's just what happened. And it has shaped me, made me who I am today. I have a fierce I'll-show-you attitude, largely due to the disparity between what my parents thought the world would offer a fat girl and what I knew I could achieve.

Between the you-should-consider-smoking statement and the size-16 fiasco, I felt I had every right to say "You are no longer my parents." For two people who had devoted their entire lives to fighting for the underdog, it always puzzled me that they couldn't see their own daughter as an underdog who needed their support.

I must admit I did scare them. I had them believing that I might never talk to them again. I hadn't shown up for any family gatherings in a good eight months. And as embarrassing as it was for them to have a fat daughter, it's even more embarrassing for a Jewish family to have that daughter skip a family function. But when my mom pleaded with me to come to my uncle's sixtieth birthday in New York, I figured it was time to extend the olive branch.

I hadn't seen or spoken to my father since I began returning his letters unopened eight months earlier. So everyone was speculating about whether I'd show up or not. It was the $64,000 question. The truth is I hated not talking to my father. I love my dad dearly and actually missed his impromptu lectures on the electoral college. I didn't want to become the cliché of the estranged youngest child. Plus it was going to be at the famous restaurant, Tavern on the Green, which I had driven past so many times before and always wondered what all the hubbub was about.

I parked my motorcycle, tucked Uncle Bill's present under my arm, and set my jaw, ready for an assault that never came. At the party, for the first time in my life, I saw my father vulnerable. He was not antagonistic but gentle. He was not confrontational but warm. He trod lightly around me, and even though he didn't apologize—and never would—his body language was very contrite. My whole life I had wanted my father to forgive me for disappointing him. But I had it wrong. That wasn't what I needed. I needed to forgive him. And in that moment, at Tavern on the Green, with my entire extended family celebrating Uncle Bill's birthday, I learned an essential life lesson. You should never give someone else the power to save you. You alone have the power to transform the quality of your life. From that day forth, my relationship with my father would never be the same. It wouldn't always be perfect, but it would evolve into a healthy father-daughter relationship.

All parents want their adult children to experience love, respect, and lucrative employment, all of which my folks thought would be beyond my grasp if I didn't lose weight. I understand their concern. In fact, sadly, in many cases they are right. The world isn't lining up to love, respect, and employ fat people.

I only hope that when I have children and make their lives miserable, if they write a book, they'll be kind.

The Road
to Wellness

The next few years were about healing. The reconnection with
my parents gave me more confidence. I was on the road to recovery, and though I had put all the weight back on, it finally occurred to me that when I'd lost the weight, I had lost myself. That
conforming to a standard that was not developed with me in mind
would be more counterproductive than good. I started to own my
body, and I felt stronger and healthier than ever.

I realized that if my happiness was contingent on my finding
work as an actor, I was not going to be happy most of the time.
Every successful actor will tell you about the ten years when she
couldn't even get arrested. Acting forces you to ask yourself, "Can
my constitution take a decade of constant rejection?" And after

ten years, you either make it or you don't. And the problem is they don't tell you in advance. You have to roll the dice. So even if you can answer yes to the constitution question, you still might wind up miserable and broke and instead of being a wide-eyed, optimistic twenty-five-year-old, you're a cynical, gnarled thirty-five-year-old with a heart full of resentment and $45,000 in outstanding student loans. One of the most important lessons my father taught me was always have a fallback plan. While I knew acting was the thing that most stirred my passions, I was no one-trick pony. I could always *teach* acting. Actors often fall into the trap of thinking that if they're not acting, or doing something related to acting, like teaching (which only makes them miserable anyway), there is nothing under the sun that will bring them fulfillment. I didn't want to be that typical actor. I knew I could explore other vocations without compromising my commitment to acting. And that didn't mean waiting tables. Can you imagine me, with my attitude: "I'm sorry, you want what? Get it yourself!"

I was determined to find something I was good at that wouldn't kill my spirit.

What I forgot to mention earlier is that I didn't go directly to the University of California at Santa Cruz but took a little detour by way of Cabrillo Junior College. I applied to UC Santa Cruz but was denied admittance on account of insufficient language credits. I had done well in all my other classes but lacked that certain linguistic gene, and thus failed both French and Spanish. Not once, but twice. I was so bad at languages I couldn't even remember the swear words.

So here was the scenario: The daughter of Jewish parents, two very proud educators, who had sent their only son to Harvard, was about to enroll at Cabrillo Community College. Which in itself isn't such a crime, but in accordance with the Jewish law: "All daughters of academic scholars must enter a top-rated university. And if you don't, you will not be allowed to be buried in a Jewish cemetery." Now, in order to get into one of those top-rated universities, you have to have passed two semesters of a language, *any* language. It seemed so easy. And I'm sure it is, if you have the gene.

When I told my parents I would be enrolling at Cabrillo Junior College to collect my language units, it wasn't pretty. But junior college was better than no college, and who knows, maybe my Russian ancestors would rise from the grave and take my final exams for me. I went to the foreign-language board. Portuguese, I don't think so. Swahili, you've got to be kidding. Chinese, not a chance. And then I spied a tiny 3 × 5 card, that read ONE TIME OFFER—SIGN LANGUAGE FOR LANGUAGE CREDITS—ONE SEMESTER ONLY! You see, sign language was never considered a language. In the past it had always been offered as a humanity. Apparently they had hired this very famous sign language teacher, but nobody was taking the class, so in an effort to save face, they were offering it as a language to boost enrollment. But for only one semester, and I needed two. So I took beginning and intermediate sign language simultaneously. Wouldn't you know it, intermediate was at 9 A.M. and the beginning class was at 2 P.M. Just one of life's ways of saying "Don't think you're getting away with anything, because you're not."

I took those two classes and somehow managed to get an A− in intermediate and a B+ in beginning. In any other situation, I would have protested the illogical distribution of those grades, but I felt like I had just pulled off the crime of the century, earning two language credits in one semester without ever having to say

"*Je m'appelle* Camryn." Don't get me wrong, sign language is a complete and complex language, but apparently one I had the learning gene for. Now I was allowed back into the Jewish Community Center and into the University of California at Santa Cruz. Phew!

Author's note: I don't know why I was rushing so fast to get into the university, because it was at Cabrillo College that I met Wilma Marcus, the acting teacher who first inspired me and gave me my wings. I vowed then, if I ever got an award, she would be the first person I'd thank.

For several years I had no occasion to use my signing skills, until one afternoon when I was walking down the street in Santa Cruz and I saw a group of police officers standing over a man who had been hit by a car. The man's eyes were wide open, and the policemen where shouting at him *"WHAT—IS—YOUR—NAME?"* "Tell us your phone number!" But the man seemed dazed and was not offering up any information. And then I knew, I *knew* why he didn't answer. I pushed my way past the blue uniforms and knelt down close to the man and signed "Are you deaf?" When his eyes lit up and he signed "Yes," for the first time my hands were not being cuffed by police officers but highly valued. I got his name, his number, his address, and his insurance information. The policeman asked, "Would you be kind enough to come to the hospital with us to help the doctors assess his injury?" I had never been asked so politely to get into the back of a police car. For the first time in my life, the police were relying on me. It was definitely a new experience.

When we got to the hospital, his family had already arrived. I was hoping that with the family there my rusty signing skills would no longer be needed and I'd get a ride back home in that cool police car. Maybe they'd even let me play with the radio and put out an APB. That fantasy was short-lived. The man's parents, brother, wife, and three children were all deaf. I spent eight hours with him and his family, doing my best quasi-interpreting, an emergency hybrid of actual sign language, finger-spelling, Pictionary, and charades. I learned more in one day than I did in most of my additional studies. After that experience, I wanted to learn sign language for real. So the next time I wouldn't be pulling my earlobe, screaming "Sounds like, sounds like!" to a room full of deaf people. What an idiot.

Thankfully in 1990 the Americans with Disabilities Act (ADA) was passed. Now there are laws that protect deaf people by insisting that all hospitals have qualified interpreters on call twenty-four hours a day.

When the ADA was passed, I was in New York City and decided to enroll in an Interpreters Training Program to study the one thing that held me back from college, a language. I loved it. All of a sudden there was something that interested me, something that would allow me to make a contribution. Interpreting is a bridge for people who might otherwise have difficulty communicating. I was honored to be a part of that bridge. When I graduated from NYU I thought my days as a student were over, but I devoted the next two and a half years to studying sign language.

The irony of it all was, now that I had found something that made me feel good about myself, I had become interesting to other people and I started to get acting work. A little work as an interpreter, a little work as an actor. Things were looking up.

Perhaps subconsciously I was drawn to sign language and the deaf community because I had always felt like an outcast. We had a lot more in common than meets the ear. As I connected with this powerful minority, I was energized by their solidarity as they struggled for their basic rights. The Americans with Disabilities Act provided the legal foundation for deaf people to demand equality. At Gallaudet University for the deaf, the students were able, through protests, to unseat the hearing president and replace her with I. King Jordan, a deaf man. Student sit-ins, the underdog prevailing, demands for human rights—it all reminded me of my roots.

Buoyed by a little employment and a good cause, I set my sights on getting more involved in the theater community. There was a wonderful casting director named Natalie Hart. She remembered me from the dreaded League Presentations and asked me to be a reader for her. A job that used to be frowned on but now is coveted by actors. I would read the play, familiarize myself with all the parts, and read opposite all of the actors who came to audition. It was a good way to spend a day with a director and watch him or her give notes to the actors. And there was always the hope that after offering your services for free for two, three, however many days, the director or casting director might actually let you audition. That's what we prayed for anyway.

I started to understand what a good audition looks like. I could have written a book on the do's and don'ts of auditioning. In fact, I became such a good reader that I was beginning to suspect that Natalie would never actually recommend me for a part because she relied on me so heavily.

About a year after I had proved myself with Natalie, she called me and asked if I'd be available to be her reader for an *entire week*. And it would pay six bucks an hour. "Sure I'm free, but what's the big commotion about?" She then told me they were casting *Merrily We Roll Along* at Arena Stage, and Stephen Sondheim himself would be casting the show. Gulp. "Stephen Sondheim would be there?" Oh my God! "Sure I'm free, when do I start?" I studied the script. I knew every part. I was going to be the best damn reader this *Side by Side* of Sondheim. And trust me, *Anyone Can Whistle* cuz I did it all the way to the studio. I remember sitting in that room when some of the greatest actors on Broadway came in to meet Mr. Sondheim. I couldn't tell who I was more enamored with, Stephen or Broadway legend Victor Garber. Natalie gave me the nod about an hour into the session—that nod all actors look for before taking our first breaths. I knew I was doing a good job.

When the week was about to wrap up, Stephen gave me a curious look and out of nowhere asked me if I could sing. I, of course, said yes. It didn't matter what he was looking for, I could do it. He could have asked me if I could juggle while hang-gliding, and I would have said, "As a matter of fact, I spent five summers at hang-gliding camp and four summers juggling with the Flying Karamazov Brothers at the Renaissance Faire." The whole point is to get the job first, then worry about your qualifications. So if, miracle of miracles, you land the part of the busty juggling hang-glider, you take the crash course then and, of course, hope you don't crash. But luckily, I *can* sing. I'm no Bernadette Peters, but I can carry a tune. So after I said yes, Stephen (may I call you Stephen?) said, "Well, have your agent call us and we'll set up an audition." OhmyGod. OhmyGod! Stephen Sondheim wants me to audition for him. OhmyGod! All I have to do is call my agent. Fuck, I don't have an agent! Fuck! Fuck! Fuck! My one chance to break out of this starving actor hell, and I don't have one of those little Satans called an agent. "Uhmmm . . . er . . . uhmmm, excuse me, but . . . I don't have . . . an agent, so perhaps I could make arrangements with Natalie to audition for you?" Stephen looked at me like I was an alien, then he looked at Natalie and calmly instructed, "Well, first *get* her an agent, then call that agent and set up an audition for her." I could see that Natalie was both shocked by the order but also proud that he took such a liking to me. And when Natalie said "I'll get right on that," I thought, "Well, I'll be darned, this is how it happens, this is how lives are changed." Stephen Sondheim has that power. The power to change someone's life. A week later I had an agent. Five years after I graduated from NYU. Finally I could begin.

Though I will be forever indebted to Stephen Sondheim, I never went on that audition. I hadn't trained my voice in two years and I didn't want to waste his time with some unrefined caterwauling. I took a rain check.

During the following year I got a few paying jobs. A tiny role in a Brian De Palma film, *Bonfire of the Vanities*, a small role on *Law and Order*, a chorus part at the Public Theater. Enough tidbits to keep me hopeful as I pursued the gypsy life.

My agent called. I so loved being able to say that. "My agent called" and told me I had an audition for a movie called *The Road to Wellville*. The part was a nurse. I had come to expect that if there was a part for a nurse or a prison warden or the best friend next door that I would be called. I spent most of my early professional career playing women whose only line was "Oh really. And then what happened?" Basically a glorified extra so the leading lady wouldn't have to deliver a bunch of soliloquies.

I've been criticized by my friends for not knowing the who's who of contemporary filmmakers, so when my agent said the film was going to be directed by Alan Parker, I really had no idea who that was. Maybe it was better that way. I walked in and met Alan

Parker, not knowing he was responsible for such great films as *Midnight Express, Mississippi Burning, The Commitments*, and countless others. So, I wasn't fazed when I went to meet him. *The Road to Wellville* was a film about bodies. All kinds of them. Fat, thin, short, funny looking, and Alan was looking for people with all kinds of body shapes. He asked me if I could ride a horse, and once again, like all well-trained actors I told him, "Absolutely." If he had pursued it, I was prepared to tell him that I spent every summer at my family's ranch in, uh, Montana, just a two-day trot from Peoria. Never mind that I hadn't been on a horse in over twenty years. Then he asked me how I would feel about getting naked. I said, "I feel fine about it, how would you feel?" He laughed, which I sensed was a big accomplishment. Finally I just said, "Listen, I'll ride a horse naked if you want me to." I got the part. That was the good news. The bad news: He really expected me to follow through on that whole get-naked thing. You'd think I would have learned by now, but knee-jerk I-can-do-it actor's instincts still get me in trouble. Like when the publishers of this book asked, "Do you really think you can write a book?" "Sure," I said. "I spend every summer at my family's book-writing camp in Montana." The problem was that they actually wanted me to write a book, which is a damned sight harder than getting naked.

I hadn't been naked in front of one person for a very long time, so you can imagine how hard it was to get naked in front of fifty people. I tried not to think about it, but the uncloaking was approaching and I was rapidly losing my nerve. The night before I had a good talk with myself and I finally came to this conclusion. If I thought about it in terms of myself and how embarrassing it would be, I'd never be able to do it, but if I thought about it on a more global level, like, if we were ever going to dispel the myths that fat women aren't beautiful, then someone had to get naked and *be* beautiful. So I did it. Over and over again. I got naked, and not just me naked, by myself, all alone, nobody else. No, I got naked next to Bridget Fonda, who, if you ask me, could use a sandwich.

Looking back on this period in my life, it seems as if I traveled so far in such a short time. I had gone from being so depressed about my weight that I risked my life, to taking it all off for millions of people to see and celebrating my body instead of hating it. I can't help but think that those old period costumes triggered some long-forgotten liberation that I had first explored at the Renaissance Faire and that Chloe Blue hadn't been left behind in the rolling hills of Agoura after all.

La
Cucaracha

I had just cleared the major hurdle of embracing my body, and now it was time for someone else to embrace my body. I wanted a boyfriend.

All actors make the mistake of believing that landing that big movie role will change their lives. That Coppola will be on Line 1, *Time* magazine will be on Line 2, and suitors will be on Lines 3, 4, and 5. Ha! *Wellville* wrapped, I went home alone, and there were no messages. You know, I wasn't even that bummed out that Mr. Coppola and *Time* weren't calling. But, damn it, where were the suitors?

Ah, dating. The perilous dance between would-be lovers that can paralyze even the most confident people. We all share the fear that there will be no love connection and we'll have to endure that awful, awkward I'll-call-you lie that signifies the end of a disastrous evening and huge waste of time. But imagine having an equal amount of fear that things will go well, that there will be some crazy chemical connection.

That total lose-lose situation is what we folk with body-image issues face every time we throw our fat on the line and roll the dice. Snake eyes! We lose. Seven! We still lose.

And yet that pull, that constant tug, that yearning for love and affection forces us to confront these fears over and over again like Charlie Brown hoping this time Lucy won't pull the football away. Just like ol' Chuck I've landed on my ass many times over the years.

*   *   *

At seventeen, after I bid adieu to sweet Adam the juggler, my summer romance at the Renaissance Faire, I met Terry Sullivan, whom I considered my first real boyfriend. He was virtually a walking, talking, singing, strumming real-life version of the boy fantasy I had first dreamed about on my family's cross-country trips. Right about the time I thought we were going to get married and spend the rest of our lives together, he moved to Portland . . . without telling me. At UC Santa Cruz, I met and fell in love with Brian Tuller. He cared so much about me that he moved in with me and fell in love . . . with my roommate. My first day at NYU I met Paul Heatherton, the blueprint of a perfect grad-school boyfriend: stunningly handsome, kind, played the flute, and was getting his Ph.D. in physics. We slept in the same bed for over a year before we finally had sex. Soon after he moved to Boston with his

pregnant neighbor. After graduation, I fell in love with Roger In-
nis, a longtime friend with whom I had a torrid tryst while he was
visiting New York. I moved to Los Angeles to be near him. (If you
haven't figured it out by now, I'm a big sucker.) Little did I
know—probably *BECAUSE HE DIDN'T TELL ME!*—Roger
wasn't interested in resuming our affair.

Good grief.

*   *   *

It goes without saying that nobody turns to the personal ads for
help unless there has been some serious disappointment accumulated over the years. And my cup of disappointment had runneth
o'er.

I decided to submit an ad to the personals section of the *New
York Press*. It is not a first option. No matter how clever or confi-
dent-sounding a personal ad is, the subtext is always screaming I
AM DESPERATE! Which, as we all know, is very attractive. So it was
with head bowed and spirits sagging that I crafted this little gem:

BIG BEAUTIFUL AMAZON

5´10´´ Nonreligious, 31. Spontaneous, sociable,
registered to vote. If you're tall, a Democrat, and
a smart ass, let's make babies.

There's nothing quite like reducing yourself to twenty-five
words or less when you've spent your whole life feeling complicated and confused. But there I was, for all to see.

Now, I had done a little research before I submitted my ad to
see what other women of size were saying about themselves. Were

they using misdirection? Were they using euphemisms? Yes, they were using phrases like "big beautiful blonde" or "big beautiful brown-eyed girl." Let's face it, "big beautiful . . ." doesn't mean you're beautiful, it just means you're fat. But you figure they're going to find out at some point, better sooner than later. So I placed "Big" and "Amazon"—two fat code words—around the pretty word in the middle and applauded myself for the forthrightness. In hindsight, if I had really wanted to be forthright, I would have said, BIG FAT BEAUTY, but I wasn't ready for that yet.

CUT TO: D day. The day the ad is scheduled to appear. I didn't yet have a copy of the *New York Press,* but I called my top-secret phone box and, lo and behold, there were seventeen messages. I found it a little hard to believe that even in a city of 10 million, seventeen men wanted to date a fat amazon. I panicked. I needed to confirm that people were responding to *my* ad, and it wasn't all a big mistake. So I called my friend Michael James at the bar he tended and recited my ad to him and asked him to relay my twenty-five words or less to a couple of unbiased patrons. I then asked him to have those customers describe the woman from the ad back to him. I waited while he conducted his impromptu survey. He came back with good news, saying the men had described me to a T. Phew!!!!

And then it dawned on me. Michael's bar carried the *New York Press.* I waited impatiently while he walked to the front door to pick one up. When he returned to the phone I asked him to flip through it and find my ad. He couldn't find it. "What do you mean you can't find it, I got seventeen calls, obviously it's in there."

"Camryn, I swear to you, I can't find it. I have scanned the entire section and it is *not* under the title 'Women Seeking Men.'"

Uh-oh. Now, I was thinking, I either have seventeen messages from soon-to-be-disappointed lesbians or seventeen messages from gay men looking for a big, beautiful, amazon drag queen to call their own. Or worse, my well-conceived personal had found its way into the section: "I WANT TO HANDCUFF YOU, TAKE YOUR MONEY, AND FELLATE A HORSE WHILE YOU WATCH."

"Keep looking, Michael!"

"Camryn, I can't find it."

And then on the other end of the line I hear . . .

"Oh, my God!"

"Oh my God, what?"

"OH MY GOD!"

"MICHAEL, WHAT THE HELL ARE YOU TALKING ABOUT?"

"Camryn, your ad is not under the title 'Women Seeking Men.' Your ad was pick of the week! It was blown up three times the size and put in the center of the page."

Wow. I have to confess that at that point I felt like I had won the personal ad Olympics. Hundreds of submissions—and scores of submissives—and they had chosen mine as pick of the week. Those seventeen messages weren't left for some desperate loser who had finally succumbed to the personals. No, they were left by excited men, hoping to land a date with the twenty-five-words-or-less city champion.

By the end of my weeklong reign as champ, I had seventy calls.

Now, let me tell you how this works just in case you've never experienced the romantic joy of throwing yourself at the mercy of total fucking strangers. I submit the ad and leave an outgoing message on a voice mailbox. Callers then pay $1.50 for the privilege of leaving me a short message. My outgoing message was: "Hi, my name is Camryn. I'm glad you called. Please tell me your favorite joke and the last book you read." Beeep!

I sat by the phone with a little chart I had created. Five columns: Name, Content of Message, Voice/Tone, Artistic Impression, and Technical Merit.

Well, although it was pick of the week, my ad didn't seem to be attracting the Men of Mensa.

Steve: Uh . . . uh . . . uh . . . my name is Steve, and uh . . . a book? My number is . . . uh. . . . Yeah, hope you'll call.

A buck fifty well spent, Steverino.

Harold: Hi, I'm Harold. I'm not registered to vote, but I am a smart ass.

Ass, yes; smart, no. Here's a little tip, Harry. If it was important enough for me to use four of my precious twenty-five words or less on "registered to vote" and "Democrat," then you might not want to lead off with "I'm not registered to vote."

The *New York Press*, however, appreciates the $1.50. *Cha-ching.*

Max: Hi, I'm Max! I don't know any jokes, but the last book I read was *How to Make Beer.*

Ah, a humorless brewmaster, just what I'm looking for. Max, ya shoulda saved that $1.50 for hops and barley.

And on and on to . . .

Dull Guy #63:
Cha-ching, cha-ching, cha-ching $$$$$$$$$$$
And then . . .

Doug: Hi, I'm Doug. I run a politically correct mail-order business. That is, if you're on the left side. *I'm a nonreligious Jew!* The last book I read was Anita Roddick's *Body and Soul,* she's the woman who runs the Body Shop, and my favorite joke is . . . uh, the personals.

It was the weirdest thing. I listened to his message, and nothing derisive or cynical leapt to mind. I played the message again, looking for that slip, that little signal that he needed to be herded into the loser corral with the others. I couldn't find it. His artistic impression and technical merit scores were quite good: 9.8 from the amazon judge. He had definitely made the most of his $1.50.

Wonder of wonder, miracle of miracles. I was going to marry Doug Schmidt. I was going to marry him with a rabbi and a *chuppah*—well, you can't have a rabbi *and a chuppah* at a nonreligious ceremony—but I definitely wanted to stomp on the glass. "Mazeltov!"

I had it all planned out. We'd be married within the year so we could work on making babies in year two. As a liberal, he would understand that all parenting duties would be shared and that I would, of course, continue my career. We would raise the children as "cultural Jews," not religious Jews, meaning they'd get all of Woody Allen's jokes but be mystified and scared by Benjamin Netanyahu. They would go to the best schools, no matter what sacrifices we needed to make. The boys and girls would have the same curfew, no double standards. They would be bar and bat mitzvah-ed just for the cash. Oh, it was going to be perfect.

But first I needed to call him back.

So with that throbbing pit in my stomach, I dialed his number and began the interrogation.

"Okay, Doug. Why did you decide to call me?"

"Well, my business partner, Sydney, brought your ad to my attention and I liked it so much I decided to call."

Note to self: Sydney is cool.

Doug continued with "So, Camryn, when can we meet?"

Oh, shit. That's right. In order to get married and make babies we'd have to meet. Damn!

"Well, Doug, I'm not really ready for that visual commitment yet. How about we talk again tomorrow?"

"No problem."

During the next day's conversation I inexplicably blurted out, "What do you look like?" What was I thinking? That only assured that he was going to ask me back.

"Well," he said, "I look like a not-so-handsome Tom Cruise." I'll take it! A not-so-handsome Tom Cruise pretty much means anyone with dark hair. Images ranging from Albert Brooks to Matthew Broderick raced through my mind, but I was pleased with his modesty and candor.

Then came the inevitable ". . . and what do you look like?"

Ugh. Now came the search for that delicate balance between euphemism and honesty. Fibbing would only lead to trouble later, but there was no shaking the nagging concern that too much *vérité* would preempt the first meeting.

"Well, I'm of good Russian peasant stock. I could work out in the fields all day and come home at night and breed. I'm a big girl, Doug. I don't know how to describe myself . . ."

"There's only one way to find out. When can we meet?"

"You know, I kind of like this you-talk-I-talk thing we've got going. What do you say we do some more of it?"

"No problem, Camryn."

And so we did. For the next week we talked about politics, family, the future, and being nonreligious Jews. The irony of the whole situation was the Sunday before I put my ad in, it was Passover, which is a very traditional Jewish holiday. Now, my very best friend is Adele Irene Agin. Her father is a rabbi. So every year I go to their house for Passover, which I love to do. And every year I ask Rabbi Agin what we're having for dinner, because I get such a kick out of his answer: "Camryn," he says, "it's been the same menu for two thousand years." Now, because I had made such a big deal about not being religious, I thought going to the rabbi's house was too much for a nonreligious Jew, so I didn't say anything to Doug. Until he semiguiltily admitted that he had been to a big Passover Seder the previous week, and we then bonded in that we-go-to-one-Seder-a-year, nonreligious-Jew kind of way.

He persisted in wanting to get together, and I was forced to be more and more creative in coming up with ways to put him off. I just wanted him to fall in love with the girl on the other end of the line first, and then we could meet face-to-face. But he was getting impatient. Monday: Breakfast? Can't, I'm running lines with my friend. Tuesday: Lunch? Oooh, no can do, got an audition. Wednesday: Dinner? Damn, tickets to the theater.

Then he said, "Look, I have a dinner engagement on Thursday night, but I bet I could get out of it early and we could meet up for a drink, what do you say?" "Oh, gosh, Doug, I can't. I also have dinner plans on Thursday." What I didn't want to tell him was that I was going to another Seder (which I had been strong-armed into by a friend) because I was afraid he would begin to question my nonreligious Jew status. He didn't press me on any of my excuses, and since I would be going out of town that weekend and had to work the following week, I managed to put off our meeting for another full seven days. Just enough time to get a facial, a manicure, and liposuction.

He said, "I don't like it, Camryn, but if I have to wait a week, I will."

So we agreed, the following Friday would be our first date.

I went to the Seder with love on my mind. Love quickly soured to exasperated crankiness when I realized the dinner was being attended by six obnoxious actors, the guests of my friend Pamela, and six nerdy business types, the guests of her roommate. That's right, a half-dozen people who can talk only about themselves and a half-dozen people who make the first group seem interesting.

Now, I don't know if you've ever been to a Passover Seder, but there's this book called the Haggadah (huh god 'duh)—which is passed around the table and people ask these questions from it like: Why is this night different from all other nights? When will Elijah drink the wine? Why do we hide the matzoh? When are you going to medical school? And because I had just come from the rabbi's house, I was showing off. "Um, excuse me, who knows what the ten plagues are?" And while the Haggadah was being passed around the table, which isn't as much fun as passing around the Häagen-Dazs, I felt like the Jew of life. The guy at the end of the table begins to read, and I'm thinking, "I know him. I've done a play with that guy." I nudge Pamela, but she shrugs and explains that he's a friend of her roommate and she doesn't even remember his name. Hmmm . . .

I indicate the girl next to him and whisper, "Well, who's his girlfriend?"

"Oh, that's not his girlfriend," she said, "that's his business partner. They run some kind of mail-order business together. I think her name is Sydney."

OH—MY—GOD! I knew I recognized his voice. There he was, Doug Schmidt.

And trust me, you can't make this shit up.

Now, he was a "not-so-handsome Tom Cruise" in the same way that I'm a not-so-skinny Carmen Electra. In other words, no resemblance whatsoever. But the coincidence factor was just too high to ignore, and I set about slipping him a note:

Are you Doug? Doug Schmidt?
What a fucking amazing coincidence.
I'm Camryn.

And I passed it under the table to Doug.

Now, I'm not sure if it's physically possible to choke on matzoh, but poor Doug just about expired when he got the note. He spilled his Manichewitz and did a remarkable spit-take with his gefilte fish before turning a lovely shade of red. On the high holidays we call it burgundy. Pam and I were cracking up in the corner like high school girls. Unfortunately, the rules of the Seder are fairly strict, and you can't just stand up any time you want, yawn, and say, "I've had enough of this Jew Exodus thing. I think I'll get up from the table and talk to *that* guy." No, you have to sit and wait. And wait. And wait. It's the law. And Seders are long.

Now, poor Doug is sitting on *schpilkes*, sending me this heavy vibe that screams, "Please don't bring up the personal ad. Please don't bring up the ad in front of these people." Of course I think it's because I'm too fat. I worried for a second that he was thinking I was too Jewish. But that would have been a little like the pot calling the kettle Moishe. I tried not to let my low self-esteem get the better of me. Besides, I told him on the phone that I was a big girl, and he said that was fine. I decided to finish the Seder, go home, and wait for Doug to call.

Friday: No call from Doug. I'm disappointed but not surprised. He was caught off guard and needed at least twenty-four hours to clear his head.

Saturday: Well, he knew I was going to be out of town. Why leave a message when he can wait to talk to me on Monday?

Sunday: See above.

Monday: Okay, what's up with that? He had three days to get over the shock. Now I'm a little annoyed.

Tuesday: Ah, Tuesday. Clearly the biggest day in the mail-order business. Now I wasn't sure if I felt hurt or felt like hurting somebody else.

Wednesday: No longer annoyed. I'm pissed!

Thursday: I get it. He's not going to call.

Gee, in my book it says we had plans for the following night. I double-checked. Yep, Friday, dinner with Doug. This would be the second time I'd know what it felt like to have testicles. Doug obviously had yet to experience it. I called Doug.

"Hey, Doug, it's Camryn. Just curious, are we still on for to-morrow night?"

"Oh, uh, yes, of course. I'm sorry I didn't call. I lost your number. Tomorrow's great, but I have to tell you I have another ap-pointment at nine-thirty."

An "appointment" at 9:30 P.M.? Would that be with your doctor, your lawyer, your dentist? Is your optometrist a vampire? Are you being arraigned in night court? People don't have "appointments" at nine-thirty at night. They have "dates." But Doug was too much of a wuss to just come out say "Oh, and I scheduled another date for the moment after we pay the check. Is that okay?" Ol' Doug apparently stacks 'em up like planes waiting to land at La Guardia. It was obvious to me that Doug was giving himself the mother of all out clauses. I'm familiar with these out clauses. If I'm no fun, ugly, and boring, he conveniently keeps the "appointment." But if I'm charming and altogether terrific, the "appointment" conveniently gets canceled. Men. Some would call that fancy footwork, but I just call it being an asshole. If he was the asshole, then I was the jackass because I agreed to meet him.

We meet at the restaurant. All the witty banter from our phone conversations is gone. The keen, penetrating interest in the other's life . . . gone. The blazing desire to marry this guy . . . fading fast. So about halfway through the meal, I decide to jazz things up with a little old-fashioned nosy confrontation. And not flirty inquisitiveness either; we're talking Nurse Ratched on three hours sleep.

"So . . . where you going at nine-thirty?"

Ah, the familiar burgundy shade of embarrassment, which I just love.

Stammer, stammer, fits and starts, then finally: "Well, uh, I don't really know what to say, uh, but uh, I have another date."

Surprise! Gee, I guess he wasn't taking his bat to the all-night vampire vet in Chelsea. Weird, those nine-thirty appointments.

Having created the awkward moment with my impertinent question, I felt sorry for him and gently tried to defuse the tension.

"Hey, that's okay, Doug. You don't owe me anything. A date? That's fine." But suddenly I was Nurse Ratched again and said, "So, who's it with?"

"Uh . . . it's . . . uh . . . with this woman I've been kind of seeing on and off for about a year and a half."

I think the kids today call that "a girlfriend."

The interrogation continued. "Anyway, Doug, if you've been

dating somebody on and off for a year and a half, why are you answering personal ads?" And then listen to what he did.

"Well, it was mostly off, until you went to visit your sister, then it was kind of on again." What kind of conversational judo was this? Oh, I get it, now it's my fault. While I was away for those three long, lonely days I had driven him back into the arms of his old lover.

"Seeing as how I abandoned you and forced you to reconcile with your girlfriend . . . why didn't you cancel our date?" Picture a five-year-old who just broke a lamp, explaining to his parents that he wasn't running in the house.

"Well, uh, you see, it's just that, uh, you're such a nice person, and, uh, and you're very knowledgeable about Judaism, and, uh, I just didn't want to disappoint you in any way, and I'm such a jerk." Sounds like you were running in the house, Dougie.

And he's going on and on, explaining and alibiing, squirming and apologizing ad nauseum.

And out of nowhere Mother Teresa relieves Nurse Ratched and I go into *comfort Doug mode*.

"Doug, stop it, it's fine. Really. I'm just sorry you really did have a date because I have theater tickets for the ten o'clock show right around the corner and I thought you might want to come."

Then he said, "Right around the corner? What theater?"

"This cool little performance space, Cucaracha."

Poor Doug, poor poor Doug. He turned from burgundy to magenta to cardinal, every shade of red you could imagine. If he were a pregnancy test, he'd be having triplets.

"I have to make a phone call," he announced.

"What's the matter?"

"I have to cancel my date."

"Why?"

Hello, freaky collision of coincidence No. 2. Of the millions of people in New York and thousands of theaters, Doug, his gal, and I were all scheduled to converge at the tiny little Cucaracha in SoHo. After another spit-take and the deepest shade of burgundy yet, Doug offers to cancel his date.

Trust me, you can't make this shit up.

Doug looked carsick. And I went into *comfort Doug mode* again.

"Doug, stop it. Go to the theater. Have a good time. You are not going to cancel your date with your girlfriend. It's a huge theater. I'll tell you what, I'll pretend I don't even know you. In fact, y'know what, let me drive you there." I should have just stayed home and carved an L into my forehead for LOSER!

"I couldn't possibly ride up on your motorcycle. My girlfriend would kill me."

"Don't be ridiculous, she doesn't have to know, I'll drop you a block away." Before I had time to really think about my offer, Doug said, "Okay."

All of a sudden I was Rostand's Cyrano de Bergerac doing my best to make sure Christian and Roxane hooked up. Looking as *pathétique* as one can on a Honda CB650, I drive Doug to the corner of Greenwich and Canal and watch him walk up to the theater. I actually sat on my bike for five minutes so that it wouldn't look like we arrived together. I used to be very cool on my motorcycle, but I was in full *loser mode*.

When I finally drove up to the theater and parked across the street, it was easy to spot Doug and his girlfriend, Jenny—Jenny Craig, from the looks of her. They were locked in a mushy, gooey, wet embrace that did not translate as "on again, off again."

THUNK! Good thing I was wearing my helmet, because reality hit me in the head like a two-by-four. The nickel dropped and the jukebox started playing "Only the Lonely." As I got off my bike, I could swear my knees were shaking. Up until that point I had fought bravely, but when confronted with that image of the happy loving couple, humiliation kicked my ass. It was time for me to get back on my bike, go home, and consume large quantities of high-caloric matter.

But before I could tear off and disappear into my bottomless well of self-pity, my friend Carolyn McDermott came bounding out of the theater and exclaimed that she was so happy that I'd come to the show. She made me promise I'd hang out after to tell her what I thought. And basically I was stuck.

So I rolled up my sleeves and reached into my deepest reserves for that courage that warriors access in the heat of battle. I parked my bike and strode toward that line, the end of which was being anchored by huggy-kissy Doug and Jenny. Well, you know I wasn't going to wait behind them, so I began scanning the line for someone, anyone I knew. That's when I saw the most gorgeous guy I've ever seen. The stud of studs, the cling clang king of the rim ram room. He had the kind of looks that would have made Michelangelo toss David and start over.

Now, when I think there is a chance of becoming romantic with a guy, I can be reserved and shy and self-conscious. But when I have no chance, I'm more aggressive than a groupie trying to get backstage at a Rolling Stones concert. And we all know how a groupie gets a backstage pass. I walked right up to him and asked, like I owned the block, "So, who are you?"

Taken aback, he replied, "Uh . . . I'm Ted." He was Ted. He was beautiful. And he was alone.

"I'm Camryn, you come here often?"

"Actually I'm from out of town, from Canada. I'm just here to see my friend Julie Moses in the show."

"Julie Moses? Julie Moses? We're thick as thieves! I can't believe you know Julie!"

He seemed genuinely happy to have met a mutual friend of Ms. Moses, never mind that I didn't know who the hell she was. With his guard down just a bit, I took the opportunity to voice the request that in some form or another would have been going through any red-blooded heterosexual woman's mind.

"Ted, I need you to do me a favor," I said, fighting the temptation to leave off the "a favor" part. "You see that guy at the end of the line, he just dissed me big time. If you could just put your arm around me, dip me, and deep tongue me now and then, it will look really good, and Julie would want you to do it for me."

Ted: "Okay."

Hallelujah, hallelujah . . . hal-le-LUUUUUUUU-jah!

I had a boyfriend for the night.

So I enter Cucaracha arm in arm with my Tom Cruise, only better looking. Like Orpheus leading Eurydice out of Hades, I was so tempted to look over my shoulder at Doug's reaction, but I played it cool.

Because Ted knew Julie, we were seated up front at a table in the V.I.P. section. Because Doug knew *NOBODY*, he was seated in the bleachers. Once we were seated, I told my boyfriend Ted that I was going to the bathroom. But I didn't go to the bathroom, instead I went backstage. I realized I wouldn't have known Ms. Moses even if she were leading the Israelites to the Promised Land. So I found Carolyn McDermott and had her make a hasty introduction. With the curtain about to rise neither one of us had a lot of time for the back story so I just said, "Hi, Julie, you don't know me, and I know you are about to perform, but try and take this in. I'm sitting with your friend Ted, and I need you to do me a favor. If you could just come out after the show and say, 'Hey, Camryn, it's so good to see you,' I'll explain it all to you later. I know you'll understand and I sure will appreciate it. Again, my name is Camryn, but if you forget it, just ask Carolyn. Have a great show, break a leg, see you later. Bye." And when I ran back to the table, my new boyfriend Ted had bought me . . . a beverage. Girls, you know what I mean. I didn't even have to ask. A real gentleman! Obviously from another country.

*   *   *

Had I not become completely immune to the bizarre during my brief association with Doug, I would have been stunned by my next discovery. On our table was a card that read: MTV SURVEY. IF YOU'VE HAD AN UNUSUAL DATING EXPERIENCE IN THE PAST FEW MONTHS, WRITE IT DOWN AND MTV MIGHT PUT IT ON THE AIR. I couldn't resist. I approached an usher and asked for a handful of the MTV flyers, then headed over to the cheap seats, the bleachers where Doug and Jenny were sitting. And there was the familiar burgundy embarrassment as I approached and said, "Hi, I'm Camryn. I work here. And I have a flyer I'd like you to fill out. It's about people who have had an unusual date recently. And you kind of look like a guy who might have had an unusual date recently. What's your name?"

"Duh . . . uh . . . uh . . . ug."

"Okay, Duh . . . uh . . . uh . . . ug. I want you to fill this flyer out and give it back to me before you leave or I will hunt you down and kill you."

Doug accepted with his familiar little stammer. I knew it was a cruel little dagger, but, man, did he have it coming. Who makes a dinner date with their personals pal when they've got a nine-thirty date with their girlfriend? A scumbag, that's who. Oh, I was so tempted to let him have it and unleash some of my well-paid-for actor's education on him.

> *Hence,*
> *Horrible villain, or I'll spurn thine eyes*
> *Like balls before me; I'll unhair thy head,*
> *Thou shalt be whipped with wire,*
> *and stew'd in brine,*
> *Smarting in lingering pickle.*
>
> —Antony and Cleopatra

Or perhaps for Jenny's edification:

> *He's a most notable coward, an intimate*
> *and endless liar, an hourly promise-breaker,*
> *the owner of no one good quality.*
>
> —All's Well That Ends Well

But I smiled through clenched teeth, swallowed the desire to rat him out in front of his girl, and returned to my new beau.

The show was wonderful and new friend Julie terrific.

When the show was over, I looked around, and Doug and Jenny were gone. I guess when the house lights came up at Cucaracha, that little cockroach had scurried for cover. Aw, fuck him, I had Ted. And in my mind, I was already buying furniture with him. As far as I could tell, Doug had not filled out his survey before beating a hasty retreat.

Just then Julie Moses came leaping out from backstage screaming, get this, "Carmine! It's so good to see you!" She had flawlessly recited about 1,000 lines in the play but blew the one line I needed her to remember to carry out my ruse. I tried to backpedal, "Uh, Carmine, Carmen, Karen, Karma . . . Y'know, all pet names." But the jig was up. I had to explain the whole Doug fiasco, and they were both happy to have played a part in my small measure of revenge. We hung out, I bought them *both* a beverage. And we had a great time. But like all fantasies, this one ended all too quickly and Ted returned to Canada the next day.

Still, he had done such a mitzvah I decided to write him a thank-you letter with an open invitation to be my boyfriend anytime.

He wrote back, which was in itself amazing.

Dear Camryn,
It was really wonderful meeting you. Thanks for the sweet let-ter you sent me. New York certainly is a wild place, and I can't stop thinking about you. I can't sleep at night. You're all I think about. I want to father your children.

Love and lust,
Ted

Alright, alright, so he didn't say exactly that. But it's my book, and it's my fantasy.

As much as I tried to read into his real missive, the only distinctive thing about it was the disturbing letterhead. Ted had replied on Philip Morris stationery.

Philip Morris. You know, in a southern drawl, "Mr. Chairman, we have no evidence or indication that nicotine is addictive." Philip Morris not only makes cigarettes, but they make Cheez Whiz and Miracle Whip too. They'll kill us if it's the last thing they do. I had to get to the bottom of this stationery dilemma, so I called my new pal Julie Moses.

"Julie, I got a letter from Ted on Philip Morris stationery. What gives?"

"You don't know? He didn't tell you?"

Now I'm thinking his dad *is* Philip Morris. Or, at the very least, Ted is the VP of distribution for Manitoba and Saskatchewan.

"Tell me what?"

"Camryn, Ted is the Canadian Marlboro Man model."

Well, fuck a duck.

Now it all made sense. No wonder I was prepared to forsake . . . well, everything and move to Winnipeg if he wanted me to. The Canadian Marlboro Man. He wasn't just handsome, he was professionally handsome. And rugged. I couldn't stop picturing him in a flannel shirt astride a horse in the high country. And then I couldn't stop picturing him without a shirt astride me on the Lower East Side. Still, I told myself that for political reasons I could never date a model. I told myself that *after* he told me he had a girlfriend. I had had my dream date with Ted and though he was just a temporary knight in shining armor, he had restored my faith in chivalry. Doug Schmidt, however, had restored my faith in chiselry.

Let's review:

Ted	Doug
gorgeous	schleppy
needs a green card	turns various shades of red
speaks French	barely speaks
a friend of Julie Moses	has a girlfriend
bought me a beverage	went Dutch
had good seats	in the bleachers
model	mail-order geek
gentle	Jell-O

So why is it I can run up to the Canadian Marlboro Man and demand a deep tongue kiss but can't ask Doug "Am I too fat for you?" I'll tell you why. Because Ted never was an option. I knew I wasn't really risking anything with him. Doug? Christ, there's nothing quite as humiliating as getting rejected by someone who doesn't deserve you. So it was risky. And it hurt. Not a lot, but enough. Enough to sour me on the personals forever. Enough to use his real name.

But I haven't given up on men. In fact, I'm still looking for a boyfriend. So if you know anyone who is looking for a . . .

BIG FAT BEAUTY

5´10´´ Nonreligious, 31(ish). Spontaneous, sociable, registered to vote. If you're tall, a Democrat, and a smart ass, let's make babies.

. . . please have him fill out the following form.

I promise the lucky winner will get a chapter all to himself in the next book.

Camryn Manheim's
Official Boyfriend Form

Do you have an on-again, off-again girlfriend? _____ (If so, do not complete this form)

Name: _____ Age: _____ Phone: _____

Height: _____ Are you geographically desirable? (indicate city) _____

Are you registered to vote? _____ Party affiliation: _____

Have you ever been in therapy? (If yes, please explain. If no, please explain.)

_____

_____

_____

Are you an employee of Philip Morris? _____ (If so, do not complete this form)

Blow job: impeachable offense, yes or no? _____

Kids? Can't live with them: _____ Can't live without them: _____ (Check one)

Are you serious about dating me, or did you fill this out to be cute? _____
(If cute, do not complete this form)

Please write a short essay: Please draw a picture of yourself:

_____

_____

_____

_____

_____

_____

_____

_____

_____

Official Boyfriend Release Form

WHEREAS, I am a relatively cute guy of sound mind and body, under no legal infirmities or incarceration, not presently subject to any impeachment proceedings in the Senate of the United States, or elsewhere, and

WHEREAS, I am a US citizen (or already have my green card and not looking for a ticket of entry), I am registered to vote and have lawfully voted to throw the bums out, I have a tape library of TV shows and movies containing Camryn Manheim (having duly paid royalties to the copyright holders thereof for said copies), I haven't torn this page out from a library book, and

WHEREAS, I am so excited to be considered for the position of "Boyfriend of Camryn Manheim,"© that I can't eat or sleep until this entry form is submitted, knowing full well that said Camryn Manheim takes on only a few boyfriends at a time from tens of thousands of entries she receives, but I'm willing to take the chance, and the mere opportunity to be considered, even if I'm not chosen, is gratitude enough to last a lifetime.

THEREFORE, I, the undersigned, hereby grant to Camryn Manheim in perpetuity throughout the known universe, in all media presently existing or hereafter invented, the right to publish my application, reproduce any letters of communications from me, the right to use my name and likeness, and the right to fictionalize any of the above. Further, I waive all rights of privacy and publicity in connection with the above, and waive and release and discharge Camryn Manheim and her publisher and assigns, from all claims, demands and liabilities, damages, costs, and expenses (including attorneys' fees), actions and causes of actions which I may now or hereafter have against Camryn Manheim in connection with the use of the rights granted herein.

Dated: _____   Name: _____

Please Print

Signed: _____

Boyfriend Applicant

Address: _____

_____

Identifying marks: _____
(leave blank if in the federal witness protection program)

Please mail forms to:

**Camryn Manheim's Official Boyfriend Form
c/o Broadway Books
1540 Broadway
New York, NY 10036**

Body Acceptance Now! • Celebrity Interviews

RADIANCE
THE MAGAZINE FOR LARGE WOMEN
FALL 1998
ISSUE #56

14th
Anniversary
Edition!

Actress
CAMRYN MANHEIM
TWO BIG STARS! Camryn Manheim
and Michael Badalucco of *The Practice*

How Do We Raise the Children?

MOVE OVER, BARBIE!
www.radiancemagazine.com

All the News That's Fat to Print

After the Doug debacle, I had a little of that Charlie-Brown-lying-on-his-back-because-Lucy-pulled-the-football-away-again feeling. Of course it had been a disaster. It's always a disaster. No matter how much Charlie Brown wants to believe that this time it's going to be different, Lucy will always pull the ball away. And no matter how much I wanted to believe that a guy was going to look past my weight and see my considerable charms, it seemed apparent that—whether right up front or at the last moment—he was going to pull the ball away and leave me alone and feeling humiliated.

The Doug Schmidt episode wasn't in itself a serious setback. But it felt a little like a final straw.

As I said, you don't turn to the personal ads as a first option. No, it's pretty far down the list. So when that failed miserably I was left wondering where to look next. Surely there was a man for me out there. Right? But where?

That is when a friend of mine told me about the size-acceptance movement. She told me there was a whole subculture in which fat was not only accepted but celebrated. I was told to check out *Dimensions* magazine. It sounded great, a magazine dedicated to fat people. As I looked for this magazine, this festival of fat, I wondered how I had managed to go through my whole life without ever having heard of it. And as I looked and looked, it became obvious. *Dimensions,* you see, is not proudly displayed between *Vogue* and *Elle.* Nor is it tucked on the row behind *Sports Illustrated* and *Newsweek.* It's most likely nowhere to be found at your local newsstand. But if you persevere and ask around, you may just find a copy of your own.

I did and was amazed.

In *Dimensions,* I found articles about fat positivism and self-love, poetry praising big beautiful women, and items on the dangers of dieting. I felt like I had discovered a parallel universe, a world in which fat was accepted, lauded, and desired. In the back of *Dimensions,* I found a list of other fat-positive magazines and newsletters: *Radiance, Fat!So?, Rump Parliament* (love that title), *Large Encounters, National Association to Advance Fat Acceptance* (NAAFA), *Metabolism, Belly Busters, BBW,* and *Super Women.*

I spent $400 subscribing to these magazines so I could familiarize myself with this subculture.

Some of these magazines had personals sections, and I thought I just might be able to find true love in this new world. But I was in for a shock. The ads weren't placed by people who accepted fat; rather they were placed by people who *wanted* fat, the more the better. Fat was the currency in this underground economy. Nobody seemed to care if you were kind or intelligent or witty as long as you weighed enough. It was the antithesis of the "real world," where I had found so much disappointment. In that world I was admired for my brains, my generosity, and gift for gab, but ultimately rejected because of my fat. In this world of "size acceptance" my fat was all that mattered; the other stuff was apparently irrelevant.

Here's what I'm talking about (ads from *Dimensions*):

SBM, 36, 5´9´´, attractive, fit, 135 lbs., professional, lives in the New York area, seeks large, lumpy, over 300-lb. female of any race for meaningful relationship.

Handsome SWM, 170 lbs., 5´8´´, wishes to meet **bottom-heavy, pear-shaped** woman over 450 pounds of any age or nationality for a long-lasting relationship.

(He paid extra for the bold face, just so there would be no misunderstanding about what was really important to him.)

Big, beautiful male, 5´10´´, 240 lbs. of prime beef, can turn into chopped liver for a tender-loined type of woman. Must be very bottom-heavy, measurements 60–56–90, 500 or more lbs., 40-inch thighs and extremely wide 25-inch calves. Race, age, marital status, location unimportant. Size is.

(I just love the cow references. Is this guy looking for a woman or a ruminant?)

These are just three examples of hundreds of ads that were weight specific, but I think you get the point.

I would never disparage a woman for her weight, nor would I condemn a man for loving her. But when weight is the only pre-requisite listed, it is just as narrow and demeaning as men who want a 36–24–36 woman in a size 4. Do you care if I'm witty? Do you care if I'm well read? Do you care if I vote? In my personal ad and subsequent outgoing message, I carefully included that I was interested in a person's politics, love of literature, and sense of hu-mor, because, to me, those are essential defining elements of a human being. Sadly, it seems that some men—whether seeking a short, 400-pound woman or a lithe blonde—don't want her to have a personality and be self-aware, for that only makes it more difficult for these men to control, possess, and dominate the woman. We are accustomed to men seeking the trophy girl, the beautiful ornament he can carry on his arm. And while I hope that most would view this as shallow and transparent, it is still a widely accepted practice. When a man specifically seeks a large woman, however, he is viewed as strangely deviant with a fetish for fat. I argue that they are equally dehumanizing. It's fine to like buxom women or thin women—we all have our preferences—but when you seek a physical type with total disregard for individ-ual character, you might as well be seeking a specifically propor-tioned mannequin.

I've been asked "What does a fat admirer do if his woman, for one reason or another, loses a lot of weight?" Well, I'll tell ya, if he's only with her because she's fat, he leaves her. Just like the man who marries the trophy girl leaves *her* if she gains weight. It doesn't matter whether he's a fat admirer or a thin admirer, the man who doesn't care about his lover's mind and soul is despicable. It is up to women to ask themselves "Would he still love me if I gained fifty pounds?" or "Would he still love me if I lost fifty pounds?" and if the answer is no, then she needs to get herself another man. Believe me, I know that's easier said than done, but it is better to search eternally for a man who respects you as a human being than to be with a man who is more interested in your dress size than the size of your spirit.

Although these personal ads are found in "size-acceptance" magazines, they really should be frowned upon by the size-acceptance movement. This is not size acceptance but "size insistence."

Of all the ads that I encountered in these magazines through my diligent efforts to find a boyfriend, there was only one that did not offend me and was somewhat intriguing. Here it is:

> Eccentric English actor, soon to relocate to the States, interested in theater, books, music, and romance, seeking a big beauty who shares a love of the arts.
> Please write:
> Stuart
> 14 Rockinghorse Road, London, U.K.

Author's note: Don't think for a second that Stuart is his real name or that Rockinghorse Road is his real address. (I got that from an Elvis Costello song.) All the names, places, and events that could connect the reader to the bloke who placed this ad have been changed. So don't even try to figure it out.

As usual, I had modest goals. We'd correspond, arrange a meeting, fall madly in love at a Broadway show, and start making babies. My first letter to him was cautious but bold enough to let him know I was keenly interested and included my 8 × 10 head shot, which hadn't gotten me much work but maybe would land me a boyfriend. But before I even had a chance to send the package, my friend Michael James called to ask me if I would submit some financial aid vouchers for him while he was vacationing in England. This is a huge responsibility, complete with checking boxes and mailing forms on specific days. They make it difficult so people can't be "collecting" while on vacation in Europe. I agreed to this clerical nuisance as long as he would conduct a little reconnaissance for me in London. Hey, I can be as shallow as the next person, and before I married "Stuart," I needed to know what the U.K. boy looked like. Michael and I exchanged instructions: I was to mail his form every Sunday and he was to go to 14 Rockinghorse Road, check Stuart out, and if he was passable, hand over my letter and photo. If he wasn't, ask for directions to Windsor.

After a week in England, Michael called to see if I had mailed his financial aid form, which I had. I asked him if he had completed his assignment, which he hadn't. I made it perfectly clear: If he did not call me before the week's end, I would not submit his next voucher. Two hundred sixty dollars is mighty motivation for an actor to get out his A to Zed book. He promised to get right on it.

Michael called later that week to give me the skinny. (Where did that term come from?) He and Andrew, the friend he was visiting, had made their way to Stuart's flat and rung his bell. Picture Rosencrantz and Guildenstern delivering a letter for Hamlet. When Stuart's voice came over the intercom, Michael and Andrew were completely flummoxed.

STUART: Who is it?

MICHAEL: Uh . . . delivery for Stuart.

STUART: Leave it on the stoop.

MICHAEL: Uh . . . uh . . . we need to see you. . . . I mean, you need to sign for it, I mean, we need to hand deliver it.

ANDREW: *(piping in)* Or perhaps get directions to Windsor.

STUART: Oh, all right.

Stuart answered the door, rightfully suspicious of the two buffoons on his landing.

Michael and Andrew sized him up and, not seeing a hump or any signs of leprosy, decided he was fit to receive the queen's epistle. They handed over my letter, but before they could turn tail, Stuart wanted some questions answered.

It was an uncomfortable situation for everybody. Michael held up the *Dimensions* magazine where Stuart's ad had run and asked if he were indeed the Stuart in question. Understandably, Stuart was a little embarrassed, but he 'fessed up to being the fat admirer who had placed the ad. Michael and Andrew told him that the letter in his hand was from an actress in New York who was responding to the ad. He thanked them for delivering it safely and politely excused himself.

As Michael and Andrew walked away, Andrew, a London actor, was certain he recognized Stuart. After several minutes Andrew exclaimed, "Stuart Templeton! He's an actor!" So my own Rosencrantz and Guildenstern decided they could find a photograph of their fellow thespian in the player's guide at the London library. Once there they discovered that Stuart was the son of Sir Clive Templeton, noted British actor. And if that wasn't enough— *Dayenu*—Stuart had starred in the British production of *Can't Tell*

You the Name, the same play Michael had just done in New York. Turns out that Michael had more in common with him than I did.

But it was great to hear that Stuart had received my package and that Michael would be bringing home a Xeroxed copy of his photograph. I waited to hear from Stu.

Two weeks later I got this note:

Dear Camryn,

So you sent your spies to check me out, you cheeky bugger.

As you've probably heard from your secret agents, I am the not-so-famous son of a famous father. I recently starred in Can't Tell You the Name *in London and hope to make my way to New York soon. It was nice to hear from a fellow actor.*

However, your photograph either is deceiving or you are not a very big girl. You might recall in my ad that I specified wanting to meet "a big girl." And while you are very pretty, I meant a B-I-G girl. So in the interest of not wasting anyone's time, if you have another photograph that you think more accurately depicts you, please feel free to send it. No messengers needed this time.

Great. In the aboveground world where the beauty myth rules, I was being rejected because I was too fat. In the underground world of fat admiration, I was being rejected because I wasn't fat enough. Since I didn't have any fatter photos, that was the end of my correspondence with Stuart.

The search continued. In the *Large Encounters* newsletter, I came across an ad for parties specifically for large women and the men who love them. It sounded perfect. By virtue of being there, the men would already be displaying a preference for large and lovely ladies. But at least they would get to see me and, yes, maybe even talk to me before rejecting me. I couldn't wait.

After some lengthy arm-twisting, I finally cajoled my friend Adele, the rabbi's daughter, to join me at a *Large Encounters* dance party in a club near Times Square. We were like nervous schoolgirls as Adele and I drove up to the club. We panicked and decided to go around the block a couple more times before committing. Then we parked and watched our fellow fat girls—dressed to the nines—enter the club. Adele kept saying "I'm not going in. I'm not going in."

And I'd say, "It's research for the play I'm writing. We *have* to go."

Adele, who's got my number, said, "Liar! You want to meet a man every bit as much as I do. But we're not going in!"

Then Adele had the bright idea to call the club from her cell phone and ask if the club was open to the public or if it was just a *Large Encounters* private party. When she learned that the club was open to everyone and that just a section was being dedicated to the private party, she said, "Okay. I've got it. We'll go have dinner in the regular part of the club, then check out the fat-girl part as if we just happen to be there."

To which I responded, "Who are you kidding? We're two fat girls all dressed up without dates walking into a club that just happens to be hosting a party for girls just like us. When they ask us if we're here for the *Large Encounters* party, I dare you to say, 'Oh no, we're just two fat single girls all dressed up to have dinner with each other.' "

I'm sure if we hadn't both been delirious with laughter, we would have been sobbing as we sat outside the club, watching our more courageous sisters walking in. I finally gave her an ultimatum, telling her that I was going in with or without her. And she realized that the only thing more pathetic than sitting in the car with me, too afraid to go in, would be sitting in the car alone wondering if I had found the love of my life.

When she said "You are such a jerk!" I knew she was coming.

We took a deep breath and strode toward the door. The doorman asked us if we were here for the party—so I guess we probably wouldn't have been able to fool him—and told us to have a nice evening. Once inside, it looked like any other club, only the fat girls weren't too self-conscious to dance. People were checking us out and for the first time I felt thin. In fact, Adele and I were the thinnest women in that room. Which, in light of my experience with Stuart, I was beginning to think might not have been such a good thing. Nobody was trying to look thin. Adele and I were the only two women wearing a long, slenderizing, unbroken line of black. As I looked about the room, I couldn't believe all the different fashions that were available to a woman my size. Everything from leather miniskirts to fishnet stockings and lace corsets.

We ordered our Diet Cokes and set up camp in the corner, trying to engage each other in that pressing manner that says to others "Please don't speak to us, we're on the verge of discovering a new way to split atoms." But once again, we weren't fooling anybody. You don't come to the *Large Encounters* dance party to discuss nuclear fission. People started to talk to us.

A couple of guys asked us to dance, but we weren't done with our science project yet and politely declined. I couldn't remember the last time I was asked to dance. It felt nice but also very scary. Maybe next time. After a while I got up to go to the bathroom. Adele stayed at the table, lest anyone steal our prime scoping position.

I was in the stall when I heard two women enter the bathroom giggling. There was a definite joyousness and carefree spirit to the evening. I liked hearing my fellow fat girls laughing in the bathroom instead of crying as usual. But then I realized what they were laughing about.

> GIRL NO. 1: ... and did you see that girl all in black with the long hair and a thousand earrings? What's she doing here?
>
> GIRL NO. 2: Yeah ... she's not super size ... she's not even midsize!
>
> GIRL NO. 1: Somebody better tell her that she doesn't belong here.
>
> GIRL NO. 2: Yeah ... those fucking midsize girls try to take the best guys.

I was mortified. There I was, with my pants down around my ankles, sitting on the toilet, listening to two super-size veterans of the scene suggesting that I was an unwelcome presence at their dance party. I seriously thought I might get beaten up in that bathroom, so I lifted my feet several inches off the ground and waited silently for them to leave. And, let me tell you, fat girls take just as long in front of a mirror as skinny girls do.

Once they left, I took a moment to sum up the last six months of my dating experience. Dissed by Doug, whom I met through the reputable *New York Press*, because I was too fat. Dissed by Stuart, whom I met through *Dimensions*, one of the more mainstream magazines for large women, because I was too thin. And dissed by the girls at the underground *Large Encounters* party for not being super size. Man-oh-Manischewitz. It made me wonder: Could I actually be the size that *everybody* hates?

It reminded me of the time that I was walking down the street in New York and these three high school girls were walking toward me. One of them was a little plump so we shared that I'm-chubby-you're-chubby glance, that smile of commiseration. Then just as we passed each other, she turned to me and said, "God, and I thought I was fat!" Though temporarily in shock that one of my own would turn on me, my survival skills kicked in and I wasted little time before retaliating. "You *are* fat! Just because *I'm* fat doesn't make *you* any *less* fat." I don't think she expected a fat girl to bounce back so fast. That happened eight years ago. Imagine somebody I don't even know, don't even care about, and will never see again having the power to poison my spirit. I don't even *know* her and she haunts me, always reminding me that I have something to be ashamed of. To this day, when I pass by a high school and see groups of adolescent girls, I am tempted to cross the street.

So I wasn't all that surprised by the disdain of the super-size women in the bathroom. To the chubby high school girl I was too fat. To those women at the *Large Encounters* party I was too thin. Now I realize that they were just projecting their self-hatred onto me, but at the time, all I wanted to do was get the hell out of Dodge.

I ran back, got Adele, and hightailed it out of there before we were assaulted for being midsize.

Although that first time was a little harrowing, in defense of these *soirees*, I have returned on many occasions—for, uh, "research"—and found the women, both super and midsize, to be very welcoming. I even got up the courage to dance and to wear primary colors. These clubs are in every city, and I encourage women of all sizes of large to check them out. There's nothing like entering this other world and seeing people who have spent their whole lives being self-conscious dancing, flirting, and kissing under the bright club lights with no apologies. And don't be mean to the midsize girls. They're fat people too.

A few weeks after I had first discovered *Dimensions*, all of the magazines I had subscribed to were coming in. One of the 'zines was called *Belly Busters*. It was a low-budget, desktop publication, mimeographed for distribution. In it I discovered this ad and many others like it:

> SWM, 39, 6´6´´, very athletic, seeks VERY FAT girl, must be very LARGE and willing to gain weight. Shorter girls under 35 preferred. Are you real FAT? Like to engage in erotic weight gain?

Erotic weight gain? What the fuck is that? And then I found this personal ad:

> Hi, My name is Cathy. I'm a 681-lb. submissive eating machine that is addicted to eating and being so stuffed I can't move! Would like to talk to anyone who is supportive of my lifestyle. I am actively being force-fed and funnel-fed, and the fatter I get, the fatter I WANT TO BE. Would like to talk to women and men who share my relentless need to be stuffed and packed with fattening foods till I can't move.

I began to realize that *Belly Busters* was basically dedicated to men and women who were turned on by erotic weight gain, a term I had never heard of nor imagined even existed.

In the back of the publication was a story about a woman who at 300 pounds met her husband Bob. Bob was what is called in this sub-subculture a "master feeder." He built her a feeding machine that is similar to the IVs used in hospitals. It's a long thin apparatus that holds one gallon of formula and a siphon that comes down into her mouth. The formula was made out of weight-gaining material, Hershey's chocolate syrup and cream. Each gallon was equivalent to 10,000 calories. In addition to her three meals a day, she consumed four gallons of formula a day. That's 40,000 additional calories. Bob measured her every three days. If she did not gain weight, he beat her. At 800 pounds, Bob built her a steel chair. She was too fat to make love to him so he built her a chair equipped with belts to hold her legs open. At 900 pounds she became voluntarily immobile. Her goal weight is to beat the *Guinness Book of World Records*, 1,200 pounds.

I was so disturbed by this story that I called my friends in the fat-acceptance movement, hoping they would tell me that that was just an isolated letter of fantasy and that this kind of behavior didn't really exist. But, sadly, I was told that force-feeding and erotic weight gain do exist in the dark corners of our society. Because its very origins are shame-based, it is a very underground practice. As a person who is trying to help women and men accept themselves and their bodies, it caught me off guard how upsetting this discovery was. That liberal, nondiscriminatory part of me wants to say "Hey, whatever turns you on is cool with me." But it really devastates me that there are women who are so lonely and so sad that they will allow and invite this kind of abuse. And it really pisses me off that there are men who are willing to take advantage of this loneliness to act out their fantasies of domination and dehumanization. I also learned that perhaps the saddest aspect of this behavior, the incredibly tragic footnote to this erotic weight-gain fantasy, is that once a woman is immobilized and physically incapable of gaining more weight, the man often loses interest, leaves, and finds a new woman with whom to begin the process all over again. Thankfully, this extreme conduct appears to be rather rare. And it's important to note that the majority of fat admirers are truly devoted spouses and lovers who would stay with their partners through thick and through thin. (Pun intended.)

I did not renew my subscription to *Belly Busters*. But I did become a card-carrying member of NAAFA and a regular reader of *Radiance* and *Fat!So?**

Even though I didn't find a boyfriend through these magazines, I did find a community in which I belonged. For the first time I could read magazines about women without feeling shitty and hating myself. I could identify with the stories; the letters were from people who had had similar experiences, and, yes, the pictures were of women just like me. So if you've ever felt overlooked and ignored by mainstream periodicals because you're not a size 4, do whatever it takes to get your hands on these magazines. You'll be glad you did.

---

*Radiance is a glossy quarterly magazine for women of all sizes of large. It is upbeat and positive and encourages its readers to live proud, full, active lives with self-love and self-respect. To subscribe, write: Radiance, PO Box 30246, Oakland, CA 94604 or e-mail at *info@radiancemagazine.com*.

Fat!So? is the 'zine that has all the news that's fat to print. It is for people who don't apologize for their size because life is too short for self-hatred and celery sticks. To subscribe, write: Fat!So? PO Box 423464, San Francisco, CA 94142 or e-mail at *marilyn@fatso.com*.

Rump Parliament is a magazine by and for people people working to change the way society treats fat people. Rump Parliament, PO Box 865137, Plano, TX 75086 or e-mail at *martin@airmail.net*.

From Here
to Anxiety

I'm not going to lie to you. I could accept myself, shout from mountaintops that I love myself, and celebrate my body until the end of time, but one thing will never change: Going to the beach is a fucking nightmare.

For the longest time, going to the beach served only one purpose: getting a tan as quickly as possible. Because we all know a tan makes you look thinner.

My uncle has a house on Fire Island, and every year I'd get that one weekend to invite all my friends out to do the *Big Chill* thing. Now, there are two things to consider when inviting a large group of people to spend quality time together on an island. First, they must be a compatible blend of people whose egos could tolerate each other for forty-eight hours. Second, and more important, they had to be people I'd be willing to let see me in a bathing suit and still be able to face when the weekend was over. These are the games that I played. This was not about my friends judging my fat, they didn't care. This was about me judging my fat, and believe me, I *did* care. And because I am a Forgotten Woman, I needed to get that slenderizing tan as soon as possible. And that's hard to do with jeans and a leather jacket on. So I went to the beach, took off my clothes, wore a damn bikini, and I pretended that I didn't care. "Oh yeah, I'm relaxed. Totally relaxed. I couldn't be more relaxed. Are you relaxed? Good, glad to hear it, me too! Glad you could all come to my beach house and *RELAX*."

And then I went into what I call Fat Survival Skills Combat. And the beach chair was the enemy.

You see, I couldn't sit in a beach chair with the back of the beach chair up, reading a book like a normal person, because this created unnecessary foldage of fat. But when I would lie with the back of the beach chair down, maintaining the linear line, presto-change-o, the foldage magically disappeared. So I ended up lying down in a very rigid position, reading with my arms stretched out and my eyes in the sun. Very comfortable and *very* relaxing.

Then, if somebody came over to talk to me, I'd go into panic mode. I would somehow get the towel that I placed by me earlier, pretend to wipe my brow so as not to look conspicuous, and then get that towel over my fat as soon as possible. All the while pretending I didn't even notice the person was coming over to talk to me. "Oh, hi, I didn't see you there." And my poor friend, who was clueless to my agony, had innocently come out of the house to ask me if I could show her where my uncle keeps the pasta strainer. And all I could think of was, "I just achieved the linear line pose, and you want me to get up? While you're watching?" That would mean doing the sleight-of-hand maneuver, the always perilous "towel off–shorts on" trick. Which is especially difficult while trying to maintain the linear line. You have to maintain the camouflage of the towel while trying to slide the shorts on up over the buttocks region, and then you have to say something in a dramatic fashion to cause a diversion, like *"Hey, look, it's Burt Lancaster and Deborah Kerr making out in the surf!"* And then roll up to a standing position. Never, and I repeat never, put a pair of shorts on while standing up—*UNNECESSARY FOLDAGE OF FAT!* Very unbecoming.

Then when all my friends decided it was time to go swimming at the beach, I'd have to think of some fabulous lie why I couldn't go swimming with them, because I needed to stay at the house and eat something. So that when everyone came back for lunch, I could eat as little as the rest of them. "Mmmmm, a mushroom. I'm full. How do you guys eat so much?" Meanwhile the Tombstone Pizza wrapper teetered at the top of the garbage, threatening to give me away.

And at night when we'd gather in the living room to play Celebrity and Pictionary, I'd have all this pent-up anxiety from my relaxing day at the beach. Everyone else was just mellow and having a beer. The fire was crackling, you could hear the tide lapping on the shore, and you could hear me screaming as I played with a vengeance.

"IT'S A TREE, GOD DAMN IT, IT'S A FUCKING TREE, AND A GOD DAMN HOUSE, YOU PUT IT TOGETHER YOU HAVE THE SWISS FAMILY ROBINSON. WHAT'S WRONG WITH YOU PEOPLE?"

My friends had all been sedated with beer and wine and I was hyped up on a twelve-pack of Diet Coke. Just one calorie. Imagine, I could drink 1,200 a day and still lose weight. I'd lose consciousness, but I'd lose weight. And that's the point, isn't it?

I don't think my friends ever noticed that when I'd go to the beach house to relax, I was totally consumed with anxiety. Going to the beach was always a horrible experience for me. And every year I'd tell myself, next time I'm only inviting people who are fat or blind.

The Unsinkable Kathy Bates

What I didn't realize at the time was that they were paying me the ultimate compliment. It was being repeated over and over again by agents and casting directors. If I heard it one more time I was going to scream. Had I only known then what I know now, I would have been properly embarrassed by the high praise.

"You remind me of a younger Kathy Bates," they would tell me. There must have been something to it because everyone was saying it. I kept nodding in agreement, saying "I get that a lot," never wanting to admit I had no idea who she was. All I knew was that she was an actor and I hoped she was a good one. Apparently she had made quite a name for herself on Broadway, but being a starving actor, my theater experience was limited to below 14th Street.

I had a meeting with yet another casting director who said "You remind me of Kathy Bates, have you seen her in *The Road to Mecca?*" I felt on the spot and didn't want to fib on the outside chance that she might test me. (Actors are very paranoid in auditions.) I could just see this exchange playing out.

CASTING DIRECTOR: Didn't you just love her death scene in the arms of her lover?
CAM: Oh yeah, that was beautiful, I wept.
CD: Ah-ha! There is no death scene in *The Road to Mecca*. I never want to see you again. Get out of my office!

So instead I just fibbed a little. I said, "I haven't seen *that* one yet, but isn't she an amazing actress?" Technically it wasn't a lie.

The casting agent said, "Well, you better hurry because it's closing this weekend."

Shit. I've got four days to find out who the hell it is that I'm reminding everybody of. On the way home, I passed TKTS, the discount ticket place, and saw that *The Road to Mecca* was on their list of half-price tickets. Seventeen fifty. A lot of money for a starving actor but a small price to pay for a glimpse into your destiny.

Sure, some people enjoy paying the extra forty bucks for center orchestra seats, but if you ask me, the best seats in any theater are front-row mezzanine. I felt like I'd won the lottery when I looked at my ticket and saw "Row A, Seat 10, Front Mezzanine."

The Road to Mecca was playing at the Promenade Theater on Broadway and 76th Street. Along with my ticket I felt like I should bring my passport, that's how foreign the Upper West Side is to a Lower East Sider. I know they think we're all freaks down in the

Village, but let me tell ya, things get plenty weird above 72nd Street. First of all, there are trees. Second, there are BMWs. And strangest of all is that Broadway becomes a two-way street, which nearly got me killed on my motorcycle by an oncoming cab. Many times I had wished Broadway ran both ways downtown, but I guess our property taxes aren't high enough to afford that convenience.

I tried to maintain my East Village cool in the lobby, but I couldn't help but be a little awestruck by the beautiful black-and-white photographs lining the walls of the Promenade. Cast photos of *Hurleyburley, Curse of the Starving Class,* and *Long Day's Journey into Night.* I was having that inspired-jealous tremble, thinking to myself "Some day. Some day I'll be on that wall."

Had *The Road to Mecca* been playing below Canal, I would have been enjoying the preshow social buzz with friends and colleagues. But since this was the Upper West Side, I looked around, didn't see any friendly faces, and went straight to my fabulous seat, right at the rail of the mezzanine.

When Kathy took the stage, it wasn't lost on me why so many agents and casting directors had noted a similarity. Even though we really looked nothing alike—there was a notable age difference, I'm much taller than she is, my hair was much longer, our coloring is totally different—we had one defining characteristic in common: We were both big women. But as I watched her sublime performance, I hoped that the comparison had more depth. I began to feel great pride in having been mentioned in the same breath as Kathy Bates. Her brilliance inspired me to write my first and only fan letter, which I include here, despite the obvious risk of embarrassment.

22 August 1988

Dear Kathy,

It must be strange to receive post from someone that you don't know, and have them greet you as Dear Kathy. But for myself, I know that any other salutation simply wouldn't do in this case.

You see, I am an actress as well, and for many years people have said to me that I reminded them of you. Unfortunately, I had never had the chance to see your work, so my stock reply was "Yes, many people have told me that very same thing," but the comparison never really meant much to me, until now.

Last week I was talking with a casting director who said, "You know, you remind me a lot of Kathy Bates." I finally felt ashamed that after all this time, I was still unfamiliar with your work. So I decided to invest in a ticket and see The Road to Mecca. *I sat in the front-row mezzanine in the center seat and hugged the piping that stretched out in front of me while I was taken on a most extraordinary journey. At the end of the play, I sat there weeping until finally all the lights had been turned off and the theater was dark.*

Have you ever seen or experienced something so profound, so overwhelming, so wonderful, that in the end, though it was a beautiful experience, you were nonetheless left with a deep sense of sadness? This was the case for me, after seeing The Road to Mecca. *Perhaps it is because I have doubts that I will ever achieve that greatness. I was in awe of your honesty, your simplicity, and your courage. Or perhaps it was simply that I wanted to embrace you, and I knew I could not.*

I have never written a letter to a performer before, so it is very possible that I am not using proper "fan" etiquette. If this is the case, please forgive my naïveté and know that these words come from the bottom of my heart.

I suppose that I would feel too uncomfortable to wait for you by the backstage door, so this is my compromise. Although I know I would be very nervous to meet you, I'm going to hold my breath and ask you anyway.

Just so you know that I'm not a lunatic, I got my M.F.A. in acting from NYU. and to pay back all my loans I am a professional interpreter for the deaf. Actually, that doesn't prove that I'm not a lunatic but I hope you will meet with me anyway. Enclosed you will find my phone number. If you are inspired, please feel free to call.

> *With much admiration and respect,*
> *Camryn Manheim*

Not wanting to entrust my bared soul to the U.S. Postal Service, I—get this—hopped on my bike and drove back into that bizarre twilight zone above 72nd Street. Acting as my own courier, I went into the theater, found the house manager, and handed him my letter with the following request: "Hi, I'm Kathy's sister, and it is imperative that she receive this letter. It's regarding an important family matter. Thank you."

Now, we've all done something like this before, half knowing that all fan mail goes into a giant pile that is slowly fed into the shredder and then into the recycling bin. But we cling to the fantasy that our letter will be read by our idol and he or she will be so touched that a personal response is in order. Who was I kidding? A Broadway actress who is closing *The Road to Mecca* at the

Promenade and opening *Frankie and Johnnie in the Clair de Lune* at the West Side Theater doesn't have time to call starry-eyed, aspiring actresses and arrange a meeting.

Rrrrrrring! Rrrrrring! Rrrrrring! Rrrrrring! Beeeeeep!

"Hi, this is Camryn, I'm not in right now, but please leave a message and I'll get right back to you."

"Hi, Camryn, this is Kathy Bates. I got your sweet letter. Sorry I missed you, but here's my home number . . . give a call and we'll get together."

How fucking cool is that? She gave me her *home number*! Not wanting to seem too eager, I waited a whole hour before I called her back, and despite my best efforts at nonchalance, I felt like the lunatic I had promised her I wasn't. She was so kind and so gracious that she immediately put me at ease. Despite her hectic schedule, she invited me to dinner and I met her at the theater after one of her shows.

I wish I could remember every single moment from that special evening with Kathy. I do remember that she was so wonderful to be around and had such a generous spirit. But mostly I just sat there thinking "Oh my God, I'm having dinner with Kathy Bates." She would share some poignant moment from her struggles of being a big woman in a thin-obsessed industry, and even while I was nodding in recognition of our kindred experience, I kept thinking "I can't believe Kathy Bates is talking to me!" I was already leaping ahead to the next time an agent told me I reminded him of Kathy Bates. "Oh, yeah, Kathy and I had dinner last week. Wasn't she just brilliant in *The Road to Mecca*?"

Even though some of the details of that dinner are a little sketchy, I left there with a renewed sense of "I can do this." I understood that because of Kathy I was going to have more opportunities. And I was right. Kathy Bates opened doors for me and all women like me that had previously been closed. She brought a unique grace, humanity, and genius to the stage and screen that forced the industry to recognize women who had theretofore been overlooked. For the first time I had someone to emulate.

Kathy and I didn't meet again until 1997, nine years after our first meeting. I had had a few small parts in movies and had recently landed my role on *The Practice*. I was having lunch with a friend when I saw Kathy walking toward my table. I gave my friend the five-second version of my Kathy Bates story and asked him if I should say hi. He said, "Of course. Don't be shy." But I was. I began to say, "Hi, Kathy, I don't know if you remember me, but I'm Cam—"

But before I could get my name out, she said, "Of course I remember you, Camryn. I've been following your rise. Congratulations."

I can't remember anything more about the exchange because I instantly snapped back into Oh-my-God, Kathy-Bates-is-talking-to-me mode. To hear your idol say she's been "following your rise"—there are no words . . .

The Women of Wrath

Hopefully by this point it's been well established that I am a theater geek. I can't get enough. When I'm in New York, I go to a show every night. Some are sublime, some not so good. But just the opportunity to see a once-in-a-lifetime performance. A moment. A live connection between actors or between actor and audience. Not something you can resurrect time and time again in your VCR. A moment. Real life. Real art.

Now, I love movies. And television has been very, very good to me. But that camera lens just isn't the same as these eyes. So I go to the theater and I laugh and I cry and I love those brave colleagues of mine on the high wire, performing without a net, no second, third, and fourth takes to get that tear just right.

I'd been out of NYU for six years when I finally started to make a tiny little name for myself in the New York theater. So going to a show was doubly fun for me now because I was virtually guaranteed to run into someone I knew and we could gab about this production or that and exchange kudos with one another.

Once I began studying at the New York School for the Deaf in 1989, I started regularly attending all the signed shows. Before I got involved with the deaf community, it had never occurred to me how inaccessible theater must be for the nonhearing. But then the Broadway producers began putting on interpreted shows. And don't get me wrong, it wasn't a philanthropic endeavor. Broadway producers are ardent capitalists, and they saw the opportunity for increased ticket sales. Deaf people's dollars make the same sweet *cha-ching* in the cash register as hearing people's. Another benefit of going to an interpreted show was that all the deaf people and the sign-language students got really great seats so we'd be close enough to the stage to see the interpreters.

So when I got the notice in the mail that *The Grapes of Wrath* was being interpreted for the deaf at the Cort Theater on Broadway, I was so excited! The Joads' cathartic journey fully realized just a few yards away. It was one of the few books I actually read in high school, and one of only two that I liked. The other one was Nancy Friday's *My Secret Garden*. I couldn't wait. I gladly coughed up the dough.

But this promised to be more than just great seats for a great story. Hey, we've all sat stageside at our high school's butchering of some otherwise wonderful Shakespeare play. No, this was going to be a great production by an amazing company, Steppenwolf out of Chicago. The alumni include John Malkovich, Gary Sinise, Lois Smith, Joan Allen, John C. Reilly, Terry Kinney, etc., and they were all the rage. Of course I must admit that my excitement was also cut with a shot of bittersweet jealousy. Ah, the joyous misery of watching others do exactly what you want to be doing. And doing it well. They were on Broadway . . . and even though I had lopped off four or five of the "offs" from my credits, I was still three "offs" from the Great White Way!

It was going to be a special night. No doubt about it.

Now, unlike most theatergoers, who hail cabs or take the subway—or roll up in the stretch limo—I prefer the independence of my motorcycle. It's easy to park, easy to weave in and out of gridlock, and you never have to give more than one person a ride. I arrived at the theater a little early to gab and backslap, not to be confused with backstab, and take in the preshow juice.

I find my seat. It's in a good spot. On the aisle, eight rows from the stage. I stuff my backpack and my helmet under my seat and begin to schmooze. I see friends and fellow actors and people from the school. There's a definite buzz. "I'm so excited . . . I hear Lois Smith is *amazing* . . . hey, you were great in such-and-such . . . and I simply loved you in blah-blah-blah . . ." And so on. I am standing in the aisle, near my seat, holding court and having a great preshow chat. These moments are precious because they all take place against the ticking clock of a soon-to-rise curtain. True theater geeks know that the pre- and postshow experiences often equal or exceed the show itself. Not tonight, though; not with Lois Smith and Terry Kinney.

As I gabbed in the aisle, a middle-age couple arrived at my row and I moved aside to let them in. They were a typical theater couple, perfectly coiffed, all decked out for the evening. We gave each other that We-don't-know-each-other, but-we'll-be-sitting-awfully-close nod as they began to make their way to their seats.

The gentleman negotiated his way without incident, but his wife managed to trip on my motorcycle helmet. From the looks of her, it was probably the first time in her life she'd come in any kind of contact with a motorcycle helmet. She didn't go down in a heap. There'd be no hip replacement surgery. There was no embarrassing I've-fallen-and-I-can't-get-up moment. But, despite the relative insignificance of the stumble, the almost imperceptible misstep, I apparently had an enemy for the evening.

"I'm so sorry," I said, moving quickly to stuff the offending headgear farther under my seat.

She didn't say a word. She just snarled, sneered, and shot me a look that my many years of acting training allowed me to interpret instantly. Her subtext was: "How unconscionable. To think of it, a motorcycle helmet in my theater! And now I have to sit next to the lesbian cow who owns it. She probably smells. Oh God, I declare it the worst night of the season here at the Cort Theater."

If looks could kill.

So I sheepishly took my seat next to her, trying desperately to melt into the right side of my seat so as not to brush inadvertently against Cruella.

As the show began, I could feel her hot wave of hatred flowing over me. This woman intended to stay pissed for the entire show. It seemed she had decided her night had been ruined and wasn't going to let any brilliant acting get in the way of her conviction. If my left arm drifted toward our shared armrest, her right arm recoiled so rapidly she risked ligament damage. But it was a small price to pay, apparently, for not having to brush up against the *Thing* with the Helmet.

She was a Capulet. I was a Montague. She was a Jet. I was a

Shark. She was Javert. I was Jean Valjean. We're talking lots of hate here.

Thank God for the artistry of the play, rescuing me from Cruella, transporting me to that dusty Oklahoma wasteland, which was far preferable to my seat at that moment. The dust bowl wasn't nearly as oppressive as a bitchy New York theater-goer. The show, as expected, was brilliant. Every nuance, every exchange perfect.

At intermission, you could feel it in the house. We were all *experiencing* something. But even if Cruella had been transported, she hadn't forgiven or forgotten. She excused herself past fifteen people to her left to avoid having to speak to me. Everyone was wondering what the hell was wrong with this lady. Could she not see that she was one seat from the aisle to her right? Boy, she was doing a really great job of making me feel bad. I wondered if she was worried that the helmet might jump out and grab her ankle again if she tried to pass my way. I also contemplated putting the helmet on for protection should she return with a mallet or baton of some sort.

She returned by the same route, inconveniencing an entire row before she'd deign to ask me to move. Her husband was quite embarrassed but followed her faithfully over twisted knees and squashed feet.

The palpable tension gave way to act two. I was right there, with those Joads, generations and thousands of miles away from my sworn enemy. I forgot all about Cruella. They actually had a real swimming hole built right into the stage. I had never even been in a play with running water. It was magical.

I was already weeping when Rose of Sharon—played beautifully by Sally Murphy—brought her dying baby to her breast. When the baby died, I lost it, sobbing like, well, a baby. And just when I thought that raw moment couldn't get any more tender, Rose of Sharon offered her lactating breast to the starving stranger in the field so that he might live. I was devastated.

And then the most remarkable thing happened.

My adversary, my nemesis for the night, reached over and took my hand. She didn't say anything. She just held my hand.

The curtain came down and the lights came up. She didn't say anything as she exited. She didn't have to.

Years later I was lucky enough to work with Lois Smith, who had been so brilliant as Ma Joad. I told her this story and we wept a little all over again.

*   *   *

The theater, however, doesn't always unite people.

After doing the show *Missing Persons,* for which I won an Obie—a coveted off-Broadway theater award—I was invited into the prestigious Atlantic Theater Company. We were to stage an open reading of Clare Booth Luce's *The Women* to benefit breast cancer research. Now, rightfully so, breast cancer gets out all the heavy hitters. So my castmates included Sigourney Weaver, Marisa Tomei, Sandy Duncan, Kristen Johnston, Ileen Getz, Kate Burton, Katie Erbe, Felicity Huffman, Dorothy Louden, Mary McCann, Mary McCormack, F. Murray Abraham, and the Grande Dame of the theater, Celeste Holm.

Celeste Holm had not only been appearing on Broadway for over fifty years beginning in 1938, she had won an Oscar in 1947 for *Gentleman's Agreement* and twice more been nominated, once for *Come to the Stable* and once for her incredible work in *All About Eve*. We were all dutifully respectful.

We would have one rehearsal during the day and then perform the reading that same night. Not a lot of time for making brave choices, but we'd do the best we could.

The role I was assigned was a Little-Old-Lady-Who-Lived-in-a-Shoe type with many, many children, one of whom I was supposed to be breast-feeding. But it was clear from the script that she cared much more about the gossip than her goslings. During the run-through, I came upon this wonderful sequence where—with baby at my bosom—I accidentally dropped a cigarette ash on my breast. When asked what it was, I said matter-of-factly, "Oh, that? That's an ash." I decided that in between those two lines, I'd blow the ash away. So it would read like this: "Oh, that?" Blow. "That's an ash." My little choice got a wonderful roar during the read-through. "Hey," I thought, "I can hang with these chicks." But apparently I hadn't scored with the Grande Dame.

Celeste Holm cornered me after the read-through and said, "I did this play years ago and I am quite sure Clare Booth did not intend for you to blow in between the lines, thereby breaking them up. Rather, you should blow after the second line for emphasis."

Wow. I thanked her for her note and assured her that I would heed her well-informed advice. I couldn't believe she had even taken the time to mention it to me. It seemed fairly insignificant, and my delivery definitely worked in the rehearsal. But, hey, she's the Grande Dame for a reason.

After rehearsal some of the girls in the company and I went out for dinner before the show. I asked them which reading they thought was funnier: line, blow, line, or line, line, blow? And they all agreed that my way was the better, funnier choice.

"Well," I said, "I've got a problem."

I explained that I had just received this instruction from Oscar-winning Celeste Holm and that I'd told her I'd do it her way.

The girls all lost it, totally cracked up, laughing hysterically. Ms. Holm, it seemed, had made the rounds, giving every single actor in the production a note here or a note there about how they should play their roles. We made a pact that we'd just pretend we hadn't understood her sage advice and do what our instincts told us.

Still, I was going back and forth: my way, her way, my way, her way. Back at the theater, I felt good about my decision to do what was in my heart and hoped she wouldn't see fit to call me out on it after the show. If she did, I would just pretend—drawing on all that acting training—that I really hadn't understood her. That was my plan. For the moment, anyway.

Before we went on stage to do this benefit reading, Celeste Holm pushed her way over to me and wagged her finger in my face.

"Just in case you didn't understand me earlier," she began, "the blow needs to come at the end. For emphasis. Not in the middle. Got it?"

Gulp. "Uh-huh, yeah, I got it!" How could I pretend to not have understood that? Twice? I was looking around for support, hoping that Sigourney or someone would interject "I thought it was funny the way she did it," but everyone seemed to be preoccupied. Probably working on the notes Celeste had given them earlier that afternoon. I was alone. Trapped. I wanted to be respectful but at the same time remain true to my instincts. "I am so grateful for your input, but I feel more comfortable doing it the way I did it during rehearsal."

"Well, you're wrong and you're a fool."

Okay . . . let me try again.

"Well, for me, it just comes more naturally in the middle. That's my instinct."

"That's the problem with you young actors. You think your instincts matter. Technique is what matters. There is no such thing as a great instinctive actor. There are only great technical actors!"

And she stormed off.

Moments later, I was standing in the wings flanked by Dorothy Louden, Sandy Duncan, and Sigourney Weaver. I looked around and realized I was surrounded by Oscars and Tonys and Emmys, and my Obie seemed suddenly insignificant. What the hell was I doing here? Besides pissing off Celeste Holm. And then the lights went down. And when they came back up this pantheon of acting goddesses strode onto the stage. *The Women* indeed!

The audience took a deep collective breath and exploded into wild cheers. I could live here. Ah, the white light of acceptance.

The reading began, and while some of my colleagues sat there mesmerized by the amazing talents on display, I was a wreck! My line that had caused a *frisson* with Miss Holm was approaching as rapidly as the A train to 42nd Street. Oh, shit, what do I do? It will just be a complete slap in the face to the Grande Dame of the theater if I ignore her advice. But I knew in my gut that my interpretation was better. I could almost feel her eyes on me, waiting to see what I'd do, daring me to cross her. Trust my instincts or bow to her Holm-liness?

Well, by now, I hope you know me well enough to know what I did. Never miss an opportunity to make waves. Or get a laugh.

"Oh, that?" Blow. "That's an ash."

The place went nuts. Laughter, applause. The next line had to hold. At a staged reading! I'm convinced even Clare Booth Luce would have approved.

I couldn't look at Celeste, but I could feel the steam shooting out of her ears. Not only had I crossed her but I'd been right. The show ended and she exited without a word to me.

*   *   *

Sometimes the theater brings us together. And, well, sometimes it doesn't. But either way, if you're lucky, you'll have a great after-dinner story. The theater is one big happy (dysfunctional) family, which is why I feel so at home there. I just hope they always leave a key under the mat for me.

Another F***ing
One-Woman Show

"So why did you write a one-woman show?"
"I wanted to create the only role for which
I would not be rejected."

In the spring of '93, things were looking up. I had my health back, a good job as an interpreter, I had tucked away a little money from *Wellville*, I was working off-off Broadway (for free) and, thanks to Stephen Sondheim, I still had an agent. Now all I had to do was go out and get some more of those paying acting jobs.

After having that great experience in *Wellville*, I was naive enough to believe that I would no longer be stereotyped. But I guess *Wellville* was an anomaly, because there was a recurring theme in the parts for which I was being considered. Can you guess? Yep, every single role I was up for was the put-upon, ugly, butt-of-the-joke fat girl. This put me in the decidedly unenviable position of either being rejected for the part or being told I was absolutely perfect. The absolutely perfect answer never came. I don't know when fat became synonymous with pathetic, sickly, lazy, homely, weak, and stupid, but by the time I hit the audition circuit, these stereotypes were firmly in place.

Sometimes I was fat enough to land the role, just not pathetic, sickly, lazy, homely, weak, and stupid enough. And sometimes I wasn't even fat enough. Once I went in on an audition for the part of Susan—"*a grossly overweight woman of 200 pounds.*" They seemed to be impressed with my audition but in the end said that I was just too thin for the part. I told them that they needed to rethink their description of the character because I weighed well over 200 pounds. They looked at each other incredulously as if they were shocked that I was able to get around without a walker. I wasn't the fat girl they were looking for. I wasn't the fat girl anyone was looking for. I came to realize that I would never get the fat-girl parts because what they really wanted was the self-loathing victim with a kick-me sign on her, not the big, powerful, articulate actor with a sign that says DON'T FUCK WITH ME.

Surely there were roles somewhere for a woman of significance and stature. But where? I scoured the shelves of the Drama Bookstore on 7th Avenue and 48th Street, looking for strong, positive roles for big women. But no luck. The only triumphant characterizations of fat women were when they lost weight and then became the object of others' desires. There was one role in all those stacks that I could find that was written for me. It was Josie in Eugene O'Neill's *A Moon for the Misbegotten*.

> *Josie is twenty-eight. She is so oversize for a woman that she is almost a freak—five-feet-eleven in her stockings and weighs around one hundred and eighty. Her sloping shoulders are broad, her chest deep with large, firm breasts, her waist wide but slender by contrast with her hips and thighs. She has long smooth arms, immensely strong, although no muscles show. The same is true of her legs. She is more powerful than any except for an exceptionally strong man, able to do the manual labor of two ordinary men. But there is no mannish quality about her. She is all woman.*

Josie, twenty-eight, strong as a horse, of the earth, the map of Ireland stamped on her face. Perfect. What I didn't know at the time was that Colleen Dewhurst had screwed it up for me by playing Josie when she was forty-eight years old. Of course she was amazing, winning a Tony in 1974 and forever changing the look of Josie. So it would be another twenty years before I would be old enough to play a character that was written as a twenty-eight-year-old. Bummer.

Faced with this grim paucity of possibilities, I convinced my agent to begin submitting me for male roles. Any time the breakdowns called for a strong, dignified, charismatic man, my agents called to ask if the casting director would consider seeing a woman. More often than not they'd say no, but occasionally they'd say sure, and I booked two parts written for men in three months. Ironically, both parts were lawyers—have I been pigeonholed?—one on *Law and Order* and the other on *New York Undercover*. As rewarding as it was to play those strong, confident characters, I wanted a chance to be tough and dignified while still retaining my femininity.

When I combined this artistic need with my newfound self-confidence, I suppose a one-woman show was inevitable. The only hitch was that I had no idea how to write it. Without any literary stratagems at my disposal, I was left with only the truth. And that's what I wrote. Or at least the truth as I saw it—or as my mother calls it, Roshomon.

So instead of waiting for someone else to write the perfect part for me, I did it myself. The character description called for a strong, confident yet vulnerable, brash but sensitive, motorcycle-riding, fluent in sign language, sexy, voluptuous, 200-pound plus, big-mouthed, big-breasted beauty. And we were only seeing one actor for the role. *C'est moi.*

Although I never considered myself a "writer," I was an inveterate journal keeper and a dedicated correspondent with friends. Still, I had never organized my thoughts into a single cohesive story. And some of the critics who saw my one-woman show think I still haven't. Hey, believe me, if Tony Kushner had written the coming-of-age story of a fat girl—*Cherubs in America?*—I would have much preferred to do his play. But I was stuck with the only writer who would tell this story for free.

Once I began looking through old journals and early photographs and letters from my family, I realized there was a surfeit of stories about how my weight had affected all of my relationships and how it defined who I was. I had been overweight since I was twelve. Subsequently my personality, my politics, my goals, my fears, and my life had all been formed and directly related to the fact that I was fat. I was on to something. I hadn't intended to confront this past that was so damaging and so painful, but I couldn't deny the one theme that kept recurring again and again. It was like pulling a thread on a sweater. Once you start, the whole thing unravels.

Conversations with My Fat: Part Three

There was no denying it anymore. My fat was right. He was my excuse for everything. So I decided to write a one-woman show and give him top billing: *Wake Up, I'm Fat!* by Camryn Manheim. I thought that might shut him up.

No such luck.

FAT: *Hey, this is so cool. We're co-starring in a show together.*

CAM: *Yeah, a show about how much I hate you.*

FAT: *Hate me? After all we've been through together? Who was there for you when Johnny Mercer called you fat in eighth grade? Who was there for you when you didn't have a date to the prom? Who was there for you when you didn't get cast in* The Three Sisters? *Who was there for you when Peter didn't return your call?*

CAM: *Exactly! Don't you see why I hate you?*

FAT: *Again with the hate. You should be thanking me.*

CAM: *For what?*

FAT: *Taking all the blame. It's all my fault: the name-calling, the rejections, the dateless nights, the unreturned phone calls. I always take the blame, but, hey, that's what friends are for.*

CAM: *Let's get one thing straight: You are not my friend.*

FAT: *I'm the best friend you've ever had.*

CAM: *Well, if you're such a great friend, why don't you get lost?*

FAT: *No can do, this is my job.*

CAM: *Well, you're fired.*

FAT: *Sorry, you can't fire me. I have a contract.*

CAM: *Contract? With whom? Who signed it?*

FAT: *You did.*

CAM: *I never signed a contract with you!*

FAT: *Oh, yes you did.*

CAM: *Oh, no I didn't.*

FAT: *Well, somebody did.*

CAM: *It wasn't me.*

FAT: *Well, who was it then?*

CAM: *I don't know. Somebody must have forged my name.*

FAT: *I highly doubt that. No, I remember, it was you. I never forget a face. The body's changed, but the face is the same.*

CAM: *Okay, when did I sign this contract?*

FAT: *Oh, about twenty-two years ago.*

CAM: *I was eleven years old, I can't be accountable for that.*

FAT: *You're accountable for everything.*

CAM: *You took advantage of me when I was vulnerable.*

FAT: *You took advantage of yourself. I'm just the result.*

CAM: *Alright, who's got this contract? Where is it?*

FAT: *You've got it.*

CAM: *I do not.*

FAT: *Yes, you do, you're carrying it on you.*

CAM: *I want to see it.*

FAT: *Got a mirror?*

CAM: *Screw you.*

FAT: *Oh, c'mon, Camryn, you like me, I can tell.*

CAM: *You are so arrogant. When are you going to get it through your thick skull that I hate you.*

FAT: *No, you don't, you love me.*

CAM: *Oh, please shut up, you're making me sick.*

FAT: *Oh, come on Camryn, say it with me: I LOVE YOU!*

CAM: *I will not.*

FAT: *Come on.*

CAM: *Why should I? I've never hated anything more than I hate you.*

FAT: *How can you hate me when I'm the one protecting you?*

CAM: *From what?*

FAT: *Men.*

CAM: *I don't want to be protected from men. I want a man.*

FAT: *No, you don't. You're terrified of men.*

CAM: *No, I'm not.*

FAT: *Really? How come you never introduce me to your boyfriends?*

CAM: *Men won't go out with me because they think I'm already involved with you.*

FAT: *Once again, I take all the blame.*

There's nothing worse than a know-it-all. My fat, of course, was always right. About everything. And literally for decades I let him dictate the course of my life, making only the feeblest attempts to maintain my autonomy. But it was during *Wake Up, I'm Fat!* that I started to figure him out and fight back. What if I stopped blaming him for everything? What if I stopped using him as an excuse? What if I stopped hiding behind him and entered into a covenant with myself that if I failed as an actor or a lover, it was my fault, my responsibility? It wouldn't be easy. I would have so much more at stake, which meant I was going to have to work harder, prepare more thoroughly, and redouble my commitment to my art. From that point forward I wouldn't let myself off the hook so easily with a simple "They didn't choose me because I'm fat." No, if they didn't choose me, it was because I didn't wow them. I stopped relying on my ever-present alibi and put all my energies into wowing them. These were my first baby steps on the journey to self-acceptance. And a funny thing happened on the way to the self-love forum: I learned that confidence, courage, and a little bit of sass can be very seductive.

*   *   *

I wrote every night for three months, telling every story I had in me. I put them all down on paper. I surprised myself with my willingness to tell stories that embarrassed me, that reminded me of all the shame that I had been lugging around lo those twenty years. Some of those stories I had buried so deeply in the recesses of my soul that when I retrieved them I could hardly believe they had happened to me: addiction to speed, battles with my parents, acting rejections, unrequited love, et al.

Bringing those memories to the surface was a wrenching experience, and my nightly writing ritual would inevitably end with me, head in hands, sobbing. It was as if I had been keeping secrets from myself and I wasn't going to pretend anymore that everything was okay. All those years I had had such a heavy heart and I never really understood why. But with each recovered memory, it became increasingly clear. After twelve weeks I had a giant pile of anecdotes, vignettes, and reminiscences. Now what?

Hello, friends.

My friend Nancy Quinn said she'd produce it. Michael Mayer, the current golden boy of New York theater, said he'd direct it. And my friend Cindy Tolan became my dramaturg. She was the first person to read it and she worked with me, tirelessly shaping the disjointed ramblings of a fat girl into a presentable piece of theater. When Michael was offered a paying gig to direct Tony Kushner's *Perestroika*—which launched Michael's career—he had to back out. But his parting gift was sublime. It was Michael who saw through the morass of recollections and captured the essence of my story. Before he left to go be a big shot, he said, "You should call it *Wake Up, I'm Fat!*" I wish I had thought of that.

I couldn't have Michael Mayer—file his name, because he'll be back—so I really wanted to "hire" someone (which was a joke since nobody was getting paid) who understood what it was like to grow up as a fat, Jewish girl in America. Enter Mark Brokaw, a tall, thin, WASPY guy from the Midwest. We had one thing in common, Illinois. And that was about the extent of our shared experience. Oh yeah, and the theater. Mark was a fantastic director. Over the years I had watched him extract some incredible performances from my peers, and I hoped he could do the same for me. I begged him to direct my one-woman show. And miracle of miracles, he agreed.

So now I had a title, a director, and hours of material. All I needed was a venue. The good folks down at Home for Contemporary Theater and Art offered me a stage. Well, not a stage exactly. They were in the midst of extensive renovations on their new theater but were willing to let artists use what amounted to a construction site in the evenings when the workers stopped pounding. There were no guarantees as to which part of the warehouse would be available and which parts would be covered with dropcloths and sawdust. But it was just a reading, no big whoop, and if there's one thing actors in New York learn, it's how to make do. Space is so limited in the city that we could put on a play in a bathroom. Or on a staircase, which is where I found myself for the very first reading of *Wake Up, I'm Fat!* With no other space available, I performed from the stairs to an audience of seventy-five invited guests seated on folding chairs in a hallway. Through a light mist of soot and dust, the reading ran three hours.

I had no expectations. I had hopes, but no expectations. No one besides Cindy had heard the material, and a huge part of me was asking "Who gives a shit?" And as I write this chapter, I find that question once again echoing in my mind. I was asking people to come and listen to me for three hours, blab on and on about the hardships of being fat and feeling inadequate. I could see how it might be relevant to my fat sisters, but would it resonate with anyone else? And I discovered, much to my surprise, the answer was yes. While all my life I had been saying to myself "I suck because I'm fat," others have been saying to themselves "I suck because I'm short . . . I suck because I'm gay . . . I suck because I'm bald . . . I suck because I'm poor . . . I suck because I'm in a wheelchair . . ." Ad infinitum. Everyone can find a reason to hate themselves, which they use as an excuse to keep themselves from moving forward. I sure had.

As I finished the reading, I could sense that something special had happened. If not for the audience, for me. I had feared that by telling these stories I was making myself vulnerable to insult and injury. But quite the opposite had occurred. I walked off that stage—I mean those stairs—empowered. Empowered by the truth. You know, the truth really *can* set you free.

When I went home that night, I wondered where the hell I had gotten the chutzpah to lay myself bare in front of friends and strangers. I'll never know. But I would never be the same. The next day the theater's artistic directors, Randy Rollison and Barbara Busackino, asked if I wanted to open up their new space in the fall with an open-ended run of *Wake Up, I'm Fat!* Not too shabby.

Days later my friend Thaddeus, who had been storing a cute little Honda 90 motorcycle in my basement, came by to pick it up. He was having a hard time getting it started, so being the savvy biker veteran that I am, I leaned in to give him a hand. Just then the handyman of my building walked by and said, "You better not get on that little thing or you'll break it." Three days earlier I would have laughed in embarrassment and said, "Oh, I know, don't worry, just releasing the choke." But the new me—posttransformation—wasn't taking any shit from anybody, least of all that asshole in 6F.

I surprised myself when I almost reflexively said, "Was it your intention to embarrass me in front of my friend? And if so, the shame doesn't belong to me, it belongs to you."

Three things happened in that moment. I was not a victim. Thaddeus did not have to feel awkward for not defending me. And the handyman was genuinely contrite. He never mistreated me again.

I was on a roll. I was feeling so strangely confident with this new self-acceptance that I was almost looking forward to people fucking with me.

*   *   *

That summer I found myself back at the beach house on Fire Island. My uncle's health hadn't been good for a few years, and he loved it when we would all gather in the small oceanfront house and be the picture of a happy family.

I was still convinced a person looked thinner with a good tan, so one morning I set out for the beach, bikini and all, to get that slenderizing bronze color. My uncle's house was in the middle-class section of Fire Island (if there is such a thing as middle-class beachfront property), far from the better-known area of the Island called the Pines, where all the groovy people hung out—the fabulous homosexuals. On this particular morning, knowing my family would never venture that way, I walked about a mile down the beach toward the Pines. I wasn't feeling that self-conscious because (a) I knew my folks would never find me, and (b) none of the boys would pay a fat girl in a bikini much mind.

I had been there about an hour. I was lying on my stomach getting my back golden brown, just about to turn over, when my mother, who must have radar, found me on the beach. I was too embarrassed to turn over while she was watching me, too self-conscious to let her see me in such an unflattering position, so instead I lay there talking to her for the next forty-five minutes or so, getting first-degree burns on my back. That's how deep this psychosis runs.

My parents had heard tell of this play I was writing, but I don't think they ever thought anything would become of it. Maybe a small run in a shoe-box theater, which is indeed how it all began.

But still, I felt a responsibility to tell them that I planned to expose some of our family secrets, and I wanted them to know it was not out of malice, just out of a quest for truth. And the embarrassment of lying there on the beach practically naked in front of my mother seemed a fair exchange for the bomb I was about to drop. Tit for tat. Humiliation for humiliation.

"Mom, do you remember when I didn't speak to Dad for almost a year?"

"Oh, yes," she said, "you were so mad at him because he wouldn't help you with your taxes."

"Well, actually, I didn't speak to him because he suggested I start smoking again, after I had gained so much weight back. Do you remember that?"

"Oh, Camryn, your father didn't mean it that way, you are just too sensitive."

"Well, Mom, I've put that story in my play. Just wanted you to know."

I could tell she was relieved that it wasn't a story about her. But then I said, "And, Mom, do you remember when I screamed at you in Bloomingdale's?"

"Oh, yes, you were so upset because I brought you the wrong color dress."

"Well, actually, Mom, I was upset because you brought me a size 16, when I had asked you to bring me a size 22."

"Oh, Camryn, it was a simple mistake."

"Well, that's in my play too."

"Oh, all right."

I could tell she wasn't too happy about it, but what makes my mother so unbelievably strong is that she has an amazing capacity to make things all right. Like a lot of mothers, she has dedicated a good part of her life to putting out all the little fires that have threatened to raze our family. And she said, "Have you ever heard of Roshomon, Camryn?"

"Yes," I said, "it means through our own eyes, we see what we see."

"Well, it's all Roshomon, Camryn. It's all Roshomon."

And then I knew it would be okay. My mother had found a way to protect herself and had given me permission to tell my story. She could see that this would be a healthy cathartic experience for me, and that even though it might be painful for her, she encouraged me to tell my story. That is the very essence of maternal selflessness. I could stop worrying that I might be hurting my family and start working on healing myself.

She finally left, and I turned my sunburned body over and sighed in relief. I was not going to alienate my family by telling the truth.

In my family, Roshomon was a way of life. If you ask my brother, my sister, my mother, my father, and me to describe the events of any holiday gathering or any family trip, you will get five wildly disparate stories. And they're all true. That's the beauty of Roshomon. But, thankfully, I was the only person writing a one-woman show.

*   *   *

The word was out. I was going to do a show called *Wake Up, I'm Fat!*, which was creating a scandalous buzz. You just don't use the word "fat" in polite company. It was a big deal, opening a newly renovated theater off Broadway. I wanted everything to be perfect. The one thing I wasn't worried about was the title.

Wake Up, I'm Fat! Pretty simple, right? You got the "Wake Up" part and then the "I'm Fat" part. No tricks. It certainly isn't as convoluted as, say, Alanis Morissette's album *Supposed Former Infatuation Junkie*. But still, people struggled mightily to get the name of my play right.

Over the course of the show's run, people would call to make reservations. In most cases for low-budget one-person shows, the reservation phone line is just the home phone number of the performer, and this was no exception. Because there wasn't a lot of advertising (advertising budget $0), I relied on word of mouth for audiences. Apparently there was a big game of Telephone going on out there, because while the title started as *Wake Up, I'm Fat!*, by the time it got all the way back to the reservation line (my answering machine), it had mutated.

I'd get messages like "Hello, I'd like two tickets for *Excuse Me, I'm Fat!*," or "Yes, may I please reserve four tickets for *Watch Out, I'm Fat.*" But my all-time favorite was "Good evening, I would like to reserve six tickets for the Friday performance of *I Woke Up and I Was Fat.*" Imagine that. You go to sleep skinny and you wake up fat. Now, *that* would be an interesting one-woman show.

*   *   *

Opening night was approaching. My parents were flying in from California. My cousins were coming from Brussels. Family and friends from all over the tri-state area had confirmed. I was a wreck. I could almost hear the roll of self-confidence I had been on screeching to a halt. The I-suck mantra was slowly but surely creeping its way back into my routine. I was really concerned that my parents would never speak to me again after the show. I had warned them that some of the material would not show them in the most positive light and suggested that they hold off on inviting all of their friends until they had seen the show. I kept falling back on what my mother had told me on the beach that summer. "It's all Roshomon, Camryn. It's all Roshomon." They took solace in their position that they had acted the way any good parents would have. I held a different view and was so nervous that by expressing it I would alienate them forever.

At this point it didn't matter. Opening night was sold out.

I arrived at the theater at 5:00 P.M. Randy and Barbara met me in the lobby with anguished looks on their faces. I slowly took in the scene. The marquee wasn't lit up. The concession stand wasn't set up. The lobby lights were dim. Something was rotten in Denmark.

All the possibilities ran through my mind. Had half the people canceled their reservations? Had the computer that operates the light board blown up? Had the theater been ripped off and all my props been stolen?

Nope. Randy explained that he had spent the whole day arguing with the fire marshal about whether the building was up to code. Randy had lost the argument, and the theater had been shut down. Not just for one night, not just for one weekend, but for a *month* while the needed repairs would be made to bring it up to code.

Fuck. I had family in from Belgium, for Christ's sake! As I stood there dazed I thought of family and friends who at that moment were driving in from Massachusetts and Connecticut and upstate New York. Fuck.

In one moment opening-night jitters became closed-for-repairs blues. I didn't know what to do. I must have seemed pretty desperate when I asked if I could use the staircase, but they told me that even that area wasn't up to code. I just stood at the front door of the lobby, waiting to break the bad news to all the people who had bought tickets to help make my opening night a success. It was heartbreaking. I tried to make light of it to ease the pain, but I was hurting. My mom arrived and comforted me with her favorite no-big-whoop saying "It's not gonna send bombs to Russia." And even if only for a moment, it worked. It did make me feel better. It was just a play, after all.

As I watched my audience file back out of the building, I wondered why my will was being tested so and what good could come of it.

I decided I was not going to let my cousins get back on that plane to Belgium or let my parents get back on that plane to California without seeing my show. I'd do it in my living room if I had to. The next morning I called every theater in New York that I had ever ushered at, done the lights for, done a reading in, or performed in, and asked if I could do my show the following night (Saturday) after their main stage show was done. Everyone was very understanding and a lot of artistic directors tried to make it happen, but it was David Esbjornson at the Classic Stage Company who came to my rescue. Not only would he let me do my show on one day's notice, but since the current show had just closed, he offered me the eight o'clock time slot.

In the next twenty-four hours, Lisa, Mark, and I struck the set at Home for Contemporary Theater and Art, moved my show to the Classic Stage Company, redesigned the lights, reblocked the show, changed the levels on the sound, and called each and every ticket buyer to alert them that the show would indeed go on.

Perhaps this was why my will was being tested. To make me prove how much I wanted it, how much I was willing to fight for

my show. A year earlier I might have thrown my hands up and sur-
rendered in defeat.

But I was driven by a strange new force that was compelling
me to fight this battle. I'd heard about this so-called muse and always nodded knowingly when others had talked about theirs, but
for the first time I was feeling the power of my own. And she was
mighty.

Once again I arrived at the theater at 5:00 P.M., prepared for
any crisis, glitch, or natural disaster that might derail my show.
And with my parents coming, there was that part of me that was
half hoping for a stay of execution, delaying the inevitable showdown. But no such luck. The doors were open, the concession
stand was stocked, the lobby lights were bright. Lisa (stage manager extraordinaire), my comrade and all-around pillar of
strength, was mopping the stage.

Author's note: You don't know Lisa Iacucci, but if you did,
you'd understand why I have to take a moment to sing her praises.
I swear she is omniscient. Midway through your question, she
gives you the answer.

"Where are my—"

"On your makeup table."

"When is—"

"Seven forty-five."

"How many—"

"Two hundred ninety-nine."

"Who—"

"Barbara."

Even now, five years and 3,000 miles removed, I can call Lisa
Iacucci and she can tell me where I left my car keys. I'd like to say
we were in tune with each other, but the truth is she was in tune

with me. There are a million things that can go wrong with a production, particularly a low-budget one, and the stage manager is
all that stands between you and catastrophe. All the fires I didn't
see, Lisa had already put out. You may think it's impossible to
move a show across town in twenty-four hours, but you don't
know Lisa Iacucci. She is my dearest friend, my most trusted confidante, and the world is a better place because she's in it.

When I walked into the theater and saw Lisa mopping the
stage, I realized that my entire life had been a prelude to this moment. She pretended it was no big deal, just another night in another theater, another show. But she and I both knew that the situation had all the earmarks of a defining moment. If not in my
career, then in my life.

I'm not going to get into my thoughts as curtain approached
because I don't have the vocabulary to adequately illustrate that
level of neurosis. But often in times of severe panic, a strange
calm sets in. I was soothed by the familiarity . . . the eight-ten
show time, the hum of anticipation in the audience, the programs
rustling and Lisa's tiny little footfalls as she came backstage to tell
me it was time.

. . . and then it was over. During the bows, I looked for my parents, but people were standing and clapping and I couldn't see
them. I went backstage to wait for the verdict. When Lisa came
into the dressing room, I asked her if she'd seen my folks. She
smiled and said, "They loved it." The fear that had prevented me
from enjoying the experience was gone, replaced by a sensation I
was altogether unfamiliar with: pride. I walked out into the lobby
with my head held high.

In the lobby, my mom and dad were holding court. People
were approaching and congratulating them. They had that look

on their faces that said more than any words could. I'm not going to get all schmaltzy here, but getting the approval you've been seeking since you were a little girl is pretty fucking great.

I had been so worried that my parents would feel humiliated and resent me for airing our dirty laundry, but they surprised me. They took a videotape of the show home with them, and every Friday night invited a group of friends over for dinner and a private screening. Instead of driving us apart, the show had brought us closer together. I had said in my play that I was doing it for three reasons: to have a cathartic experience, to catapult my career, and to get a boyfriend. But perhaps the most significant accomplishment of my show was that it forged a new relationship between me and my folks. And I've got to say, there aren't too many parents out there who could have handled my show with so much grace and class.

*   *   *

The next day David Esbjornson invited me to finish my month run at the Classic Stage Company. From there the show moved to Second Stage, where it continued to pick up momentum. During its run at Second Stage I allowed myself the fantasy of performing *Wake Up, I'm Fat!* at my favorite theater in New York.

From those first awestruck days in New York City, I had dreamed about performing at the Joseph Papp Public Theater. It was half a block from NYU, and I passed it every day always pausing to acknowledge its grandeur.

It was five years after I graduated from NYU that I first stepped on the main stage at the Public Theater. Not in front of an audience, mind you, but just for rehearsals. I was an understudy in

Henry IV, Parts 1 and 2, and Ruth Maleczech never got sick. But I didn't care. I was working at the Public.

The following year I got a job in the chorus. Though I had few lines, they were in front of a live audience. The next summer when I was cast as Lucetta in the Public's production of *Two Gentlemen of Verona*, I knew I was moving up because they had cast me as a character with a name. But still, I never truly expected to have my name above the title on a poster in the lobby.

Two years after I first performed *Wake Up, I'm Fat!* on the staircase, Rosemarie Tichler, the associate artistic director of the Public Theater, called to invite me to perform my show on one of their prestigious stages. My reality had exceeded my dreams. Not only would I be performing at the Public, but they'd be paying me what seemed like a fortune: $400 a week. Sweet.

As I think back to those long nights, crying in front of my computer, it seems hard to believe that the show went anywhere, much less the Public. It's really pretty surreal: that reading on the stairs, the fire marshal as grim reaper at Home for Contemporary Theater, saved by Classic Stage, and arriving at the Public.

As I said, I had set three goals for the show: have a cathartic experience, catapult my career, and find a boyfriend. Two out of three ain't bad. In case you missed it, the boyfriend form is on page 117.

If I Were
Thin . . .

Like most fat girls, I have spent way too much of my life contemplating how things would be different if I were thin. What a fucking waste of time!

While writing my one-woman show, I pored through the archives of my life and came across lists and lists of "If I were thins . . ." in my journals. Here, now, I am disposing of them once and for all.

12/20/73: *If I were thin, I'd sit on Santa's lap and lift my feet up off the floor.*
—First of all, I'm Jewish. Second, I'm all grown up now and the only lap I'm interested in sitting in is the lap of luxury.

12/23/74: If I were thin, I'd skate out to the middle of the lake.

—During those brutal Midwest winters, I'd think about this one a lot. Gee, now that I live in Southern California, where the only ice skating is at the mall, I hardly think about it at all.

7/16/75: If I were thin, I'd love the summer.

—I *do* love the summer: barbecues, sailing, outdoor concerts, long motorcycle rides, Shakespeare in the Park, the Renaissance Faire. In fact, I love it so much, I can't even be sarcastic about this one.

7/19/75: If I were thin, I'd ride a horse—no, a pony.

—Who needs a horse when you've got a hog? I ride a Honda CB650.

8/7/75: If I were thin, I'd jump on a trampoline.

—Yeah, it's been tough. I can't tell you how often this one comes up.

9/14/81: If I were thin, I would have been beautiful enough to be in the Miss California Pageant.

—See cover.

6/23/82: If I were thin, I'd slam dance.

—Slam dance? Who slam dances? Oh, right, Billy Idol was huge in '82.

6/29/83: If I were thin, I would have been accepted to the Yale School of Drama.

—And had to spend three years in New Haven, Connecticut. No thanks. If my fat saved me from that fate, I am forever grateful.

6/29/83: If I were thin, I would have been accepted to Juilliard.

—And I'd still be trying to unlearn those haughty speech lessons.

10/22/83: If I were thin, I wouldn't hide the Hershey's chocolate syrup behind the oatmeal.

—That is crazy talk, hiding the Hershey's syrup. You've got to have quick access to that nectar of the gods.

3/9/84: If I were thin, I could be on top.

—Turns out, if you're fat, you can be on top too. Been there, done that, loved it, hope to do it again real soon.

6/22/84: If I were thin, I'd drink regular Coke.

—Woo, imagine the fun. Truth is, I don't even like regular Coke.

4/16/85: If I were thin, I'd never say "I am powerless over fudge."

—a) I can't believe I actually ever said that. b) Which, of course, isn't to say that I *do* have any power over fudge. Particularly if it has nuts.

11/3/85: If I were thin, I'd play an ingenue.

—Done it, thanks Tony Kushner.

8/7/86: *If I were thin, I wouldn't have to depend on my cleavage.*

—If I were thin, I wouldn't have any cleavage. And that, Theodore Dreiser, would be *An American Tragedy.*

9/3/86: *If I were thin, I'd fit into the paper gown at the doctor's office.*

—What I've learned is if you wear two gowns, your butt doesn't flap in the breeze.

11/27/87: *If I were thin, I wouldn't hold the towel rack when I got on the scale.*

—Easily fixed. Now I don't own a scale.

1/15/88: *If I were thin, I would have participated in those trust exercises at school. You know the ones where you stand on a table and fall into people's arms.*

—In retrospect, I think that was a good instinct. Fat or thin, you shouldn't be falling off tables on purpose.

6/1/88: *If I were thin, I'd go to my high school reunion.*

—July '99, you know I'll be there. (Is it tacky to bring your Emmy? Just curious.)

8/31/88: *If I were thin, I wouldn't be jealous when friends lost weight.*

—Sure I would. If being thin was that important to me, I'd never be thin enough not to be jealous.

2/13/89: *If I were thin, I could see my feet.*
—Seen 'em. No big whoop.

5/12/89: *If I were thin, I'd wear horizontal stripes.*
—Why? They look crappy on everybody.

5/12/89: *If I were thin, I'd tuck things in.*
—Well, I'm not and I do it anyway. Hips, hips, hooray!

7/11/89: *If I were thin, I could go to all-you-can-eat restaurants.*
—Not sure I understand my reasoning on this one. Thin people don't go to all-you-can-eat restaurants. Besides, I can live without Sizzler and the all-you-can-eat salad bar at Bennigan's.

4/4/90: *If I were thin, I'd win a daytime Emmy!*
—Little did I know that if I were fat, I'd win a prime-time Emmy.

5/30/90: *If I were thin, I'd put an ad in the personals that said, "I'm smart, I'm funny, I'm beautiful, I was a beauty pageant contender, I love to travel, I love to take long walks on the beach, I love romantic evenings by the fireplace, and I'm thin . . . impress me."*
—And wouldn't that be nauseating?

7/30/90: *If I were thin, I'd bungee jump.*
—Apparently, I was under the impression that weight loss would drive me insane. Which, as we know, it did.

3/8/91: If I were thin, I'd be more forgiving.

—Are you kidding? I'm so forgiving that at the last minute I cut out the "These Are People I Hate" chapter from this book.

6/22/91: If I were thin, I wouldn't have to take a Valium before I went shopping for a swimsuit.

—Which would eliminate the only fun part of shopping for a swimsuit.

9/2/91: If I were thin, I'd take a cooking class.

—Well, that would be a pretty big waste of time since I cook about once a year.

5/14/92: If I were thin, I wouldn't buy lingerie from the catalogs.

—I'd buy it online like everybody else.

10/1/92: If I were thin, I'd stop wishing I had other women's bodies.

—What was I thinking? Even thin women wish they had somebody else's body. That's why it's called the beauty *myth:* The perfect body doesn't exist.

I can't believe how much time and energy I devoted to not only wishing I were thin but actually writing those ridiculous wishes down.

11/6/93: Wake Up, I'm Fat! opens at Classic Stage. I guess I woke up, because this marked the end of my "If I Were Thin" journal entries. Hallelujah.

Déjà Vu
All Over Again

During rehearsals for *Wake Up, I'm Fat!* at the Public, I got a call from Michael Miller, the Director of the Graduate Acting Program at NYU. I figured I was in trouble. Had I forgotten to return a textbook? A costume? A wig? Nope, it turned out Dean Miller wanted me to sit on a panel of alumni and address the grad students with career advice. At this point in my career I found that rather ironic. Or perhaps I was being held up as an example of what not to do.

Joining me on the panel were two other NYU grads, my dear friend Marcia Gay Harden, who had gone on to star in many feature films, and a woman who had quit the business altogether. I was obviously somewhere in the middle, far short of stardom but still plugging away. It was clear that Dean Miller had set it up this way, showing three possible futures to the wide-eyed students.

Marcia and the former-actress-turned-editor, we'll call her Kate, sat on either side of me. The students were most interested in what Marcia had to say, since they were all convinced that they would follow in her footsteps, not mine, and certainly not Kate the quitter's. Marcia, who is an amazing storyteller, held the audience rapt with tales of Hollywood and movie sets and famous directors. I talked about the downtown theater scene below Canal Street, which had always seemed sort of glamorous to me until I heard Marcia's stories. Kate discussed the joys of having health insurance.

When we got around to the Q and A, the first question was "What's the best advice you can give us?" Marcia explained emphatically the importance of always looking your best, adding that you never know who you were going to bump into at the supermarket. As I listened to her, it occurred to me that we must shop at different markets, because I couldn't imagine running into someone who could change my career at the Grand Union on Bleeker and Lafayette. My advice was to work hard, see a lot of theater, and have an appointment scheduled for 10 A.M. every day so as to not sleep the day away. Kate's advice was the most simple: Get out. She said it like a character in *Poltergeist*. There was such horror in her voice as she explained why it was imperative to get out of the business. I have to admit, she made a lot of sense.

While they didn't want to see it that way, I knew that most of those students would follow in my footsteps, the great gray in-between. It's just a mathematical truth. Most actors are not stars. Most actors are not as beautiful and talented as Marcia Gay Harden. Most actors do not even have health insurance. And most actors have a nonacting job to pay the rent. That's how it's always been and that's how it always will be. Of course, those young pups all believed that they were the chosen ones. And it's just that optimistic naïveté that can get you through the lean years.

I really enjoyed addressing the students, and, in fact, it helped clarify a few things for me. As I asked them how hard they were willing to fight for their dreams, I was forced to ask myself the same question.

Every year after that when Dean Miller called to ask if I'd do the panel again, I jumped at the chance. One year Marcia was off doing a film and Kate couldn't make it, and I ended up giving the presentation on my own. Three hours of "Is There Life After Graduate School?" by Camryn Manheim. I took this very seriously. I prepared diligently, creating a list of twenty-five guidelines for jump-starting your career. I had handouts and assigned homework. My professor parents would have been so proud.

What had started as a "Sure, whatever" favor to Dean Miller was becoming something of a passion. I really appreciated the opportunity to steer those kids clear of some of the hurdles I had run smack dab into. I started giving the seminar every year, not just at the graduate acting school but to undergrads, at Playwrights Horizons, the Atlantic Theater, the Learning Annex, and privately as well. Here I was, the one-time teacher's nightmare, now up at the front of the room telling people not to be late. (But I didn't make a federal case out of it if someone needed to get up to use the bathroom.)

While back at NYU, I became reacquainted with a former classmate who was now on the faculty. Let's call him David. He congratulated me on my one-woman show, saying that he had really enjoyed it, but remarked that some of my complaints about NYU were thankfully no longer valid. David told me about a recent faculty meeting at which the teachers had gathered to discuss each individual student, their strengths and weaknesses.

"Camryn, I wish you could have been there," he said. "When it came time to evaluate one of the students with a weight problem, you could tell they all wanted to say something about it, but nobody did. Your presence was palpable. You had been so critical of the teachers in your one-woman show, and I think they just wanted to be sure that if this student ever wrote one, they wouldn't end up in it."

That was music to my ears. In a perfect world, the faculty wouldn't be ignoring a student's weight for fear of repercussions, but rather because it's not an issue as long as she can act. But this was a start.

And good for NYU, which is one of the few elite drama schools that now routinely accepts plus-size actresses into their programs.

I had the privilege of meeting one of these actresses after a lecture I gave to the soon-to-be graduates. And trust me, she didn't need her teachers telling her to lose weight. Like me, she had parents and a thin-obsessed society to do that. She approached me after class and said, "Hi, my name's Ryan. I just had a bad experience and I was wondering if I could get some advice from you."

"Sure, what's up?" I said, already guessing what the underlying issue was.

"I was doing really well and feeling great about graduating," Ryan began, "until I saw myself on film during an on-screen camera class. I was so taken aback at how full my face looked that it made me totally depressed."

Ryan continued as her eyes welled up with tears, echoing every sentiment I had experienced nine years earlier on the precipice of graduation. Am I good enough? Will I work? Will there be a place for me in the business?

Talk about striking a chord. I knew I couldn't undo the decades of self-hatred that had accumulated in her. Hell, I was just trying to figure it out for myself. I saw so much of me in her. I gave her my card and we began a friendship that continues to this day.

Ryan came to see *Wake Up, I'm Fat!* and we began a very open dialogue about women, self-esteem, self-acceptance, self-love. Nine years earlier I wouldn't have been able to engage in such personal conversations about issues that caused me such deep, profound pain. I just wasn't ready to share that with anyone. I had always kept a lid on those dark caverns, where the bogeyman lived. But Ryan was very open and, in that way, courageous. I learned so much about who I had been through seeing myself in her. It was a revelation.

As Ryan prepared for the League Presentations, which nine years ago had completely devastated me, I felt very protective of her. She would face those same daggers, those same judgmental eyes. I worried that the experience might crush her spirit as it had mine.

At the time, my friends David Houts, Daniel Elias, and I were making a documentary about fat acceptance. I thought it would be really interesting to follow Ryan through this potentially traumatic experience to see if anything had changed in nine years.

We filmed her rehearsal for the League Presentations, then interviewed her afterward about her hopes, fears, and expectations. It was as if I had pushed "play" on a tape recording of myself in 1987. I guess I shouldn't have been surprised. Did I really expect things to have changed so much?

She too wanted to change the beauty standard, but when I asked her if she felt beautiful, you could see the pain register on her face. She clearly didn't. I remembered having to trick myself into thinking I was beautiful to make it through the nude scenes in *The Road to Wellville*.

She talked about older women coming up to her and saying "You have such a pretty face . . . if only you could lose some weight." How that reminded me of the yentas at the Jewish Community Center when I was growing up in Long Beach. "*Oy, rachmonos* to the family, she has such a pretty face. What a shame."

Ryan spoke with such tenderness and caution about her mother, careful not to implicate her. In one breath her mother would tell Ryan how beautiful she was, but in the next breath her mother would suggest she try liposuction. Was that so different from my mother who had suggested hypnotism, psychotherapy, and bribery? Liposuction must not have been around yet. Mothers and daughters have such a fragile relationship. Moms want their babies to be beautiful and daughters want to make their mothers proud. The psychotherapy profession would collapse if it weren't for mother-daughter angst.

In keeping with our parallel experiences, while speed was my drug of choice, Ryan had turned to the only-slightly-more-socially-acceptable drugs, fenfluramine and phentermine (fen-phen). We all know that speed is bad for you, but it wasn't until they discovered that people were developing heart valve defects that fen-phen was taken off the market. I asked Ryan how she had first heard about fen-phen and who had provided it. My heart sank when she told me that her mother had suggested it and her father, a doctor, had reluctantly prescribed it. Again, no different from my father suggesting I keep smoking to suppress my appetite, except, of course, the medical community was unaware of the dangers of fen-phen at the time.

The interview was an embarrassing and painful yet courageous confession for Ryan and a rugged trip down memory lane for me.

When I asked Ryan if she had felt pressure from the NYU faculty to lose weight, I was surprised—and a little envious—when she said no. I guess David had been right. The times were changing. Which isn't to say that Ryan was operating in a shame-free zone. She more than made up for others' reticence with her own self-flagellation. She recounted story after story of how her weight had impeded her growth as an actor. Often it was all she could think about. Even while rehearsing for the League Presentations, this shame was at work. Ryan was performing this zany comedy piece with large movements and, midway through the scene, while reaching above her head, her shirt became untucked. But as a fat girl who understands the importance of never showing your belly, I knew that this seemingly innocent, organic glimpse of skin was far more disturbing than anyone but a fat girl would understand. Because Ryan is so technically skilled, however, she didn't let it compromise her performance.

After the rehearsal I asked her about that moment, and she admitted that as ludicrous as it sounded, it had completely disrupted her concentration. Ryan laughingly recalled the entire sequence, which probably lasted less than five seconds, an eternity for an embarrassed fat girl. She said that it was okay if her belly showed while her hands were above her head because that created the long, sleek, slenderizing effect. And it was okay while she was lying outstretched on her side, which also had a slimming effect. But her mind had already skipped ahead to the approaching moment when she would have to lean over and expose her back. "And there was no way I was going to show my back fat." So she had deftly tucked her shirt back in and proceeded to wow us.

Can you believe the things that go through our minds? In a scene where an actress is supposed to be thinking "What is my objective? What do I want from this person? How can I get it?" Ryan was aware of the absurdity but nonetheless was momentarily overcome by the competing objective: "Don't let anybody see my fat."

So even though NYU had apparently softened its stance on plus-size women (and I say women, because it was never an issue with the men), Ryan was providing plenty of harsh judgment for herself. With the League Presentations just a day away, I was going through this incredible nervousness all over again. I knew she was prepared and I knew she was a great talent and I hoped that the agents would be able to recognize that. The League auditions had undergone several significant changes. First of all, the League had disbanded, so although they were still referred to as the League Presentations, it was really just NYU and Yale presenting their graduating acting classes to the industry. And second, there was no longer the great humiliating Wall of Lists, where you could search endlessly for your name to appear on an agent's must-meet list. In the new, much-more-humane system, actors would be handed a packet of interested industry folk who wanted to meet them. So you could still get shut out, but just not for all the world to see.

I wished her luck and waited to hear how it went. I had seen her scene and I knew she was fantastic. If they didn't want to meet her, the shame and loss was theirs.

To my surprise, relief, and envy, Ryan called to tell me that many agents wanted to meet with her. I was so proud of her but couldn't help remembering my own shame and disappointment when nobody wanted to meet me. And she was off on her whirlwind tour of the best agencies in the business.

I didn't hear from her for a couple of weeks so I figured things were going really well. Finally she called me. Apparently all of those agents who had been so interested in her talent were reluctant to sign her. Ugh. That dull *thud* was the sound of the other shoe falling. One agent said, "You have the face of a leading lady and the body of a character actress. You aren't fully either one. So you will either have to lose weight, or cut your hair and gain weight. You're not pretty enough to be Lucy and you're not ugly enough to be Ethel. I'm curious to see what happens to you in the future." Talk about brutal. The truth is when they saw her act, they recognized her talents and were inspired. But when they got back to the office and started thinking about making money off her, they realized that there are just no roles for beautiful young fat girls.

What I say in my seminar and what I reminded Ryan—partly to ease the pain but also as genuinely good advice—was that sometimes not getting an agent is the best thing that can happen to you. It forces you to develop fighting skills that will serve you throughout your life. Too often young actors sign with a big-time agent and stop fighting their own battles, assuming that the agent is fighting for them. And by the time they figure out that the agent is not, their own muscles—the ones that got them into a great drama school and got them a good agent—have atrophied. I told Ryan that I didn't have an agent for five years after graduating, but in those five years I learned how to write a play, how to produce a play, how to become involved in different theater companies. Basically I learned how to hustle. I know that if William Morris had signed me right out of school, I would have sat back and waited for the phone to ring.

Still, it seemed a little ridiculous that she had just come out of the finest drama school in the country and couldn't even get an agent. I knew that my words may have provided only a small comfort to her, but I also knew that if she persevered, eventually she would discover the truth in them and her talent would shine through.

I spoke with Ryan recently. It had been two and half years since she graduated. Again I heard myself in her words. She had just booked a chorus part in *Twelfth Night* starring Helen Hunt at the prestigious Lincoln Center. She had just done a guest spot on a network TV show. But most important, I could hear in her voice that she was starting to fight, starting to hustle, starting to raise a little hell.

But learning how to fight for yourself doesn't necessarily mean you've accepted yourself. Ryan told me that she was still plagued by weight issues. She reluctantly confessed that she was taking Meridia, the latest diet drug, but worried that it wasn't working because she had built up a tolerance to it.

Every time Ryan shares a fear or hope or desire with me, it sounds to me like an echo of my own life bouncing off a not-too-distant mountain. I try to spare her the hopeful platitudes that I ignored for years because I remember how hollow they sounded. But listening to Ryan gave me the courage to admit that I too experimented with diet drugs, even after my near-fatal overdose on speed. It's amazing the lengths we'll go to to be accepted. The last thing we seem willing to do is accept ourselves. The irony, of course, is that once we do accept ourselves, others accept us. There is nothing more seductive than someone who respects and feels good about herself.

Before I hung up with Ryan, she said that she was lamenting getting her new head shots taken because she felt that she was not yet at the weight she wanted to be. And in the same breath laughing at how absurd that sounded.

She then told me that many years ago her mother went to see a psychic. Before her mother could ask about her daughter Ryan, the psychic said, "Don't worry about your daughter. When the time is right she will come into her own." Her mother brought this prediction back to Ryan, who interpreted the supernatural advice to mean that when the time is right, she'd lose weight. And as she was telling me the story she had her own revelation: "It never occurred to me that it could've meant when the time is right, I'd accept myself."

Ryan recalled a quote from *Henry IV, Part 1*, right before he becomes king, that she had always used to comfort herself.

Yet herein will I imitate the sun,
Who doth permit the base contagious clouds
To smother up his beauty from the world,
That when he please again to be himself,
Being wanted, he may be more wond'red at
By breaking through the foul and ugly mists
Of vapors that did seem to strangle him.

Then she added, with a bit of a laugh, "I've always thought, 'When I lose weight, I too will shine.' "

You're shining already, sister.

*   *   *

Although Ryan has started to get noticed for her talent, she is still seeking representation. So if you know anyone who wants to represent a big beautiful actress, call her service, (212) 769–8204. Trust me, I'm not doing her a favor, I'm doing one for you.

Air
Camryn

You know, life is about defining moments. Sometimes you think you've had a defining moment and then you look back and realize it was just another insignificant moment onto which you tried to project some kind of gravity. But occasionally you really are at the crossroads. And when those two roads diverge, your creature-of-habit self starts to push you down the path most taken, but your gut tells you that maybe this is that defining moment when you need to take the road less traveled. It happens in an instant. There is no deliberation, no analysis of the consequences, no contemplation of the repercussions. You just do it.

Your entire life has informed this moment, and if you've been paying attention, you will be prepared. This moment came for me on January 16, 1996.

Let me give you the back story.

November 1995: *Wake Up, I'm Fat!* is selling out at the Joseph Papp Public Theater. Not because it was good, but because I had been seeing five plays a week for the last eight years and those people owed me. *Uncle Vanya* in the Village, *Macbeth* on the Upper East Side, experimental Mac Wellman kaleidoscopic odysseys on Walker Street below Canal. Site-specific Engarde Arts, Karen Finley at Dixon Place, Luna Lounge, Surf Reality, West Bank Cafe, ad infinitum. And now it was payback time! And payback is a bitch with a one-woman show. I called them all. Not once, not twice, but three times. Beep . . . "Hey, Bob, loved you in *The Cherry Orchard* . . . so listen, you've got six weeks to see my show or we're never speaking again. Love ya." *Click.*

Having Bob there is all well and good if I want to play Olga in *The Three Sisters,* but if I was going to catapult my career I needed to put some important asses in those seats, and telling the bigwig casting directors that you'll never speak to them again if they don't come to your show just doesn't work. Besides, I had managers now, and they were on a first-name basis with all the important asses in show business.

Maryellen Mulcahy and Peg Donegan were and are much more than managers to me. They have been teachers, supporters, advocates, and comrades-in-arms. They were the first people who didn't pepper me with these refrains: "Camryn, don't set yourself up for disappointment, understand your limitations"; "Camryn, be realistic"; "Camryn, set reachable goals"; "Camryn, don't expect too much." Those voices had been steering me toward that road most taken seemingly since my first steps. But Peg and

Maryellen were different. When I first met with them, I kept waiting for them to tell me what I couldn't have, but they never did. They understood the road less traveled.

Peg had a good friend over at Twentieth Century–Fox, Randy Stone, the vice president of casting. As the story goes, he was coming to New York to run in the NYC Marathon, all twenty-six miles of it, and was flying in the night before. Peg suggested he come to see my show. Randy, as politely as he could, said something along the lines of "I'd rather stick a fork in my head than see a one-woman show the night before I run a marathon." Peg, diligent manager that she is, said, "If you don't see it, we're no longer friends." I guess that strategy *does* work at the higher levels. A not-so-happy Randy Stone came to my show.

Everything was working against me. He was jet-lagged, cranky, had been coerced, and had twenty-six miles to run in the morning. Not late morning, we're not talking brunch. We're talking early, crack-o'-dawn early. So I'm sure he was ready to hate it. But he didn't. Thank God!

Randy knew that David E. Kelley was writing a new TV pilot called *The Practice* and that he was looking for a sassy, streetwise kind of gal. Hello! Streetwise and sassy? I know where all the crack houses are and "fuck" is my favorite word. How much more streetwise and sassy can you be? Randy thought David should meet me. But before he agreed, he wanted to see some of my other work. So we sent over a tape of scenes I had done in the past. Including two shows where I had played lawyers. David wasn't impressed. He told Randy that I was too conservative. Randy replied by saying, "Okay, she is so *not* conservative. The girl has twelve holes in her ear, rides a big bad motorcycle, and has a tattoo. The one thing she isn't is conservative." Yeah, for Christ's sake. The lawyers I played on those two shows were *supposed* to be conservative. Duh! That's acting!

So David agreed to see me despite his overwhelming gut feeling that I was all wrong for the part. For most of us a gut feeling means we're getting an ulcer. For David it means another Emmy is going up on the mantel. My job was to convince him that this particular gut feeling was just indigestion.

You'd think that Randy would have had the decency to lie to me and tell me how excited David was to meet me. Ya know, a little support for the girl who is paying her own way out to meet Mr. Michelle Pfeiffer. But noooooo! Randy tells me that David thinks I'm all wrong for the part but that he is willing to meet me anyway. Let me get this straight: If I pay my own way, fly 3,000 miles, rent a car, get lost in El Segundo, but still find my way to your office on time . . . you won't have security throw me off the lot. Gee, thanks!

Still there was that faint scent of a defining moment. So I fly out to L.A. to meet with the mysterious Mr. Kelley. First thing that tripped me up was that he was so handsome . . . and he looked about twelve. Second thing that tripped me up was he was the worst interviewer in the history of mankind. "So you're an actor," he says. "Yep, that's why I'm here." It was the worst. And to add to the gruesome remains of my dignity, Randy was over in the corner piping in "Tell him that really funny part in your one-woman show." A sure way to ruin any punch line.

Well, just about the time that I figured out I was never going to see the inside of a David E. Kelley studio, I started to get up to leave. When I was about halfway out of my chair I noticed that David had a cribbage board sitting by the side of his couch.

This was it. I could walk out that door, the road most traveled, never see David Kelley again, and watch some other, less sassy, less streetwise actress get *my* part, or I could seize the moment. Imagine you're Michael Jordan, and the person you are trying to impress has no idea you're the world's greatest basketball player. And just when you think the opportunity to impress has passed you by, you see a basketball in the corner. That's how I, Air Camryn, was looking at that cribbage board. And the thing about defining moments is: You don't deliberate, you don't contemplate, you don't analyze. You just blurt out, "Hey, do you play cribbage?"

And for the first time in the entire meeting David showed some signs of life and said in the most challenging of all tones, "Yeah, but I don't think you want to go there with me." Wow, he actually had a pulse! Now, I'll tell you a little secret. I majored in math, and I'm a tournament bridge player, so the one thing you don't want to do is challenge me in a game of cards. It just came out, there was no stopping it. "Y'know, David, I could continue to have this conversation with you, and I could continue to try to impress you, like I'm doing unsuccessfully now, *and* I could beat the shit out of you at cribbage at the same time." The dynamic had changed . . . forever.

With a curl of his lip he said, "I don't think you understand, I play the computer!"

"Well, I don't think *you* understand," I shot back, "I play for money!" The whole atmosphere had changed; it was charged. I even got a glance of David Kelley's teeth through his half snarl, half smile. I could feel the playing field leveling. And then I said, "Look, I'll make you a deal, David, why don't we fuck this audition, and I'll play you right now for the part. If I lose, you will never see me again. No *Chicago Hope*, no *Picket Fences*, no *Ally McBeal*, no *Practice* . . . but if I win, I walk out of here with the script." How's that for sassy and streetwise? Then he hemmed and hawed a little bit and finally said, "I think you have a better chance of getting the part if you actually audition." I quickly pounced on his bravado and said, "Now I can actually taste your fear." It wasn't about the part anymore, it was about my pride. David just laughed, which was a far cry from the man taking a nap in the earlier portion of my meeting, and said, "Look, I haven't even written the script yet, but when it's finished, I promise you, you'll get a copy." *Ding ding ding.* End of round one. I never even had to pick up a basketball. (Of course I mix my sports metaphors. I'm a fat Jewish girl who hated gym.)

When I left the meeting all I could think about was kicking David Kelley's ass in cribbage. I could have cared less about *The Prosecutors* or whatever his stupid show was called.

Three weeks later I got the script. And the description of my character was something like: big, ballsy woman walks in. I knew I had won a much bigger battle than a cribbage game. I had managed to change the description of the character. Now I had to convince them that I was right for the character that they were basing on me. Slam dunk!!!

When I got the phone call from my agent saying that I had gotten the part, I sat down in the middle of my kitchen floor, holding the phone, and wept. No experience in my life had prepared me for these feelings, the depth of joy, and the wondrous relief of victory after a twenty-year battle fought with no end in sight.

But I wasn't going to let David Kelley see this tender side of me. No way. I sent David a cribbage board and a note that said, "I challenge you to a duel, you big fat wuss!" Still he wouldn't play me. At the end of the first season, David had yet to step up to the plate. So during our final read-through I made a little announcement to the cast and crew: "Just want to let you all know that though I've challenged David again and again to a game of cribbage, he's too afraid to play me." Having been called out in front of everybody, David finally agreed to come into my dressing room and fight this battle once and for all. The stakes were established, 25 cents a point. He told me stories about skunking his mother in cribbage. Like that psychological ploy was going to intimidate me? I invented the cribbage psych-out! Twenty minutes later it was over. David emerged from my dressing room and went back to his office as if nothing had happened. Some of the cast and crew were circling around trying to get the results. For all I knew there were some bets being made. I don't really need to tell you the outcome of the game. All you need to know is that the very next day, David circulated a memo throughout the entire studio and it read:

> As of December 16, 1996, cribbage playing is no longer permitted in the dressing rooms. Hearts and gin rummy are still acceptable. P.S.: It is reminded that unauthorized gambling is illegal in the state of California.

Talk about a poor loser. Since David refused to cough up the dough after our game, I figured I better respond to his little outburst. In a letter dated December 17, I wrote:

> Dear David,
> I am in receipt of your memo stating cribbage is no longer allowed to be played on the set of The Practice. In keeping I would like you to pay your debt to me in full, since you will have no recourse to win it back. Please make the payment in check form, as it will be suitable for framing.

I guess David didn't think it was as funny as I did, and on December 20 he wrote:

Dear Camryn,
As of Wednesday night, I had decided to rescind the ban on cribbage, opining that the game need only be regulated rather than squashed. I thereby appointed myself Commissioner and ruled that the games continue.

Unfortunately, I received a rather flippant note from you on Thursday and, as Commissioner, I feel I have no choice but to suspend you indefinitely from playing.

Moreover, I am fining you one dollar and thirty-five cents for the flippancy. You may expect to be paid the debt owed to you by me, minus the $1.35. As a show of good faith, since I continue to believe in you as a person, I am appointing you as Treasurer of the Cribbage Association. You will be expected to open up an escrow account and deposit the $1.35 accordingly.

> *Sincerely,*
> *David E. Kelley*
> *Commissioner*

As if he has nothing better to do with his time. But apparently I don't either, because I couldn't let him have the last word.

Dear David,
I am pleased that you are taking our cribbage enterprise seriously and that it is now under supervision and regulation.

I am accepting the position of Treasurer and I have opened an escrow account as you directed. However, I want it to be

*known that I accept this under protest and ask that the Com-
missioner distribute the rule book before playing resumes.*

Sincerely,

Camryn Manheim

Treasurer TCA

There are only a few things that David Kelley and I have in common. It certainly isn't writing, because he seems to actually enjoy it, and it's certainly not our paychecks. But we do share a fierce appetite for competition, and for that I love him.

Things seemed to die down for a while. I was playing cribbage on the sly with my fellow castmate Steve Harris whom I taught how to play the very first day I met him. (And soon realized I had to stop teaching him all my tricks because he was treacherously using them against me.) It hurts me to confess that he would go on to beat me over and over again, and part of my debt was to call him "El Capitán" and say "You are my master and I will always serve you." I only tell you this now, because if I didn't, he would find a way to publicize it to the world. This way I can control the damage by 'fessing up only to the people who will read this book, which I'm sure is considerably fewer.

Somewhere along the line, people got this idea that I would make a good host or emcee at political events, and I got my first request to emcee the Center for Law in the Public Interest's annual fund-raising dinner. Apparently, if you honor a celebrity and you have a celebrity hosting the thing, you have a much better chance of selling tickets. Guess who they were honoring? My boss, David E. Kelley. Knowing I was going to be standing up in front of a group of lawyers, I flashed back to the moment when David had paid me the money I had beaten him out of in the famous cribbage game. Unfortunately for him the transaction had been photographed, and where better to expose David's illegal transferring of funds than before 500 lawyers at a legal event?

I agreed to expose David Kelley . . . I mean to host for David Kelley.

The dinner was great. Steve Harris jumped on board and co-hosted the event with me. We started by saying "Before Steve and I tell you all of those wonderful anecdotes about David Kelley, let me first say that we both have a contract for twenty-two episodes of *The Practice* and there are 500 lawyers in this room who can attest that no matter what we say here tonight, that contract is binding!"

David Kelley is one of the most provocative, pioneering, uncompromising, and brilliant men in entertainment. His wife, Michelle Pfeiffer, is equally intelligent, fearless, and arguably the most beautiful woman in the world. You've got to wonder what a conversation would be like between the two of them on a Saturday night when the kids are in bed, and they have some time to themselves. Steve and I decided to do a little reenactment of what we thought their private moments would be like. (Recall that during the '96–'97 season, ABC had buried *The Practice* on Saturday nights.)

STEVE: So I'm going to be David.

CAM: So I'm going to be Michelle.

STEVE: Great, so honey . . .

CAM: Wait, could you not talk for a second, I want to be Michelle for just a little longer. . . . Okay, you can continue.

STEVE: Did you like the chicken from Boston Market?

CAM: It was alright, no potatoes?

STEVE: I thought we'd try the corn.

CAM: You know I love the potatoes!

STEVE: Alright, next time I'll get the potatoes.

CAM: Would you like to go to the movies tonight?

STEVE: Michelle, it's Saturday night. *The Practice* is on at ten o'clock.

CAM: David, be reasonable. Nobody watches TV on Saturday night.

Even with the stinging reminder of our terrible time slot, David thought our dramatic reenactment was funny. He took it like a champion.

Now we know about David Kelley the great writer, we know about David Kelley the great thinker, but what about David Kelley the great sport? And I turned to Steve and said, "I'm just curious: How much money have you won off David playing cribbage?" And without missing a beat, Steve said, "Does he beat anyone?" (Laughter.) "I hear he beats the computer, but there really isn't anyone to verify that. Plus David writes everything longhand so the only computer he's ever had was a Commodore 64."

And then I launched into the story of the Great Cribbage War. And we passed out the color Xerox copies of David paying off his debt.

"You were right, David, gambling is illegal in the state of California, and frankly with this physical evidence, you could use a good lawyer." And fifteen people handed him their business cards.

The next day Steve and I received the following letter:

Dear Steve and Camryn:
Just a note to say how moved I was by your mastering of the ceremonies. I look forward to returning that favor but thus far

I have been unable to find an organization willing to honor you.

Sincerely,
David E. Kelley

For the remainder of the first season, David and I would pass in the halls with a healthy dose of mutual respect and a glint of challenge in our eyes.

Although I'm sure he wishes it would go away, I have been keeping the story alive and well. Magazines, newspapers, talk shows . . . anyone who wanted to hear it. And then invariably they would ask, "Do you think your cribbage challenge got you the part?" I had no idea. Until a year later, at the end of our second season, when we were all asked to sit on a Q & A panel at the Museum of Radio & Television. As we approached the stage in no particular order, I noticed that all the actors were sitting in the center of the stage and the producers were off to the side. There were no more seats left by my friendly costars, and as I passed by David, he said, "What's the matter, you afraid to sit by me?" And with my ever-present fuck-you attitude, I plopped down in the chair flanked by David Kelley and our executive producer, Jeffrey Kramer.

During the panel discussion David and I took turns jabbing each other. I made fun of how quickly he writes scripts, and he said we'd be seeing less and less of my character. But the one clarifying moment for me in that symposium was when he was asked if he wrote the characters first and then found the actors, or did he meet the actors first and then write the characters. He said, "I wrote the characters first." Pause. Long pause. "Except for Camryn. I found her first and then I wrote her character." I smiled as if

I had known it all along. But the truth is, I had never really fully believed that he had written the part for me. For me, the fat girl from Peoria, Illinois. But when I heard the words "Except for Camryn, I found her first . . ." it took my best acting skills not to burst into tears.

And then I knew. On January 16, 1996, I hadn't made it up, I hadn't projected undo importance onto it, but that it truly was a defining moment in my life. I may have beaten him in a cribbage game—hell, who hasn't?—but there is no doubt in my mind that David Kelley is my hero.

Red Diaper
Baby

In my family, being an activist wasn't something you chose. It was genetic. My mother's father, Sam Nuchow, was an early organizer of the Millinery Workers Union. My mother followed in her dad's footsteps and worked as a receptionist for the Communist Party. Her brother, my uncle Bill, organized the New York taxicab drivers in the 1950s. He eventually became secretary-treasurer of local 840 of the Teamsters Union. My brother, Karl, was deeply involved in the antiwar movement during the Vietnam War. My cousin Bobby got thrown out of the army for organizing a soldier's union. My cousin Laura was the illustrator for a socialist newspaper.

Ironically, my father, whose side of the family was much less politically active, suffered the most serious repercussions as a result of his perceived political affiliation. He was working on a communications system for ITT in 1951 when he was summarily dismissed as a "security risk." He filed an appeal and was summoned to Washington, where he was ordered to appear before a Senate committee. He was told that he was deemed a security risk because he was in possession of a book called *Political Economy* by Leontief. It was true that he owned that book, but he had never read it. The scary part for my father was the realization that someone who had been in his house was reporting to Joseph McCarthy's thugs. They told my dad that they knew that he was the leader of the Communist Party in Hartford, Connecticut, even though he'd only been to Hartford once, for two hours at the government's request to see if he qualified for further benefits under the G.I. Bill. Eventually the trumped-up charges were dropped, but he was blacklisted from all industries that might in some tangential way be connected to the military, which, during the Korean War, was pretty much all industry. He returned to teaching.

Perhaps that taste of tyranny sparked the activist in my dad, because he started speaking out and marching against injustice.

We have pictures of my father, holding me in one hand and a picket sign in the other. I am so proud of those photographs.

It's in my blood to be an activist. Ever since I was beaten up in sixth grade for voting for George McGovern in my elementary school's mock election, I have been a committed liberal. For a long time while I was following my dream of being an actor, I had severe guilt about not joining the Peace Corps. I knew I would never forgive myself for not making a more significant, tangible contribution. But as I began to make it as an actor, I realized that just because I wasn't on the "front lines of activism" didn't mean that I couldn't lend my strength to the good fight. And besides, while I'd really love to go out and dig an irrigation ditch, I just look better in Anne Klein than Gap Khaki. Just kidding.

I've been arrested for civil disobedience and uncivil disobedience, interpreted for the deaf at countless rallies and political events, and have had the privilege of working alongside the Reverend Jesse Jackson for racial equality. In fact, it was at a rally against Proposition 209, which would end affirmative action in California, that my family's activism came full circle. I had been asked to join Jesse, Ed Asner, and Mike Farrell to stand in support of affirmative action, which I gladly did. My brother, Karl, meanwhile, had been working tirelessly on the legal end to quash Prop. 209. So it shouldn't have surprised me that when I arrived to stand on Jesse's left, Karl was standing on his right. The two Manheim kids, the real lawyer and the one who plays one on TV, united in the good fight. I was and am so proud to be his little sister.

It's easy to fight the good fight when you're a celebrity. People listen. Don't ask me why people care what we think, it's just the way it is. It would be just fine with me if no one paid any attention to Arnold Schwarzenegger (Conan the Republican), Bruce Willis, and Charlton Heston, at election time, but, sadly, they do. It's a hell of a lot harder to sway people when no one's listening. And before I landed my role on *The Practice*, no one was listening to me.

Two years after *The Road to Wellville*, I got cast in *Romy and Michelle's High School Reunion*. Not only was I psyched to get the job, but on my thirty-fifth birthday, I found out I'd be playing an eighteen-year-old. I'd spent my twenties playing sixty-year-olds and now in my thirties, I'd be playing a teenager. Talk about your Hollywood irony.

After the audition, the next step was to have a costume fitting. And the best thing about costume fittings is, if you like the clothes, you can buy them at the end of the movie for half price. Unfortunately, prior to that I had played a lot of frumpy next-door neighbors so I was never much interested in taking advantage of the 50 percent off sale. But now I was going to be playing a teenager. Fantasies of Calvin Klein jeans and lip gloss made me remember to bring my checkbook as I walked out the door to go to my fitting.

I had a nice chat with the costume designer about nothing in particular before we entered the fitting room. And as we strolled toward the room where I'd be trying on all the newest fashions, I caught a glimpse of a floral muumuu. When we turned the corner, I was confronted with a huge costume rack full of primary-color floral, polyester muumuus. And then she said something like "Hey, why don't you try these on?" She might as well have said "Hey, why don't you perpetuate the stereotype that fat people don't know how to dress?" I was so upset. By this time I had learned how to be confrontational without my head exploding into tiny pieces (and getting all over those muumuus, which would certainly make them a lot harder to return). I just said, "Look, I can't wear these clothes. I have a political, emotional, and spiritual aversion to them."

Then any good impression I had made on her in our prefitting chat was forgotten, and she said, "This is the Midwest, these girls don't know how to dress!" And I said, "It's not the Midwest, it's Tucson, Arizona, and these girls have magazines, and they have television. I bet they do know how to dress. Besides, the fat girls are always trying to fit in by wearing the latest trends." Then I got the Well-I'm-going-to-have-to-talk-to-the-director response, which I think was supposed to scare me, but it didn't. I said, "Yes, please do talk to him. Tell him to call me at home if he has any objections," and I walked out without ever having my skin touch a polyester muumuu.

CUT TO: Me buying my extremely cool costumes at half price.

After narrowly escaping the humiliation that comes with a polyester muumuu, it became clear that *Romy and Michelle's High School Reunion* was going to test my mettle again and again. It was, to its artistic credit, very much like a real high school reunion. And what could be more terrifying and potentially humiliating than spending three and a half months in that fishbowl of judgment? It was a perfect re-creation of Woodrow Wilson High School in Long Beach. There were the pretty cheerleaders, the nerds, the jocks, and me, the fat girl who didn't fit in. And it wasn't like I could start pretending to drop acid to win the crew over. On most films, it's easy to know where the lines are drawn between who we are as people and who we are as characters. But, again to the film's credit, those lines got blurred and my teenage insecurities made an unwelcome comeback.

Some people get very nostalgic about high school—you know, the good old days—but I closed that chapter, hoping I would never have to revisit it. Imagine my surprise when I got that familiar knot in my stomach as I yearned for acceptance from my peers on the set. I was terrified that I wouldn't be popular, which is a pretty absurd position for a thirty-five-year-old woman to find herself in.

On the very first day of shooting we broke for lunch and everybody else seemed to have somebody to sit with. The camera crew sat at one table, the producers at another, the extras at the very edge of the cafeteria, the wardrobe people and the prop people, the sound guys, the grips . . . the only group I recognized as actors were a perfectly coiffed, outfitted sixsome of cheerleaders, laughing and smiling at a table together. I stood in the middle of that cafeteria, holding my tray, looked at them and actually had this thought: "I bet they don't want me to sit with them." There I was, seventeen years removed from high school, thousands of dollars of therapy later, and I was having a flashback to when the cheerleaders really didn't want me to sit with them. Just before I turned and headed to a deserted corner, I caught myself and said, "Camryn. What are you thinking? You're thirty-five years old. Those girls are actors. They're not really cheerleaders. You can go and sit with them. It's okay." And so I did.

They couldn't have been nicer. Phew. Day 1: lunch hurdle cleared.

My character, Toby Walters, was that absolutely annoying girl that every high school has, who talked way too loud and way too close, invading everyone's personal space. My objective was simple: Annoy Janeane Garofalo's character at every turn, forcing her to tell me to "fuck off." So even though I knew in my head that this was fiction, every time she said that to me, I felt a little wounded, because it reminded me of being dismissed so summarily by the popular girls in high school.

After a particularly painful scene in which I had to say "Will you sign my yearbook, and please don't tell me to 'Fuck off' because it really hurts my feelings," I went to lunch, feeling a little fragile. I'm such a big baby.

Now I realize that I've become an unofficial poster child for fat girls, but at that time in my life, I was trying to eat fat-free. But as some of you may know, if all you're going to eat is a salad, it's gotta be a pretty fabulous salad. Luckily, the caterers had a great salad bar, replete with artichoke hearts, black olives, hearts of palm, mushrooms, cherry tomatoes, etc. So I made myself a salad grande. (It was after all, just a salad, so I could sit with the cheer-leaders and not be embarrassed. Or so I thought.)

I had barely placed the last cucumber on my salad when one of the caterers said rather apologetically, "Uh, excuse me, could you be a little more careful about how much food you take? We're concerned that there won't be enough for everybody."

I was shocked. I probably would have been okay with that if I had overheard him saying it to everybody, but he wasn't, he was just saying it to me. Perfect, single out the fat girl and tell her to take less food. I stammered out an "excuse me?" And he contin-ued, "There's been a lot of food wasted and it just doesn't look like you'll be able to finish that."

"It's a fucking salad! Not only could I finish it, but I could fin-ish you, you little fuck!"

But that was my inner monologue. Outwardly I was stunned. Finally I said, "I find it so insulting that of all the people here, you single me out. Don't you see how offensive that is?"

He apologized and said he was only following orders. I literally stood there with my mouth agape. Following orders? Had there been a big catering summit where it was determined that some-one just had to tell the fat girl to make a smaller salad?

I was practically catatonic. I was paralyzed with rage, humilia-tion, and general bewilderment. I stood there holding my tray, half expecting sirens to blare and a spotlight to shine down on me and my offending salad. I obviously wasn't masking this torrent of emotions because Lisa Kudrow came up to me and asked me what was wrong. I recounted my exchange with the catering Gestapo and she asked, "Who said that?"

Before I could answer, the head caterer, who apparently had given the order, stepped forward and said almost confrontationally, "I did. Look, we've been having a big problem with people wasting food and our budget is too small to feed everyone if people keep throwing food away."

It's not like I had eight slices of prime rib on my tray. I had a fucking salad.

Lisa was incredible. She had sized up the situation, seen that I was too overwhelmed to speak for myself, and leapt to my defense. She told the catering fascist, "Look, if you're having a budget problem, you should talk to the producers. It's not acceptable to have this conversation with an actor."

And then the most amazing thing happened. He apologized . . . TO LISA! Not to me, but to her, for making her feel uncomfortable. Lisa wasn't about to let him off that easy. She said, "I think you owe her the apology."

It rolled off his tongue when he was saying sorry to the star, but it stuck in his throat when he tried to spit out an apology to me. He continued to lament his small budget and the constraints he was working under. He just wouldn't give it up to me. Finally I walked away, no longer excited about my fabulous salad.

I called my managers, who, in turn, called the producers, and there was a big brouhaha. When my managers called me back, they asked if I wanted the caterer fired. Part of me wanted to say yes, but I'm not a vindictive diva. Diva, yes. Vindictive, no. It turns out he thought I was an extra, which, apparently, would have made his actions excusable. In other words, had I been an extra, he could have walked all over me with impunity. Like a lot of actors, I started as an extra. And like all extras, I was often treated like a second-class citizen. On a Hollywood movie set, the caste system is very much at work, the pyramid narrowing all the way up to the star. And in that hierarchy, extras are below the caterers, below the production assistants, and below the interns. Extras can be dismissed at the drop of a hat. No matter how much good fortune I have, I will always remember what it was like to be an extra and will always treat extras the way I wanted to be treated, with courtesy and respect.

So when the caterer came to me that afternoon and apologized for the mix-up, explaining that he thought I was an extra, that didn't fly with me. As if I were going to share a good laugh with him and say "An extra? Hah, that's a good one. No wonder you treated me like shit. Those silly extras . . . why should they get to eat?" He continued to apologize profusely, groveling and thanking me for sparing his job. It was pretty unseemly, the change in his demeanor once he was told that I was a principal actor. But I felt sorry for him and let him believe I forgave him. He did his best to make it up to me over the next two months, but each time he did something nice for me, I knew he would never do that for an extra.

Just for the record: Extras are oftentimes remarkable people who've led rich, full lives as attorneys, rabbis, nurses, entrepreneurs, writers, etc. You'll often find me in the holding area playing cards or charades with the extras because, frankly, they're just more interesting.

I never realized the scope of this battlefield. I was just clearing obstacles one at a time: getting naked in *Wellville*, the muumuu lady, the nasty caterer. In the beginning, my survival instincts led me to defend myself and my dignity. But little by little I realized that the battles I was fighting would someday be considered activism.

I didn't set out to be a crusader. Like all actors, I just wanted to work. And like all people who are discriminated against, I wanted fair and equal opportunities. True, I had been an activist for the poor, the disabled, immigrants, the environment, and countless liberal causes, but it had never occurred to me to fight for my own rights. Like a lot of people in this country I had erroneously assumed that all my rights were guaranteed. But I had learned otherwise. I had been discriminated against by teachers, employers, casting directors, agents, and now the caterer. I had begun to fight back. Once you get over your own self-loathing, it feels pretty good to stick up for yourself. And there is no turning back.

When I found out I had been cast in *The Practice*, I nearly threw my back out jumping for joy. At every turn people had told me I would never be on TV. "Just not the TV type, I guess." For ten years I rejected their close-minded worldview and relied on that I'll-show-you attitude.

The pilot was going to take three weeks to shoot. One week in Boston, and the rest of the time in Los Angeles. I had never even flown first class before. Something I would struggle with as my career took off. And contrary to my old beliefs that first class was much ado about nothing, I finally got a taste of warm pistachios just before take-off.

The day I arrived in Boston was such a thrill. My hotel room was a suite. Five people could have slept there. So different from the road trips I had taken before when six people would get a single room and sleep on the floor. There was a basket of fruit and chocolate from David Kelley Productions and an enormous bouquet of flowers from ABC. *La Dolce Vita*, indeed. I went to the makeshift production office in the hotel and they handed me a wad of cash—per diem. I pretended not to look too ecstatic.

The next morning I was picked up and taken to the Boston courthouse where we would be filming for the next five days. The first scene in the pilot had Dylan McDermott and me walking briskly through the courtyard, discussing the day's events. The prop guy gave me a cup of coffee and a doughnut to hold. Dylan was holding files. Already it had started. I tentatively approached the director and told him I wasn't really comfortable eating a doughnut on screen, especially since it was the introductory scene for my character. He said, "Oh, you don't have to *eat* it, I just want you to *hold* it. It gives that we're-rushing-to-work feeling to the show." Although I had become more comfortable speaking up for myself, it was my first day, and I wasn't sure if I should whip out my "Fat Police" badge just yet. I acquiesced. I may have dropped it with the director, but my mind was racing a mile a minute. How was I going to get out of this bind? I walked over to Dylan and said, "Hey, what do you think about this? I'm your right-hand woman, right? Don't you think that I'd be holding your doughnut and your cup of coffee and all your files while we walk up to the courthouse?" And Dylan, with whom my only encounter prior to that moment was a starstruck "hello," said, "That's a great idea." And if you were to look back at the first episode of *The Practice*, your first glimpse of Dylan McDermott will be of me stuffing a doughnut into his mouth as we give you that rushing-to-work feeling. Small battles, huge victories!

After we finished in Boston, we headed back to L.A. I remember when they showed me my dressing room. Not only did it have running water, but I had my very own bathroom, TV, couch, desk, telephone. *Free* telephone. I thought I had died and gone to heaven.

I was shown the different sets: McCall's Bar, the witness room, the judge's chambers, and the permanent courtroom, where I would be the big, ballsy, sassy, streetwise attorney Ellenor Frutt. The name doesn't exactly roll off the tongue, now does it? Had I been as cocky then as I am now, I would have said, "Hey, David, what's up with Frutt?" Then they showed me the office complex, where if all went well, I'd be spending the next five years. And then the director showed me Ellenor's desk, and I don't know why I was surprised, but there was a big bowl of candy on it. A big ol' bowl. A fishbowl. Well, I guess the week in Boston had toughened me up, jaded me, because I turned to the director and said, "Let me tell you a little secret, fat girls don't keep candy on the desk, they keep it in the drawer. So if you want to have candy on someone's desk, put it on the skinny girl's desk, and I promise I'll give it a little glance every time I walk by." Before the director could tell me he was trying to get that we're-rushing-and-don't-have-time-to-eat-lunch feeling, the prop guy took the candy bowl off my desk and put it next to the coffee machine. If you ever get a chance to see old episodes of *The Practice*, check out the candy bowl by the coffee machine. It's huge, you can't miss it.

With the doughnut victory and the candy dish conquest behind me, I was feeling more confident in my advocacy for fat acceptance. In the first two seasons of the show, I won a few more battles and lost a couple too. But all along I knew I was being heard and my concerns were taken seriously. Friends in the business have told me that that is incredibly rare, but it doesn't surprise me, since everything about David Kelley is unique.

Toward the end of the second season, I was delivered a script that introduced a possible love interest for Ellenor. The first thing I did was call the casting directors, Janet Gilmore and Megan McConnell. They must have been waiting for my call, because they had already put together a list of potential suitors. I wanted this boyfriend to be attractive, and my concern was that the prevailing sentiment would be "fat people only date other fat people" and that they'd cast to type. But Janet and Megan were way ahead of me. They cast J.C. McKenzie, who is not only handsome and charming but a great actor. Damn, I was all ready for a good knock-down, drag-out brawl, but I had been given the spoils of war without ever having to engage in combat.

All was well. For the moment. J.C. played tall, blond Dr. Spivak, who had carried a torch for Ellenor ever since they met in college. In his first episode, there was some cautious flirtation and a peck on the cheek, and the anticipation of bringing sensuality through Ellenor to prime time was really exciting. Then I got the next script.

When I got to the scene where Ellenor tells Lindsay, "We made love last night," I thought, wait a minute, did I miss a scene? Because I don't remember reading the action line, "Ellenor and Dr. Spivak embrace and crawl underneath the covers as the fireplace crackles." I flipped back through the script, but sure enough, it was nowhere to be found. I set the script down, picked up the phone, and called the producer. Poor Bob Breech, the guardian angel of *The Practice*, unwittingly took my call and said, "What's up, Cammy?"

"Bob, have you read this script?! Something seems to be missing. If Dylan and Lara Flynn have sex, you not only show it but you promo it as being the most exciting part of the episode. But when the fat girl finally gets some, she just gets to talk about it?!"

"Cammy, calm down." (By the way, unless I really love you, like I love Bob Breech, do *not* call me Cammy.)

Despite Bob's best efforts to soothe me, I was not going to capitulate on this one. I had to explain to Bob that no matter what the intention was, the effect of this glaring omission would be a loud and clear message: We don't want to see a fat girl have sex! Bob recognized that I was not going to budge on this issue and took my concerns to David.

When the next day's rewrites came out they included not one but two sensual and romantic scenes between Ellenor and Dr. Spivak. All my little victories on *The Practice* had been gratifying, but when J.C. kissed me—whoa, what a kisser—there had never been a battle so wisely fought.

Ten years earlier at NYU I had been afraid to kiss a boy in rehearsal. And now I was insisting on it. This triumph was just an extension of that epiphany I had while working on *The Road to Wellville*. I realized then that if we were ever going to dispel the myth that fat people aren't beautiful, then someone was going to have to get naked and be beautiful, and I realized on *The Practice* that if we were ever going to dispel the myth that fat people aren't sensual, then someone was going to have to be sensual. In *Wellville* it was an act. I never felt beautiful, I only pretended. But with J.C. it was no act. I felt it.

*   *   *

I never intended to become the spokesperson for the fat-acceptance movement. But I did want to provide an alternative role model to young girls so they wouldn't feel such pressure to emulate the unrealistic beauty standard in our society. At a very early age, girls in this country are subjected to images of leggy supermodels and emaciated waifs, distorting their perception of what women—real women—actually look like. I came across a wonderful did-you-know list of truths on the Internet that I think should be required reading for all young women.

Did you know . . .

- There are 3 billion women who don't look like supermodels and ONLY EIGHT WHO DO.
- Marilyn Monroe wore a SIZE 12.
- If Barbie were a real woman, she'd have to walk on all fours due to her proportions.
- If shop mannequins were real women, THEY'D BE TOO THIN TO MENSTRUATE.
- The average American woman weighs 144 pounds and wears between size 12 and 14.
- One out of four college-age women has an eating disorder.
- The models in the magazines are air-brushed . . . THEY'RE NOT PERFECT!
- A psychological study in 1995 found that three minutes spent looking at models in a fashion magazine caused 70 percent of women to feel depressed, guilty, and shameful.
- Models, who twenty years ago weighed 8 percent less than the average woman, today weigh 23 percent less.

Many billion-dollar industries are invested in perpetuating women's self-hatred. If women began accepting that we come in all shapes and sizes, a lot of businesses that bank on the beauty myth would go bankrupt.

Imagine this crazy little fantasy: Women all over America wake up tomorrow morning and say "I love myself just the way I am." It's crazy, I know, but what would happen? The first batch of casualties would be plastic surgeons in Beverly Hills and Scarsdale. N.Y. Therapists' offices would be thrown into chaos as no-longer self-loathing women filed out and the CEOs of Jenny Craig, Weight Watchers, and NutriSystems filed in, begging for antidepressants. Richard Simmons would become even more neurotic. The pharmaceutical companies that make Dexatrim, Meridia, Chitosan, Ionamin, and Pondimin would have to restructure their goals and actually produce something that helps people. *Vogue, Cosmopolitan, Elle, Harper's Bazaar,* and countless other magazines that promulgate unattainable body images would have to radically alter their whole mission. If women took the billions of dollars they spend on the futile pursuit of the beauty myth and poured it into their communities, we could house the homeless, feed the hungry, and put a computer on every kid's school desk.

End rant.

*   *   *

While political activism seems to be in my DNA, I had to learn about fat activism. And some of those lessons I learned the hard way, after inadvertently offending people.

When I performed *Wake Up* at the Public Theater, an official from the National Association to Advance Fat Acceptance called and asked me if I had "fat-friendly seating." "Uh . . . uh . . . uh . . . well, what exactly is fat-friendly seating?" I could hear her here-we-go-again sigh on the other end of the phone. "You gotta have seats that super-size fat people can sit in comfortably. And that doesn't mean pulling out the first row and putting a bench there. You've got to scatter seats throughout the entire auditorium so super-size people can sit wherever they like and not only in the front row where people can say 'Hey, look at all those fat people.' " "Oh," I said, "I'll see what I can do." It wasn't easy including fat-friendly seating, but it was worth it.

Before I could teach fat acceptance, I had to learn it myself. The first thing I had to figure out was what was the proper, in-offensive term for large-size people. Rubenesque? While it's very romantic and complimentary, try saying it 100 times in an inter-view. Overweight? Over *whose* weight? Obese? That gives you that I'm-just-about-to-die feeling. Large and big are pretty safe, but morphologically ambiguous. Real weight? As opposed to fake weight? And then there's "fat." Short, to the point, and if we're re-ally trying to say that there isn't any wrong body shape, then there shouldn't be anything wrong with the word "fat" either.

*   *   *

In the past year I have been honored by several organizations for my activism, but the credit really belongs to my family for teach-ing me how to fight for what I believe in. Whether it's lobbying their congressman, protecting a clinic, or doing *pro bono* work to protect people's civil liberties, my family continues to inspire me to keep shouting, to keep fighting, and to work hard to live up to their example.

I'm so happy I didn't change my last name.

"I Really Think You Should Lose Some Weight"

This is basically what everybody's been telling me since puberty. If I had a nickel for every time someone thought they were imparting some incredible advice and empathy with this sentiment, I could buy out Jenny Craig and open Lane Bryants in all those locations. The most annoying part of this unsolicited advice—and unsolicited advice is almost always annoying—is that these people actually believe they are telling you something you don't know, like it's going to be completely revelatory. It's as if they are unlocking some mystery and bestowing some arcane knowledge upon you, allowing you to go forward in life, unfettered by ignorance. Well, wake up! Fat people know they're fat. For many of us, it's the first thing we think about when we open our eyes in the morning and the last thing we think about before we fall asleep at night. And whether we think we should lose some weight, or want to lose some weight, or are trying to lose weight, it is entirely our business. So the next time you have an impulse to suggest that a friend or family member lose weight, take a minute to ask yourself why it is important enough to you to risk humiliating someone you care about to give this profound advice. Most people argue that they are merely looking out for the well-being of their loved ones, but I suggest that some other factor is at work here. Am I to believe that their concern is that I'll get heart disease twenty-five years from now? Or is it something else? Could it perhaps be embarrassment? Do we as a society just hate to be seen with fat people? Why is it so offensive? People have a harder time telling someone they have bad breath than they do casually pointing out the latest diet craze to a fat person.

In my experience, there are two basic types of people who feel obliged to tell me I should lose weight. One is the person who is embarrassed by my weight; the other is the erstwhile fat person who recently lost weight and suddenly can't wait to proselytize.

My friend Joanna falls into the latter category.

Some time ago I went out to lunch with her. We had been roommates while I was attending NYU. She had also been overweight her whole life so we bonded in that fat-girl kinda way. I hadn't seen her in awhile, but we had talked on the phone. She told me that she had been quite ill and lost weight as a result. And I said, "Oh, I'm sorry that you're not feeling well, but that's great about the weight." That was always a secret fantasy of mine. When I was younger, I would wish that I would get into an accident and have my jaw wired shut so I couldn't eat. Or have some near-fatal disease so that I would be hooked up to an IV and wither away to nothing, or at least a size 8. But that was the whole self-destructive side to me that I've left behind.

I waited outside the restaurant for my friend, and when she walked up my inner monologue began: "Oh my God, she got so thin. She looks beautiful. I hate her. I've got to get me one of those ulcers. They do great work."

Job number one was to not let on how jealous I was. "Joanna, you look wonderful. Oh, you must feel great. I can't believe how stunning you look."

There was, of course, the awkward, pregnant moment that follows an unrequited compliment. She couldn't even muster a "you too." But I remained chipper, determined not to let on that I was much happier being her friend when she was fat.

As we walked in, I reflexively said, "Come on, let's go in and *eat* something," remembering the times we'd bonded over food. She asked if we could sit in the smoking section and I said, "No problem."

Oh yeah, that old trick, smoking as an appetite suppressant. So now, not only was I jealous of her because she was thin, I—a former smoker—was going to have to sit through lunch jealously watching and smelling someone smoke.

We talked about health, hers and mine. She had had the good fortune to come down with an ailment that took forty pounds off, but otherwise didn't leave her the worse for wear. Me, never sick a day in my life. Nope, strong as a horse. I was so fucked up at the time that I was actually interpreting my sound health as not being able to catch a break.

Lunch was going fine, but it was clear that the dynamic had

changed. It was like an addict hanging out with an old friend who was in recovery. We weren't two fat girls trading war stories. We were two very different people tiptoeing around the differences. Until . . .

Joanna reached across the table, set her hand on top of mine in the most gentle, solicitous manner, and said, "I really think you should lose some weight."

My smiling, congenial countenance disappeared. Who was she to judge me? I let her have it.

"You have a lot of nerve. You, who have been fat just as long as I have, should know better. You were sick, for God's sake, you didn't even try to lose the weight. And just a reminder, when I was quitting smoking and we lived together, did I ever say 'Sure wish you could put down the cancer sticks. It would really improve your health.' No. And now, today, sitting in the smoking section, me, a nonsmoker, did I reach my righteous hand across the table and say 'You know, Joanna, I wish you would quit smoking.' NOOOOOO, I didn't! And you know why? Because you know that smoking is bad for you. You don't need me to remind you of all your faults, and I don't need you to remind me of mine. But thank you for reminding me that I've failed. Thanks for pointing out that you lost weight, and I didn't. Thanks for reminding me that I'm still fat."

She recoiled and took the it's-just-that-I'm-so-much-happier-being-thin, I'm-sure-you-would-be-too position. The irony, of course, was that if I had suggested to her one year earlier that she lose weight, she would have flown into a rage and cursed me out. I thought I was fairly restrained given how pissed off I was.

Does it make people feel better about themselves to point out what they perceive as your inadequacies? If so, that sucks. Rest assured that no matter how much you care about me—or pretend to care about me—nobody cares more about the way I look and feel than I do.

Except maybe Kathy Smith.

After I won my Emmy, I got some more unsolicited advice, this time from someone I've never even met and who obviously falls into the category of "embarrassed by fat people."

Kathy Smith is a fitness guru, who took it upon herself to write about my acceptance speech at the Emmy Awards in a newspaper column headlined "If Fat Becomes Hip, We Are in Extreme Trouble." Really? How so? What kind of trouble? I'm just trying to figure out what kind of chaos the world would be thrown into if fat became hip and hips became fat. Would there be chocolate rationing? Would Wall Street buckle under heavier brokers? Would all the pork in the federal budget actually be appropriated for pork? It's hard to imagine exactly what this "extreme trouble" might be.

I have hypothesized that fat acceptance would cripple the industries that rely on the beauty myth for their billions. Which would be just fine with me, but we know that that is not what Kathy Smith is worried about. Of course, one thing that would surely happen is that people like Ms. Smith, who write fitness columns and books and sell millions of exercise videos, would be out of work. Maybe that's what she means by "extreme trouble."

In her column she laments a news story about "a 'fat' people's association, whose motto is 'Love us the way we are.' " And then goes on to say that my Emmy acceptance speech was contributing to this problem. "One joyous winner was an actress from *The*

Practice. Camryn Manheim. A heavy woman, Camryn waved her award and proudly announced words to the effect that this was 'for all the fat people in the world.' " No. What I said was "This is for all the fat girls." Now I'm not a journalist, I don't even play one on TV, but the disclaimer "words to the effect . . ." just means Kathy was being either (a) lazy or (b) disingenuous. If the former is the case, Kathy just didn't take the time to find the actual quote. If it's the latter, Ms. Smith knew what the actual quote was but found that it didn't support her hypothesis quite as well as her casual paraphrase. But being misquoted isn't what upsets me about this piece.

Ms. Smith goes on to write: "That we don't live in the time of Peter Paul Rubens—the 17th-century Flemish painter whose corpulent models were considered the height of beauty—works to our healthful advantage, since the desire to look good and be sexy is usually the most powerful motivator to keep extra weight off. . . . But if the motivation were eliminated by a growing acceptance of fat as desirable or even just ordinary, we'd lose vanity as a weapon in the health wars and our obesity rates would climb much faster than they are already."

Vanity as a weapon? Health wars? That Ms. Smith would choose to use violence as metaphor to illustrate her point should come as no surprise to those of us who are familiar with being beaten by the vanity club. Still, I must say that her shamelessness is remarkable. She literally seems to be saying that it's more important to be thin than to feel good about ourselves, lest we lose our vanity.

There's more. She writes: "People who rationalize their weight gain and eat indiscriminately without regard for how much they eat or what kinds of foods are ignoring one of the most compelling ways to manage their health and retard the aging process. It's an undeniable fact that better eating translates to a better quality of life."

Undeniable fact? Well, I feel a little uncomfortable questioning an "undeniable fact," but I wonder where Kathy obtained this "fact." For whom does it translate to a better quality of life? If I am presented with the choice of a rice cake or tiramisu, I know that Ms. Smith would so desperately want me to choose that rice cake so as to enhance my quality of life. But it's not going to happen. Because I know that tiramisu improves my quality of life. Life is about tiramisu. It's about indulging and partaking and embracing and enjoying. Sure, we could go live as ascetics on top of a mountain in Tibet, perhaps for 120 years, avoiding all contact with red meat, dessert, and people's germs. But that's not living. That's merely existing. And I want to live . . . in a world with tiramisu.

*   *   *

Sometimes the reminder that I should lose weight comes from the most unlikely sources.

About five years ago, I was hanging out with my sister's six-year-old son, Noah. At one point he turned to me and asked, "Auntie Cam, why are you so fat?" I said, "I don't know, Noah. It's just the way I am." Then he continued, "Well, can't you get unfat?"

I wanted to be honest and gentle with him because he was just a little kid, asking little-kid questions, but part of me wondered where this line of questioning originated. So I asked him, "What's so bad about being fat?" And cute Noah said, "It's just when I ask my mom if I can have a cookie, she says, 'No, you can't have a cookie, Noah, or you'll grow up to be fat like Auntie Cam.'" Ouch!

I sat with that for a while, and it made sense. My sister was a fat kid who admits she was self-conscious and uncomfortable with her self-image. It is totally understandable and completely natural that she would not want her sons to suffer the way she had. However, to be held up as the image of what *not* to be in her household was very hurtful. Although I understand where that comes from, it doesn't ease the pain.

My sister and I had a bizarre intersection of morphology. For the first eleven years of my life, I was a skinny kid. For the first sixteen years of her life, she was fat. But as I entered puberty and she completed adolescence, we traded bodies. It was like a bad sci-fi movie. Every five pounds she lost I gained. By fifteen I was officially fat and she was thin and getting married.

Naturally, being sisters, this was a source of conflict. I envied her for being thin, and I suspect she was embarrassed that I was fat. Perhaps it reminded her of an aspect of her childhood that she'd just as soon forget. No doubt because of these unique circumstances, Lisa and I have had a long-standing awkwardness when it comes to weight, and we continue to struggle to find a place where we can discuss it comfortably.

My sister is a vegetarian who eats very healthily, and, quite frankly, it's a little intimidating. I get embarrassed thinking that she's judging me, even if she's not. I find myself eating before I visit her, so I can pretend to be satiated by small portions. My other defense is to not visit at all, and that extends to my entire family. Because I am fat, I always feel like I'm disappointing them when we're together. But since I actually like everybody in my family, it hurts me to not be in touch with them. So over the years I've accumulated a lot of frequent flyer miles with MCI's Friends and Family. The phone is a nice safe way for me to enjoy my family's company without feeling judged.

While Lisa and I haven't completely solved this food puzzle, we don't let it define our relationship. Because I love and admire my sister, obviously I want to hang out with her, her husband, and their two beautiful boys. But it's still a work in progress. And I still eat a Snickers bar on my way down to visit.

Look, I can understand why Joanna, Kathy Smith, Lisa, and millions of other people are horrified at the prospect of being fat. There is nothing worse than being fat and hating yourself. I know. I lived there. But there is nothing more liberating than being fat and accepting yourself. It is the purest form of self-acceptance, loving yourself in a society that loathes you.

All I'm saying is Wake Up, *I'm* Fat. I'm not saying you should be fat. You should love yourself just the way you are. And if you want to lose weight, great, go ahead, but don't impose your agenda on anybody else. Trust me, they won't appreciate it, no matter how well meaning you are. But if I have bad breath, I hereby give all of you permission to tell me.

Life in
the Fat Lane

By now I'm pretty sure everyone has woken up to the fact that I
am fat. Hooray! And part of the reason I've wanted to shout it
from the rooftops is so that reviewers will no longer have to point
it out. And believe me, they have.

Even my good friends at *People* magazine couldn't pass up the
opportunity to refer to me as "the plus-size star," which prompted
this letter to the editor from my new best friend, Chris Cummings
of Sacramento:

> *Shame on you! In your write-up of the Emmy Awards you*
> *merely gave the names of the people in the article until you*
> *came to Camryn Manheim. With her, you felt compelled to*

add "the plus-size star." Why? You didn't describe Michael J.
Fox as "short." Or Helen Hunt as "slender." Or Calista Flock-
hart as "long-necked." Please stop making an issue of size.

If you ever need a thesaurus for the word "fat," look no further. Here is the definitive list of fat synonyms and fat euphemisms, all culled from reviews about me. These are from actual reviews. Many of these critics took it upon themselves to alert people that I was fat, just in case they wouldn't notice. And it's obviously really important to these critics that people do notice.

Rotund	Robust
Big boned	Oversized
Frumpy	Big
Fat	Zaftig
Buxom (we like this one)	Full-bodied
Heavy	Wide-ish
Colossal	Large
No Slenderella	Immense
Plump	Tremendous
Ample	Generously proportioned
Heroically proportioned	Enormous
Overweight	Grand
Couch potato	Plentiful
Stout	Corpulent
Hefty	Heavyweight talent
Matronly	Gravitationally challenged

Now, just so you don't think I'm making this up, here are quotes from the actual reviews these words are taken from.

On my performance in *Two Gentlemen of Verona*, Michael Feingold writes in the *Village Voice*, ". . . a fat Lucetta (Camryn Manheim) flapping wet sheets in the air . . ."

Have you ever seen Michael Feingold? Well, that's the pot calling the kettle fat!

David Richards, the *New York Times*: ". . . and her buxom waiting woman (Camryn Manheim) beat their laundry in the shallows . . ."

Thank you, that's exactly the description I was looking for when I wore a very tight corset that created enough cleavage to hide a small child in.

Clive Barnes of the *Post* on *Missing Persons*: ". . . plus the fat, husband-hungry widow (played by Camryn Manheim) from next door . . ."

I guess I should be honored that the legendarily sleepy Mr. Barnes stayed awake long enough to notice I was fat.

Jan Stuart of *New York Newsday* on *Missing Persons*: "Gemma, the plain-Jane widow from next door with three kids . . ."

With all due respect, Jan, I am not a plain Jane. Please. Just look at all the other reviews; I'm fat, for Christ's sake!

Thomas M. Disch on *Triumph of Love* for *NY Entertainment*: "Harlequin, who falls for the princess's heroically proportioned valet (played by Camryn Manheim) . . ."

While I would like to discourage reviews based on physicality, if your physical characteristics must be pointed out, "heroically proportioned" is okay by me.

Clive Barnes on *Sin*: "Her couch potato friend Camryn Manheim must be assured she is fat and terrible . . ."

Gee, I don't know, a guy who regularly falls asleep in the first act calling me a couch potato . . . who's projecting here?

Jeremy Girard in *Variety*: ". . . the fat best friend Avery's moved in with . . ."

Uh, I know I'm new at this writer thing here, but I remember in high school when we learned about the superlative, you know, like "best." It meant, there could only be one. Or was I merely the best fat friend? Or did that sneaky Avery have a "skinny best friend" that I didn't know about?

Frank Schock from the *Hollywood Reporter*: "the best moments are provided by Camryn Manheim, hilarious as Avery's defiantly overweight friend . . ."

Once you've said the best moments are provided by me, you can say whatever you want.

Jennifer Dowling, *Daily Pennsylvanian*, on *The Road to Wellville*: "To its credit, an early voice of the sexual revolution is heard in *Wellville* as the ample Virginia (played with unsurpassed sensuality by Camryn Manheim) tells the friend Eleanor that 'the only thing harmful about sex is when women don't get enough of it or don't get to enjoy it when they do.' "

Unsurpassed sensuality! That's right! Michelle Pfeiffer used to have the title, but I apparently usurped her throne. As for Virginia's pithy views on sex, I couldn't agree more.

Peter Stack, *San Francisco Chronicle*, on *Wellville*: "... Broderick fights against the spa's rigorous codes but his wife digs the place and is soon glommed onto by sex-minded men, as well as befriended by a stout female guest, wonderfully played by Manheim, who nearly steals the show."

No offense, Pete, but I'm too tall to be stout. Teapots are stout. You know, "I'm a little teapot . . ." I'm 5´10´´, for Pete's sake.

***Variety* on *Wellville*:** "... fairing a bit better is Fonda's Eleanor, who is awakened to the notion of liberated female sexuality by her hefty friend, Virginia (jovial, insinuating Camryn Manheim) . . ."

Hefty, nice. Now I'm being described like a kitchen garbage bag.

Ellen Futterman, for the *St. Louis Post-Dispatch* on *Wellville*: "Camryn Manheim, as Eleanor's confidante, a rotund feminist who questions many of Dr. Kellogg's practices, including his belief in celibacy . . ."

Rotund feminists are the best kind. We get more done and can intimidate conservatives more effectively.

Joe Baltake, *Sacramento Bee*, on *Wellville*: "Eleanor, with a matron, scene-stealing Camryn Manheim, who enlightens her protégée by introducing her to two quack doctors . . ."

Once again, when you include the "scene-stealing" modifier, you get a lot more slack.

Janet Maslin, *New York Times*: "Camryn Manheim and Michael Lerner as the robust sidekicks of Ms. Fonda and Mr. Cusack, respectively, do what little is possible to provide comic relief . . ."

Isn't coffee robust?

Gannett News Service: ". . . particularly robust . . ."

Yes, I think Taster's Choice is particularly robust.

The *Courier Journal*: "Eleanor explores sexual liberation as practiced by her plump friend Virginia (Camryn Manheim)."

Chubby girls: They plump when you cook 'em.

Kenneth Turan, *Los Angeles Times*, on *Happiness*: ". . . Allen has an admirer of his own, the seriously heavy Kristina (Camryn Manheim) . . ."

Seriously heavy? As opposed to ridiculously heavy or giddily heavy?

In the book *Prime Time Lawyers*, edited by Robert M. Jarvis and Paul R. Joseph. "Frutt (Camryn Manheim) is, to be perfectly honest, a frump."

I can't reprint the whole chapter here, but, to be perfectly honest, it sucked.

The Globe writes: ". . . big and beautiful star . . . healthy and happy to be pleasingly plump . . . Camryn's a big gal now and proud of it."

Two bigs and a plump in the same sentence. That's got to be a record.

Wayne Murphy, the *West Australian*: "... she is not blonde, curvaceous and with impossibly long legs, she is shortish, wide-ish and not beautiful ..."

Shortish? How tall do they grow 'em Down Under? C'mon, Wayne. My whole platform is that I'm big *and* I'm beautiful. Don't blow it for me.

Howard Kissel, reviewing *Wake Up, I'm Fat!* for the *Daily News*, writes: "To begin with, Camryn Manheim isn't all that fat. She's no Slenderella, but she's not even as heavy as, say, Roseanne."

Slenderella? That's priceless. Howard managed to insult not just me but someone who wasn't even in the show.

Michael Sommers from the *Star-Ledger* on *Wake Up, I'm Fat!*: "... Manheim also just happens to pack some extra pounds around her person."

Some people pack extra underwear; I pack extra pounds.

Brian Scott Lipton in *The Manhattan Insider* on *The Triumph of Love*: "... the differences between Margaret Welch and Camryn Manheim hit you in the face. Welch, who plays the beautiful, manipulative Princess Leonide, is blond, blue-eyed and just shy of model-thin; Manheim, who plays her cheeky servant Corine, is dark-haired and, to put it delicately, corpulent."

Delicately? Gee, I'd hate to catch Brian on a day when he felt like being harsh.

The caption on the photo that accompanied Mr. Lipton's article read: "She's not heavy, she's my servant."

Some editor thought this was clever. Now, he could have said I was chewing the scenery; *that* would have been clever.

*   *   *

I want to say for the record that there are a lot of classy critics out there. Here are a few of my favorites:

Gail Shister, *Philadelphia Inquirer:* "... big-boned co-stars Camryn Manheim, Michael Badalucco, and Steve Harris look refreshingly like regular people on ABC's lawyer drama, a hit in its new slot."

Kinney Littlefield, *Orange County Register:* "... vibrant, vigorously intellectual Manheim lives life her way, no apologies. A full-bodied woman, she bucked Hollywood's preference for tissue-paper waifs to win the compelling role of Ellenor on *The Practice.*"

Michael Sommers in the *Star-Ledger:* "... have they cast Cherry Jones' successor yet for 'The Heiress'? Who's playing Cordelia to F. Murray Abraham's Lear? Wake up, Camryn Manheim's a gifted actress who could use a good role."

William Stevenson, *Backstage*, on *Wake Up, I'm Fat!:* "Wake up everybody; she's talented, so who cares if she's fat."

New York magazine writes: "Calling a show *Wake Up, I'm Fat!* is the best example of American straight speaking since Harry Truman."

Cynthia True in *TimeOut New York:* "... her hilarious and moving one-woman show, *Wake Up, I'm Fat!* at the Public Theater ..."

And my all-time favorite, from Peter Marks of the *New York Times*: "Forget about butter substitutes. The real breakthrough for fat people this year is Camryn Manheim."

*   *   *

Look, I don't mind being described as fat. In fact, that's the whole point. But I hope there are more interesting aspects to my performances, and I would hope in the future reviewers will focus on my acting and not my dimensions. The reason they don't mention that Tom Cruise is 5´8˝ in reviews is because it doesn't matter. And I hope that some day, my weight will be regarded as equally irrelevant.

Fashionably Late

Ever since I was a fat twelve-year-old trying to hide in my Levi's, I've had what you might call dress-a-phobia. Dresses were to me what a crucifix is to a vampire.

I went all the way through junior high without wearing a dress. The only time I wore a dress in high school was in a production of *June Moon*, and even then I protested. As a motorcyclist and a wanna-be lesbian in Santa Cruz, the whole dress thing didn't come up a lot. I don't think I even *owned* a dress. At NYU I wore sweatpants and baggy shirts. I did have to wear dresses in a couple of productions, but I drew the line at panty hose. And as you know, my bad dress mojo climaxed in Bloomingdale's with the showdown with my mother.

Perhaps part of my aversion to dresses and fashion in general stemmed from my being a "Forgotten Woman." You know, one of the millions of women size 16 and up whom fashion forgot. And, quite frankly, I got pretty accustomed to being forgotten and never really developed a relationship of any kind with fashion.

So when Loree Parral, the wardrobe designer of *The Practice*, called to discuss her ideas for Ellenor's look, the first words out of my mouth were "Please don't make me wear dresses."

Loree (whom, by the way, I love) told me that the Boston court system was very conservative and that she'd have to talk about it with David Kelley. Somehow I didn't think David would understand the complexity of the issue or the depth of my contempt for dresses. So I told Loree to be sure to tell David that it was a federal law that women were allowed to wear pants in court. I also asked her to point out that I have a tattoo on my ankle and since I'm allergic to nylon and wouldn't be wearing hose (good one, eh?) a dress would reveal my tattoo, making me look less conservative than I would in a pantsuit. And besides, I thought the whole point was that Ellenor was *not* conservative.

Loree laughed and assured me she'd take my concerns to David.

"Oh, and by the way, Loree, I have twelve earrings in my right ear. I imagine that's quite a lot for the conservative Boston court system, but Ellenor might be just sassy enough to get away with four or five."

I think at this point Loree thought I was messing with her: no dresses, tattoo, twelve ear piercings. I made it sound like she was going to have to outfit a member of the Red Hot Chili Peppers. When I hung up with Loree, I thought for sure David would just fire me. It would be so much easier than trying to make *me* look like a lawyer.

To my surprise, Loree called me the next day and told me that David had said yes to the pantsuits, yes to the tattoo, and yes to the twelve earrings in the right ear. How cool was that?

During that first season, Loree put me in some incredible suits—Tamotsu, Jones of New York, Dana Buchman, Anne Klein, Emmanuel. "Fabrics and textures and colors, oh my!" I had always had an adversarial relationship with clothes, but suddenly I was starting to look forward to my fittings. For the first time in my life, I didn't have to worry that the clothes wouldn't fit, thanks in part to the plus-size designers but mostly due to sweet Anoush Yergan, the show's talented and tireless seamstress.

In those first weeks at *The Practice*, when we were all being invited to various network meet-and-greets, I realized I didn't have anything to wear. On more than one occasion, Loree bailed me out, loaning me a designer suit for an event. This was all very new to me. I hadn't been to too many functions where my picture was taken or where I'd been asked who had made my outfit. Before Loree, the answer would have been "Levi Strauss." Now I was strutting around in Marina Rinaldi, Nira-Nira, and Carol Little. It was hard to believe I was the same girl who used to think getting dressed up meant wearing Wranglers.

As fun as it was to be wearing these great designers, I always felt a little bit like Cinderella, having to get the clothes back to *The Practice* if not by midnight, then at least by noon the next day. At the parties, I would look at the other cast members and realize that I was the only one who didn't own my clothes. I was the only one at any of these gatherings that felt like she could actually get in trouble for spilling salsa on her blouse. I bit the bullet and bought a few suits.

Ellenor survived that whole first season without once being

forced to wear a dress or skirt. But in season two, Ellenor had to argue a case in front of a federal judge. And since federal judges are appointed for life and tend to be old-school fuddy-duddies, Loree felt Ellenor should show them the respect they believed they deserved. I begrudgingly relented like a little kid agreeing to put her jammies on. But Loree made it painless. She outfitted me in a long dark (slenderizing) skirt with tights and cool boots. Not only did I not mind wearing the skirt, I bought it.

By the third season of *The Practice*, I could be overheard asking my dresser Susie Roberts (whom I also love), "Why doesn't Ellenor wear more skirts?" To which she would roll her eyes and say, "Oh my God, I can't believe I heard you say that!" But it's true, one of the unexpected results of this whole self-acceptance thing is allowing myself the desire to look pretty.

Another by-product of my self-acceptance was that I began seeing other women of all sizes of large as beautiful too. Which is why it bothered me so much that the clothing stores that made their millions catering to women size 12 and up always used models at the small end of the plus-size spectrum in their ads. It was as if they were saying "Sure we make clothes up to size 26, but our clothes look much better if you're a size 12." I got so frustrated that I actually wrote a letter to Lane Bryant asking them why they didn't use larger models who were more representative of their clientele. Their thoughtful response opened my eyes to a deeper problem. Here it is:

> *Thank you for your letter expressing your feelings on the models we use in our catalogues. We do understand and we want you to know that your complaint is not unique. The comments we have received in the past two years have caused*

*us to take a second look at the way our catalogues are pre-
sented. We are moving in the direction of more mature and
fuller figured models, however, we are sure we are not where
you want us to be and we may never get there. Please let us explain.*

*In early January we ran a newspaper insert ad in various re-
gions of the country selling one of our most popular shirts. Half
of the inserts used a size 12 model and the other half used a
larger size model. Everything else in both ads was identical.
The final result showed that the ad with the size 12 model sold
50% more merchandise than the ad with the large sized model.
This response was not a surprise. Similar tests conducted during the past few years have yielded similar results. As an organization, we appear to have a serious dilemma. Our customers
ask for fuller figured models, yet when we use them, these same
customers don't respond as well to the fuller figured models. As
a result, our business is left with no choice.*

It is a sad commentary on our society that the beauty myth is so
pervasive that size 22s, who know they will never be a size 4, still
dream of being a size 12.

It turns out that the problem is not with them (Lane Bryant)
but with us (plus-size consumers). In fact, Lane Bryant has kept
its vow to employ more mature fuller-figured models by hiring
yours truly (size 22) to model the fall lineup. Now is our chance,
sisters. If we want to see more fuller-figured models in the future,
then we need to reward the companies that employ large-size
models with our patronage.

It still seems weird to me that the self-hating, clothes-hating fat
girl I once was could grow into a self-loving, clothes-loving fat

woman who shills for Lane Bryant. Of course, part of the reason I had no affinity for clothes when I was growing up was that there was nothing to wear. When I was thirteen years old and didn't fit into Ditto's or Sassoons, my options were seriously limited. Don't get me wrong, I would have liked to have worn cool clothes, but the Long Beach malls didn't exactly cater to girls like me.

But, thankfully, times have changed. This past year I have been asked to model for *Mode* magazine and designers Tamotsu, Anne Klein, and Liz Claiborne. I never thought I'd have anything in common with Kate Moss, least of all a modeling agent. Models desperately want you to think that their job is really, really tough. Pssst, it isn't. You basically have a team of people buffing you, pampering you, and photographing you all day. They put on cool music and spend hours shouting "That's beautiful, baby. You're fabulous." Wow, really tough.

But before I knew how much fun it would be, I was a little apprehensive. When I got that first call from *Mode* magazine telling me they wanted to do a feature article and a fashion photo shoot, my biggest fear was that I'd get to the studio and none of the clothes would fit me. They'd have racks and racks of size 16s and we'd all stand around embarrassed as the stylist ran down to Fifth Avenue, searching for my size. But this was *Mode*, baby, the fashion and style magazine dedicated to plus-size women. And there's a reason it is the fastest-growing magazine in the country.

The shoot was like a fairy tale. Everything they gave me to wear fit perfectly, even the shoes. I guess it was a big deal because CNN and *Extra* came to the shoot to interview me. Was it really newsworthy? "FAT GIRL HAS PICTURE TAKEN!" Story at eleven. Maybe it is newsworthy, a fat woman being portrayed as an object of desire. It certainly doesn't happen every day. And in order to make it an everyday occurrence, I ask you, the reader, to insist that your doctors, dentists, lawyers, and every other professional with a waiting room subscribe to *Mode* magazine. To subscribe, call: 1–888–610–MODE. Those coffee tables should include every image of beauty so as to represent all the different types of beautiful women who flip through those magazines as they wait for their appointment. Who knows, maybe if we get *Mode* in every waiting room, eventually there would be clothes that actually fit us in every store. Because that sure isn't the case now. And if you think it's bad here in the States, try shopping for plus sizes in Europe. I did, and it's not pretty.

Every couple of years I like to schlep over to London to catch all the new plays so when they come to Broadway I can say "Seen it." You certainly don't go to London for the food, and I warn you now, if you're over a size 12, you certainly shouldn't go over there for the fashion.

I was traveling with my good friend Jane, who is a size 6, and let me tell you, she spent a fortune. Blouses, skirts, jackets, dresses, even a gown. It became clear to me why fat women have so many pairs of shoes and so many accessories. Earrings fit everybody. Dresses don't.

After the trip to Buckingham Palace, the hours at the Victoria and Albert Museum, Piccadilly Circus, Leicester Square, Big Ben, etc., Jane and I left a couple of days exclusively for shopping. What a mistake. Now, don't get me wrong, I like to shop every bit as much as the next gal, but one of the really special features of shopping is being able to purchase something that actually fits. Sure, the vicarious thrill of watching Jane find the perfect jacket and the perfect suit held me over for about an hour, but after that I started feeling sorry for myself. At Harvey Nichols and Marks and Spencers there wasn't even anything to try on. Harrods had a plus-size section, but it was a joke. Back to the muumuus and stretch polyester.

Come on, England! If the national food is deep-fried fish and chips, you'd think the clothes would reflect the culture.

I ended up buying lots of fabric, so I could make my own clothes and still be able to say "Oh, this, I picked it up in London." Nothing ruins a vacation more quickly and more completely than not being able to shop.

Though things have definitely improved here in the States, fashion has always been a little slow in accommodating large women. Some of my favorite stores still haven't gotten on the plus-size bandwagon. So it is now my personal crusade to start a letter-writing campaign to Banana Republic, Donna Karan, the Gap, and countless others to get them to expand their catalogues and clothing lines to include the same fashions in larger sizes. Let's let them know that there is a substantial consumer population that they're not reaching. Send an e-mail or even a snail mail to the corporate headquarters of the store you'd most like to see include plus sizes. Dollar signs always seem to get their attention. We're not asking for philanthropy here. Wake up, we're fat, we like nice clothes, and we've got cash.

Still, I'm never too far from a pair of Levi's. There's a pair in my dressing room, a pair in the trunk of my car, a pair in my gym bag, and a pair on my body as I sit here typing this chapter. Maybe some day there will be a federal law saying that lawyers can wear Levi's to court.

Wake-up Call

RING!

Who the fuck is calling me at five-thirty in the morning?

Isn't it amazing how many thoughts can race through your mind in the two seconds between being awakened from a deep sleep and answering the phone?

Damn, I'm late for work. The alarm didn't go off. Eighty-five crew members, two hundred extras, directors, producers, co-stars, and guest stars are all standing around in the courtroom, looking at their watches, wondering "Where the hell is Camryn?"

I look at the clock and I look at the top of my script for my call time and realize I'm not due on set for another three hours.

Oh, shit, somebody's hurt, or worse . . . No, that's crazy it's too early for anybody to be *up* to get hurt.

It's probably just one of my New York friends who thinks if she's up the whole world must be up, never mind the three-hour difference.

Maybe it's that cute Liam O'Shaughnessy I met in Ireland last month. What time is it in Dublin?

RING!

Should I let the machine get it? What if it's one of my friends prone to early-A.M. *faux* crises? "I'm sorry I woke you, but now that you're up . . ." It better not be AT&T asking me to switch. Oh, Christ . . .

"Hello?"

"Congratulations."

The voice was familiar, friendly.

"Who is this?"

"It's Jeffrey Kramer."

Oh, shit, my producer from *The Practice*. Maybe they really were all gathered on the set waiting for me. I double-checked the clock and my call time.

"Jeffrey, I'm not late. My call time's not until eight-thirty."

"Camryn, congratulations. You were nominated for an Emmy Award for Best Supporting Actress in a Drama."

And *that* is the only acceptable excuse for waking somebody up at five-thirty in the morning. My articulate, well-crafted response went something like this: "OH MY FUCKING GOD! OH MY FUCKING GOD. JEFFREY, I CAN'T FUCKING BELIEVE IT! ARE YOU FUCKING SURE? DON'T FUCK WITH ME! OH MY FUCKING GOD!"

Then came the soothing voice of reason. "Yes, it's true. Isn't it fantastic? Congratulations, Camryn. You deserve it." Jeffrey swears a lot less than I do.

I never imagined I would have responded this way, but the second it registered, I burst into tears. My reaction was not a conscious evaluation of the wonderful news but a physical response to the fulfillment of the desperate desire to be accepted. I had spent the previous twenty-five years erecting defenses and developing a sheet of armor and still had the scars from battles lost, and in that moment, for the first time I could remember, I didn't feel like an outcast.

"Camryn, you were nominated for an Emmy Award for Best Supporting Actress in a Drama." I was still trying to wrap my mind around those words.

I put the phone down, trembling with joy. A kind of joy I had never known. My brain didn't even know how to process the information. All I could do was hold my head in my hands and weep. I was very familiar with the flip side, the disappointment of rejection, the hollowness of defeat, the churning in my stomach from being passed over. But this . . . this was something new. To have my peers say "We recognize your work." If I ever told you that that didn't matter to me, I was lying. Because it does matter. Big time.

So there I was, weeping like a schoolgirl who just got crowned prom queen. And all of a sudden five-thirty didn't seem so early anymore. I guess there are two excusable reasons to call someone at five-thirty in the morning: One is to tell her that she's been nominated for an Emmy, the other is for that person to tell her parents.

My mom answered the phone with that wee-hour combination of sleepiness and concern, and I was little help in assuaging her fears that something was terribly wrong because I was hyperventilating and screaming unintelligibly "IWASNOMINATED-FORANEMMY!!!!"

"Honey, slow down, take a deep breath. I can't understand you."

"Okay . . . Mom . . . listen . . . IJUSTFOUNDOUTIWAS-NOMINATEDFORANEMMYAWARD!!!"

And then she screamed at me, "Camryn, stop it, you're scaring me! Is something wrong?"

When I was finally able to compose myself enough to convey my news, my mom woke up my father, shouting "JERRYCAM-RYNWASNOMINATEDFORANEMMYAWARD!"

Soon we had three-way hysteria. My parents must have awakened the whole neighborhood with their shouts of *"Oh ich hob naches."* Then the call-waiting beeps started. I had never received so many calls before 6:00 A.M. in my life. And with each call more tears, more mucous. By six-thirty I was exhausted, and I still had to go to work.

Not only had I been nominated, but the show had been nominated for Best Drama. So everyone was already in high spirits. I was greeted by shouts and hugs. When I walked into the makeup trailer, my castmates Lisa Gay Hamilton and Kelli Williams threw their arms around me. The entire trailer erupted into celebration. I burst into tears again. How could there be any left?

Michael Badalucco, who plays Jimmy Berluti, sparred with me playfully about being a big star, and Dylan—whom *People* magazine touted as one of the sexiest men alive—gave me such a hug, he managed to squeeze out some more tears. And sweet Steve Harris, who had been kicking my butt in cribbage since the first day I taught him, paid me the ultimate tribute: He came to work on his day off to congratulate me. As Steve hugged me and I began to cry, I could see a pattern emerging. I had become a congratulations-activated faucet.

Just when I thought my heart couldn't be touched any more, I went to my dressing room and found it filled with flowers. Calista

Flockhart had sent me a beautiful bouquet. What time do flower shops open anyway? The red light on my phone was telling me I had messages. Friends and network executives had left congratulations. Lara Flynn Boyle wasn't working that day but she left me some incredible sentiments that ended with a stern warning: I expect you to thank me in your speech or you'll have to wash my car for the rest of the season. And in his own inimitable style, David Kelley left this little gem: "Hey, Camryn, it's David. Just calling to say 'Hi.' See ya." Yeah, calling to say, "Hi" at 8:28 A.M. Good ol' David, never one to use twelve words when eleven will do.

*   *   *

I was aware that I had been the only cast member nominated, but my coworkers were so supportive, so gracious, and so cool that they gave me permission to revel in the moment and not feel like I had to downplay it. Everyone should get to work with people like these.

By 11:00 A.M. the entertainment reporters were on the set. *Entertainment Tonight*, *Access Hollywood*, E! Entertainment Television, all wanting to know what it felt like to be a first-time nominee. "Indescribably delicious!" I could hardly contain myself as they set up their cameras. Someone from *Access Hollywood* asked me if I was going to be as excited on camera as I was off camera. I didn't realize there was a difference between off-camera exhilaration and on-camera blasé. I clearly had a lot to learn.

Entertainment Tonight asked if they could follow me while I shopped for an Emmy dress. This book got its title from a horrible experience shopping in a clothing store, and there I was contemplating having cameras follow me while I tried on clothes. Boy, have I changed! "Free publicity. Heck, yeah, I'll do it!"

I had just had this great experience doing a layout for *Mode* magazine so I called Michele Weston, the magazine's fashion and style director, and asked if she would help me contact designers. Several designers had already called my managers asking if I was interested in wearing one of their gowns to the 50th Annual Emmy Awards. My first and only criterion for entertaining their offer was "Do you make plus-size clothes?" The most common response was "No, but we'll be happy to make a gown for you." Sorry, no dice. What good does it do for me to wear your dress if people like me can't buy one? Basically, what these guys were saying is "Hey, if you're fat and you want to wear one of my dresses, all you have to do is get nominated for an Emmy." I looked to Michele to guide me to the designers who do make plus-size clothes. That is when I discovered the gowns of Anne Klein, Emanuel, Ferre, Nira-Nira, Tamotsu, Marina Rinaldi, and others. I was Cinderella and for the first time in my life the glass slipper fit.

I flew back to New York to meet designers. Hold on. Let me just write that again. I—flew—back—to—New—York— to— meet—designers. Nope, still doesn't seem possible. But it was.

When I returned from New York, Armand from Harry Winston jewelers called. "We would love for you to wear our diamonds at the event." Had I gone into Harry Winston the day before, I probably would have been ushered out. I think they have a retina scan at the door that tells them instantly if you can afford their jewels. In the spirit of keeping things positive, let's just say their finery wasn't for me. (Stage whisper: Too gaudy.)

Next stop on Rodeo Drive, Van Cleef & Arpels jewelers. I made the mistake of asking for something in silver. "Oh, no, we don't use the 'S' word here. It's platinum." Oh, okay, well . . . I kinda had my heart set on the "S" word.

How could shopping for free diamonds be this depressing? So many carats, so much to learn, so little interest.

I left sort of bummed out, wondering if I'd be able to find anything that suited me that didn't make me feel like I was posing. I continued down Rodeo, which is not exactly my stomping grounds, and then I stumbled upon Frances Klein's Estate Jewels. They were beautiful. Simple, elegant, tasteful. They had been lived in and, in some cases, died in. I had found my Emmy jeweler. The only problem was they didn't have enough matching diamond earrings to fill the twelve piercings in my right ear, but I respectfully accepted the gorgeous diamond necklace and the long diamond earrings they offered to lend me for the evening. Phew.

*   *   *

I was about midway through my whirlwind week when I got a letter from Jeffrey Kramer. Had I received a letter from Jeffrey the week before, I would have assumed it was a notice of termination. Nobody gets letters from their producers. You see them every day. But I was lucky enough to get this one.

Dear Camryn,

I have never made a more exciting phone call. It is truly a moment I will never forget. My thoughts go back to that first meeting with you in David's office and the wonderful feeling that you left with us both. I am so proud of you, your ability and your advocacy for women. You are an inspiration for us all. Congratulations!

Love,
Jeffrey Kramer

I guess at this point I don't have to tell you that it made me cry.

*   *   *

I spent more time on fashion in the next six weeks than I had in my entire life up to that point. Dresses, jewelry, shoes, purses, undergarments, hair, makeup, decisions, decisions, decisions.

Now, I don't want to say that this wasn't all great fun, but I had these nagging responsibilities. You see, David Kelley still expected me to show up for work even though I had been nominated for an Emmy. What a meanie! And, get this, he still expected me to produce Emmy-nominated acting. Then there was this little matter of Camryn Manheim, author. A month earlier— before all hell broke loose—I had signed a book deal, not realizing that I would actually have to *write* a book. The signing of the contract was easy. Signature, date, triplicate. Where's my check? Then came the hard part.

"It was a dark and stormy night . . ." Crumple, crumple, toss in the trash.

"In the beginning, there was Camryn and she was fat . . ." Crumple, crumple, toss in the trash.

"It was the best of times, it was the worst of rhymes . . ." Crumple, crumple, toss in the trash, go to bed.

Wake up. Call editor. Ask for extension.

So instead of partying and basking in my nominee status, I was trying to write a book. I felt like all the other kids were out playing and I was grounded, forced to do my homework. Imagine my surprise when they told me it had to be 250 pages long. I had been planning on just fixin' up my one-woman show and turning that in, but my show was only 41 pages long. Yikes! That meant I'd have to write 209 new pages in four months. That's 52.25 pages per month, or roughly 13 pages a week. And with a full-time job and all, I figured out early on that my weekends would no longer be the respite I looked forward to.

So I've got the book hanging over me and this Emmy thing approaching and my life is what I call mitzvah madness or, in other words, good stress.

With all the attention and good wishes, I decided I wanted to be a nominee forever. My category included *ER*'s Laura Innes and Gloria Ruben, *Touched by an Angel*'s Della Reese, and *NYPD Blue*'s defending champion Kim Delaney. I didn't want Emmy night to come and go. On the Big Night, you're either a winner or a loser, but in the weeks before, you are a nominee, a potential winner, a hopeful. I thought Laura Innes deserved to win but I had a feeling her talented co-star Gloria Ruben would. And I was really dreading writing the chapter about losing at the Emmys and "how honored I was just to have been nominated."

*　　*　　*

Let me back up a little bit here. Do you have any idea how someone gets nominated for an Emmy in the first place? Because I didn't. The way it works is you pay $125 to join the Academy of Television Arts and Sciences. Then you get a form in the mail asking if you want to nominate yourself and in what category. Yep, so all those people who pretend they're above it all and treat these things as a public service, let me remind you, they nominated themselves. The Academy receives all the self-nominations in March. My manager called and asked me if I wanted to do an Emmy campaign. A what? Believe it or not, most potential winners spend $15,000 to $20,000 on a PR campaign to garner a nomination. Yep, 15 to 20K. This campaign includes having your favorite episode copied and sent to all 1,300 Academy members. Here's the rub. Nobody watches the tapes. Think about it. In one month an Academy member receives over a hundred tapes of shows that have already aired and will likely be on again that summer. Don't get me wrong, I'm grateful for the HBO, TNT, and Showtime movies they sent me (and of course all the ABC shows), but the rest of the tapes went in a big box in the lobby of my building in New York so my neighbors could watch them. They were priced to move—*FREE!*—but people still weren't interested. My manager told me that most people who end up getting nominated had run these costly campaigns. I had a better idea.

No TV personality wants to do publicity in the middle of the summer. Their shows are in reruns, their movies aren't out yet, they are all on vacation or making another film. Who's got the time for a photo shoot and a lengthy interview? *I* do. I love the press. And they are largely responsible for my nomination. It's weird. These hardworking people in the print and electronic media do so much to promote our careers and our medium and yet many people in show business resent and dismiss them. Ninety-nine percent of the reporters I've met have been really cool people that I'd like to hang out with. I'm not talking about the paparazzi, I'm talking about journalists, and it's an important distinction.

Maybe I'm just a geek from Peoria, Illinois, but when I arrived at the Emmy nominees dinner and stepped onto my first red carpet, it was really a thrill for me to see all those flashbulbs popping.

At the dinner, we all went up one by one and Dick Clark gave us our nominee certificate. Now the heavy hitters, your Kelsey Grammers, your Helen Hunts, weren't there, and let me tell you, they missed out on a basket of goodies. Every nominee was given a gift certificate for a Frederick Fekkai full-day massage, designer sunglasses, crystal, a Mont Blanc wallet, Harry Winston silver bookmarks . . . as I said, I wanted to be a nominee forever.

ABC's fall season launch party was scheduled for later that same night, but I had been to that party the year before and felt lost in a sea of TV stars. But my dear friend Patrick Breen, who was my date for the evening, assured me that this year would be different, and boy, was he right. Now, I can schmooze with the best of them, but it just felt a little different, people going out of their way to schmooze me. As I said, I wanted to be a nominee forever. But alas, the big night was approaching. Damn!

*   *   *

The Emmys always fall on a Sunday afternoon, so you have all day Saturday to panic—I mean prepare. I don't know what other nominees were doing on that day, but I'm quite sure I was the only one teaching a class at the Learning Annex. Three months earlier I had agreed to give my seminar, Advancing Your Career on Your Own Terms, and a commitment is a commitment. So there I was, at the Doubletree Hotel in Santa Monica, in the Marquis Room, doing my best Tony Robbins, trying to inspire people. I kid, but I've given this seminar at least fifty times, and every time I'm reminded that we all have the power to transform the quality of our lives.

*   *   *

It was now Emmy eve. Michael Mayer had flown in from New York for the weekend to be my date. He is not only one of my dearest friends, but he is one of the only people I would trust to chaperone my parents on the outside chance that I had to go up to the stage for some reason or another.

I'm not saying my folks are a handful, but you don't just dump them on anybody. And Michael is family. I had done most of the work already. I had explained to the folks what was to be expected of them. No embarrassing me by accosting the TV stars, no snapping photos on the red carpet and no organizing a protest if I lost. We had already cleared the wardrobe hurdle. My dad had called and said, "Your mom says I don't have to wear a tux, that a nice suit will do."

"Well, Mom's wrong." Now that that was cleared up, there was the little matter of my mom's attire. She called me to tell me that she had bought a beautiful dress from Saks. "Oh, Camryn, I've never had anything so beautiful. It's a designer dress by Dianna Buchanan."

"That's great, Mom. I've never heard of Dianna Buchanan, I've heard of Dana Buchman."

"Yeah, that's what I said, Dana Buchman."

I offered her a little walk down Rodeo Drive to find some jewels, but she had her own plan. She had invited all her girlfriends over for brunch and told them to bring their finest. So Elaine and Lynn and Joan and Ingrid all came over with their *bijoux*. I was going to have to trust that they'd hook my mom up.

I had booked my folks a room at the Regency Beverly Wilshire (*Pretty Woman*) Hotel. My limo would pick them up on Sunday afternoon before picking me up and we would all go to the Shrine Auditorium together.

Now that my parents were taken care of, Michael and I went to a dinner party hosted by Jonathan Pontell, a producer of *Ally McBeal* and *The Practice*. Among the many guests were my boss and his wife, Michelle Pfeiffer. Now, as my date, one of the requirements is to pay attention to me. But even though Michael is a proud homosexual, he couldn't take his eyes off Michelle. And even though I'm a proud heterosexual, neither could I. That's how beautiful she is. We had an amazing time joking about the slim chances of *The Practice* winning the Emmy and practicing our gracious-loser smiles. We left at a reasonable hour, and in the car, all Michael could talk about was that Michelle Pfieffer spoke to him. He kept saying "She actually made eye contact with me, called me by my first name, and we had a conversation."

That night Michael and I lay in my bed staring out the skylight, reminiscing about how we'd always promised to fly on each other's wings. Earlier that summer I had had the privilege of being his date when he won the Drama Desk Award for directing *A View from the Bridge* on Broadway. The following week, however, I was not on Michael's arm at the Tony Awards. Rather, I was Alan Cumming's date. Michael lost, but Alan took home a Tony for Best Actor in a Musical for his role in *Cabaret*. Coincidence? I don't think so.

As we drifted off, I turned to Michael and asked, "What does it feel like to lose?"

I just wanted to know because I wanted to be prepared.

He said, "The worst part is that my parents were there, and I felt really sad for them."

So I fell asleep with thoughts of consoling my parents the following night after I had lost.

This Is for All the Fat Girls

Sunday (Emmy) morning arrived and my eyes popped open like a kid at Christmas. And I'm Jewish. That's how excited I was. It was hard tiptoeing around while others slept when all I really wanted to do was scream "WAKE UP! I'M FAT AND I'M GOING TO THE EMMYS!"

Even with my loud, pretend-quiet antics, setting down coffee mugs, singing, moving dressers, Michael didn't wake up for another hour. How could anyone be sleeping at a time like this? Didn't he realize we had to be at the Shrine Auditorium in seven hours? I guess I was a little excited.

Because I was a nominee, the television studio provided hair and makeup artists, who came to my house at ten-thirty. Did I mention that I wanted to be a nominee forever? Emmy crisis No. 1 was in full swing: hair up or hair down? For weeks I had been planning on wearing my hair up, but an ABC exec had told me just days earlier to wear my hair down because the statistics showed that winners always wore their hair down. I told her that the votes had already been counted by Ernst & Young and there was no possibility of my hairstyle influencing the outcome. And yet she'd got me thinking. Up? Down? Down? Up? Ah, the huge decisions in life.

Makeup, on the other hand, was going smoothly.

Michael had gone to Noah's for bagels, step one of our daylong nourishment strategy. Step two would have him picking up sandwiches for the limo ride. You see, the limo picks you up at 2:00 P.M. and takes you to the end of the endless limo line, where you sit and wait, moving fifteen feet every ten minutes. The reason it takes so long is that everyone needs to get a picture of Kevin Sorbo, who plays Hercules, as he steps out of his stretch. If you're lucky (and aren't having a hair crisis), you arrive at the Shrine at three. You walk the red carpet for a good forty-five minutes, then make sure you pee *before* the four-hour telecast begins. And here's the kicker. There is no snack bar, no beverages, no guy yelling "Peanuts," in the Shrine. So the preshow nourishment strategy is essential to survival. With preshow and postshow responsibilities, you can go eight hours easy without a morsel of food. This is why it looks like a Who concert when they open the doors to the banquet room for the Governor's Ball. But I had been warned by several Emmy veterans not only to eat in the limo but to limit liquid intake for fear of pulling a Christine Lahti at the '98 Golden Globes.

2:00 P.M.: My folks arrived. They looked amazing. My father

was adorable in his tuxedo, not the one that he wanted with the ruffles, but the one I had instructed the store to rent him. And my mom looked radiant with Lynn Perlman's gold necklace, Ingrid Aall's earrings, and Elaine Quillian's purse adorning her Dana Buchman designer dress. It was the first time in my entire life that I had seen my father in a tux. Tuxedos and socialists don't often mix. But I think he really liked getting all done up, and I could tell my mom was proud to be swinging on his arm.

Me, I was a mess. The phone hadn't stopped ringing, I still wasn't dressed and I hadn't decided on up or down. And it was now ten past two. Michael, the makeup artist, the hairdresser, the hairdresser's assistant, my brother, our neighbor, my managers, and my parents were all gathered around, voting on up or down.

"It looks beautiful up, Camryn."

"Wear it down, you have such beautiful hair. Don't hide it."

"Do whichever you want, Cam."

That's when I told Michael it was time to usher everyone into the living room and instruct them to speak in quiet tones.

My hairdresser made one last attempt, and as she pushed the final bobby pin through, I looked at it, liked it, and said, "Up it is. Let's go!"

As the white stretch limo pulled up, I had to give myself the first of many reality checks. Okay, let me make sure I've got this right. This is my limo, taking me to my first Emmy Awards ceremony, where my name will be read as a nominee. These are my parents in a gown and tuxedo. This is my dream. This is my life. Somebody pinch me.

As I rode in the back of that limousine, it could easily have been a fantasy. I needed proof that I wasn't dreaming the whole thing. And Michael produced it in the form of a turkey sandwich. Everything else could have been dreamed, but when you're lying a bath towel over your Emanuel gown so the mustard won't drip on the velvet, you know it's real. No fantasy would include that scenario.

As we rambled toward the Shrine and the red carpet, it struck me that my parents used to look down their noses at TV and kept one in the house only to watch the news. They couldn't understand my obsession with "Gilligan, the skipper too, the millionaire and his wife, the movie star, the professor and Maryanne . . ." and when I was out of line they would withhold television from me as the ultimate punishment. No chores, no David Cassidy. TV rationing was part of the standard penal code in my house. How ironic that now my parents call me every Wednesday morning after surfing the Net to update me with the Nielson ratings.

> MOM: Camryn, you were number thirty-six nationally but the show came in seventeenth in San Francisco. Isn't that fantastic?
>
> DAD: Yeah, and you more than held your lead-in, improving on *20/20*'s number in the eighteen to forty-nine demographic.
>
> MOM: But I don't think you're getting the viewers from the *X-Files* like ABC had hoped, because their overnights were still much higher than yours.

Years after not being allowed to watch *The Twilight Zone*, I was living in it. These same two people who had rationed my television viewing to two hours a week were now explaining to me the marketing reasons behind why *Dawson's Creek* was the WB's breakthrough hit. And now we were on our way to the biggest television event in the world.

While they were incredibly savvy regarding the TV ratings game, there were still a few things my parents didn't know. Like what to do when the limo pulled up in front of the Shrine. We went over the details of disembarkation. My dad would help my mom get out of the limo and then they would join my managers, who had arrived in the car in front of us. Peg and Maryellen would escort my folks down the red carpet and make sure they got to their seats safely. Michael would help me get out and escort me on that magic red carpet ride. Nourishment strategy, arrival strategy, and in-case-of-separation strategy had all been covered and/or implemented. We were the most prepared first-timers ever. We wouldn't have been good Jews had we not invited our sweet limo driver, Jerry, to help himself to a sandwich.

As we neared the Shrine, I flashed back to a week earlier when Lara Flynn Boyle and I were on location for *The Practice*. We were outside a seedy motel with a flashing neon sign that kicked on at dusk. It would be thirty minutes before the crew had reset the lights, so we sat in my convertible underneath the flickering neon sign and admitted to each other how lucky we felt. Lara had been to the Emmys as a cast member on *Twin Peaks*, and I grilled her for information. She gave me one piece of sage advice: "Don't wear knee-highs. When you step out of the limo and your skirt is hiked up, they'll snap that photo and it's the only one you'll ever see splashed across the papers." When I saw that phalanx of photographers I silently thanked her. Had I not had that conversation with her, I very well may have worn knee-highs. That's how much of a geek I am.

The limo slowed to a halt and Jerry the driver called back, "Ms. Manheim, you've arrived."

Fortified and as ready as one can ever be for such an occasion,

I took Michael's hand and let him lead me out into the afternoon sun. As my heel touched down on the red carpet . . . (Begin dream sequence, only it was real.)

Flash, flash. "Miss Manheim, over here!" Flash, flash. "Miss Manheim, look left!" *Click, click.* "Camryn, to your right!" *Pop, pop.* "Strike a pose!" *Snap, snap.* "Who's your date?" Flash, flash.

As the words "Who's your date?" echoed in my mind, I had reality check No. 2. "Michael Mayer," I shouted. "M-A-Y-E-R!" Yes, the same Michael Mayer with whom I had come of age in New York. Had he not been there, it all could have been a dream, but with him at my side, I was grounded. The first seven plays we did together we didn't earn a dime, only subway tokens. I looked at him, proud to be his friend, and remembered those late nights in the West Way Diner, sharing our dreams over hot, open-faced turkey sandwiches and mashed potatoes with gravy, all for $3.99.

My nostalgia was interrupted by more shouts and screams and flashbulbs. Fans yelling from the bleachers, lining the red carpet. "We love you, Camryn!" "I hope you win!" The frenzied atmosphere was unlike anything I'd ever experienced, and I walked as slowly as I could down that red carpet to drink in every moment.

I had dreamed of this moment for as long as I could remember. I had rehearsed it a million times. The elbow-elbow-wrist-wrist wave to my adoring fans, the gracious smile, the sincere thanks. In my little-girl fantasies, I had been on Johnny Carson, Dinah Shore, Mike Douglas, walked down countless red carpets, accepted many awards. But now it was happening. Frame by frame my dream was coming true. I was overwhelmed, filled with a happiness unlike anything I had ever felt. There haven't been that many moments in my life that I just wanted to yell "Freeze" and have them last forever. But this was one of them.

As if it weren't intoxicating enough, Tom Hanks brushed by me. Then Mary Tyler Moore. Then Mel Brooks. And as I looked around, trying to seem unfazed, I realized I was sharing that carpet with people I had admired all my life.

There I was looking around at all these legends and I had an attack of impostor's syndrome. As if I were going to be found out any minute for the fraud I was. What the hell was I doing there? As I looked around for my parents, as children instinctively do in panic situations, I couldn't find them. I remembered I had given our tickets to my parents just in case we got separated. I honestly began to worry that they wouldn't let me in without my ticket. I thought of the story of Gerald Ford running to catch Air Force One and the Secret Service having to assure him it wouldn't leave without him. But surely they could hold the 50th Annual Emmy Awards without me.

My psyche was on overload, juggling the ecstasy of the moment with the anxiety that somehow it could all be taken away. We become accustomed to the idea that every action has an equal and opposite reaction, and, on cue, I was spun around, a microphone was shoved in my face, and there was Joan Rivers.

"What designer are you wearing?"

I so feared this moment. I was afraid that I would welcome her into my heart and she would unleash her acerbic wit on me as soon as I was five paces away. I remembered vividly how cruelly she had taunted Elizabeth Taylor about her weight. Even as I met with designers I had Joan on my mind. I wanted to wear something that even she couldn't criticize. But we were both in for a bit of a shock. Me, because she was so genuinely kind. And she, because I was wearing shoes from Payless. She looked at my velvet high heels and asked, "Are you serious?"

And right on live television, I said, "Why pay more, when you can pay less?"

More photographers, more microphones, Army Archerd from *Variety*, more shouts from the bleachers as the walk to Wonderland became ever more surreal.

Annie Fort, the amazing ABC publicist, took my arm and said, "No more questions. Camryn, we have to go in." It was time. More deep breaths and Michael and I were ushered to the doors. As I saw that you had to pass through those red velvet ropes, my well-worn insecurities would not allow me to enter the aptly named Shrine without another pang of I-don't-belong-here-itis. I worried that the gatekeeper, manning the velvet ropes, would say "Hey, you can't go in there, you're too fat." But as he pulled the rope aside and welcomed me in, I realized those days were over.

Michael, my mom, my dad, and I were led to our seats, fourth row, center aisle. Was I on the aisle for a reason? Does Ernst & Young arrange the seating? No, don't read too much into it. Gloria Ruben is going to win and she deserves it. Just enjoy the moment.

Meryl Marshall, the president of the Academy of Television Arts and Sciences, was sitting right in front of me. Billy Crystal, that "mahvelous" mensch, sat down right behind me. Maybe the big stars get used to it, but my head was pivoting—as discreetly as possible. Ellen Barkin was sitting two rows in front of me. Damn! She's sexy. Ellen Degeneres, whom I simply worship, was to my left. Andre Braugher, a dear old friend from my New York theater days and one of the best actors on the planet, was to my right. Calista Flockhart, whom I had known when we were both scrounging for off-off Broadway roles, now a confirmed star, was in the front row.

Emmy winners John Lithgow and Christine Baranski were

within spittin' distance. Oscar winner Olympia Dukakis approached me, wished me well, and gave me that firm squeeze of the hand that says "I really mean it." She is so cool.

The show was starting in three minutes so I had to compose myself and stop gawking at the sea of celebrities. Once again, what the hell was I doing there? In those final few minutes before the curtain went up I read through the program and experienced reassuring reality check No. 3. There on page 123 was my category, my photo, and my name: M-A-N-H-E-I-M.

Good thing I checked because I had been told that Best Supporting Actress in a Drama was the first category. Had I not perused the program, I would have been puzzled by the choice of Lisa Kudrow in a dramatic series. But my category wasn't due for another ninety minutes.

Starting with Lisa Kudrow's upset in the Best Supporting Actress in a Comedy Series category, the prognosticators were taking a beating. Still, I never for a moment thought I was going to win. In fact, it was torture waiting to lose. I was already doing the math. A four-hour ceremony meant that after I lost at the ninety-minute mark, I'd have to sit there for two-and-half hours wearing my it's-a-privilege-to-be-nominated smile. Thank God for those turkey sandwiches.

As my category neared, I recalled what Michael had told me the night before about what it felt like to lose. So I leaned over to my parents and whispered, "Please don't feel bad if I lose. I don't want you to worry. I'll be okay." They assured me that they'd be fine and that they knew I'd be fine, that the relatives would be fine, that our dog Lefty would be fine, that the whole world would be fine. There was a whole lot of reassuring going on . . . and we all braced for the big whammy.

I was so convinced I was going to lose that my body sort of shut down. I was excited but also strangely calm. It's a lot less stressful to smile and applaud than it is to address 600 million viewers. I was kind of relieved that I was going to lose. That's when Michael whispered in my ear, "If you win, do not run up the stairs. Do not let your heels touch the steps. Go up on the balls of your feet." Sage advice.

Hector Elizondo and Mark Harmon emerged to present the Emmy for Best Supporting Actress in a Drama. A cameraman knelt in the aisle, ready to capture my reaction. I was thinking "Don't shoot me from below. It gives me a double chin." And: "Whatever happens, look happy."

Hector began reading the nominees. "Kim Delaney, *NYPD Blue*." Last year's winner, and the Academy loves a defending champ. "Laura Innes, *ER*." My personal favorite, whom I had worked with another lifetime ago at the New York Theater Workshop. And then he said, "Camryn Manheim, *The Practice*." Damn, I should have worn my hair down. Keep smiling. "Della Reese, *Touched by an Angel*." Would she be touched by an Emmy? "Gloria Ruben, *ER*." She had had an incredible story line, delivered beautifully. I'd be shocked if she didn't win.

And then Mark Harmon said, "And the Emmy goes to . . . Carmen Manheim." Now, at a moment like that, I would much rather have him mispronounce *my* name than pronounce someone else's correctly. I sat there stunned, not completely certain that there wasn't a sixth nominee named Carmen. But when Michael threw his arms around me and I could feel my father's hand on my shoulder I knew it was true. As I made my way to the steps all I was thinking about were Michael's words of wisdom about walking on the balls of my feet. "Ball . . . ball . . . ball . . . ball. . . ." I negotiated the steps without incident, and Hector greeted me with my Emmy. <u>My</u> Emmy. I squeezed that beautiful trophy with all my might. And, man, those suckers are heavy. If ever I needed a reality check, it was right then. But I got the furthest thing from it. I turned and looked out at 5,000 of the most famous people in the world. I'd come a long way from the half-empty ninety-nine-seaters on 42nd Street. My reality had been altered—forever, I think.

I looked to the balcony, where I'm usually sitting, and screamed, "This is amazing!" Which, of course, it was. And my fifteen years on the stage paid off as I was able to get through my speech without a stumble. I want to reprint my acceptance speech here because it only lasted thirty seconds then, but here it can last forever. And my thanks to these people is eternal.

> *I have always felt like such a misfit and to get this award from my peers is such a huge victory. I must thank Wilma Marcus who taught me, Maryellen Mulcahy and Peg Donegan who fought for me . . . David Kelley who believed in me—you are my hero! I need to thank Jeffrey Kramer, Bob Breech, Jonathan Pontell, Randy Stone, the Gersh Agency, the incredible cast I get to work with every day, the unbelievable crew headed by the sublime Dennis Smith, and my mother and my father who are here with me tonight, and who paid for every cent of acting school. I brought my autograph book. I hope you all will sign it, especially the four women in my category, I am honored to be counted among you. . . . This is for all the fat girls!*

I held that Emmy high overhead in a pose that friends told me looked like Lady Liberty because I was clutching my autograph book in one hand and the luminous statuette in the other.

I was whisked offstage, where Annie Fort and Kim Sandifer, the publicists for *The Practice*, greeted me with elated hugs and congratulations. It was so great to see these two familiar, friendly faces, knowing that they would guide me safely through the press gauntlet. I could tell by their expressions that they were every bit as thrilled at my victory as I was.

First stop: Mary Hart, *Entertainment Tonight*. I asked her to autograph my book, and she laughed and said she'd be happy to. Before I could be led off for the mini–press junket, Lara Flynn Boyle ran up to me crying, threw her arms around me, and gave me the sweetest, wordless congratulations. Next stop: Photographers and more Flash, Flash. Camryn, look left. *Snap, Snap*. Camryn look right. Stop No. 3: More photographers, this time more regimented. There was a walkway with marks, signifying where you would stand and pose with your Emmy. Stop No. 4: The interview room. And I went right up to the microphone and said, "Hello, press, I am so happy to see you!" Someone asked me if I had prepared the speech, and I told them, "No, the speech I prepared said, 'This is for all the men I ever loved who never loved me back.' "

Whisk, whisk out the back door of the Shrine, where I was greeted by the warm night air and a circuslike array of white tents. E! Entertainment, *Good Morning America*, *Access Hollywood*, *Entertainment Tonight*, local TV stations—basically anyone with a signal interviews you.

After the whirlwind one-hour tour through the media maze, I was escorted back to my seat. On the way, I snagged autographs from Ellen Degeneres, John Lithgow, and Billy Crystal. I was also waylaid by the crew of *The Practice*, who were sitting at the very back of the auditorium. They saw me coming and leapt out of their seats to congratulate me. I wanted to jump up and down with them for a while because I knew once I got back to my seat I'd have to act like an adult. It just wouldn't be very gracious to continue my victory dance in the fourth row.

When I got back to my seat, I became a little disoriented. Someone I'd never seen before was sitting in Michael's seat . . . right next to my folks. And then I figured it out. I leaned past the seat filler in Michael's seat (I think he was in the bathroom) and hugged my parents and let them heft that beautiful statue. You have never seen so much *kvelling* and *shepping naches.* When you've been trying your whole life to make your parents proud, and you see them beaming for you, for your achievement, the feeling is indescribable. And better even than winning an Emmy.

Now, the Academy expected me to sit still for ninety minutes. Yeesh. At least I could relax, kick my shoes off, and watch my old friend Andre Braugher win his long-overdue award for Best Actor in a Drama. Never have I enjoyed an hour that was not about me so much. I just sat there clutching my winged trophy. When Andre returned to his seat, he slipped me a piece of paper and asked for my L.A. number. One side of the paper had been written on, so I turned it over and began jotting down my number. But before I had a chance to return the paper, James Garner began reading the nominees for best drama: *ER, Law and Order, NYPD Blue, The Practice,* and *The X-Files.* I had my it's-a-privilege-to-have-been-nominated face on but got the second biggest surprise of my night when Mr. Garner said, "And the Emmy goes to . . . *The Practice.*" Holy shit! Twice in one night. Only this time, the presenter said it right. He didn't say *The Prosecutors.* From all corners of the Shrine, the producers, cast, and crew stood up and made their way to the stage. David gave the acceptance speech and for the first time ever I didn't listen to a word he said. I was too busy sharing the euphoria with my castmates.

We were momentarily whisked off the stage, then promptly asked to return with all of the night's winners for a group photograph. It was the first time I had ever been to the Emmys and I had been brought to the stage not once, not twice, but three times. There I was between Helen Hunt and Christine Lahti, whose mantels are lined with Emmy Awards in addition to your odd and sundry Oscar and Golden Globe.

Helen had just done *Twelfth Night* at Lincoln Center, which not only featured my sweet friend Ryan but just happened to have been stage-managed by none other than dear friend Lisa Iacucci. Small world, eh? So there on that Shrine stage amid a Who's Who of Hollywood, I had my final, perfect reality check. There was no way I could drift off too far into that rarefied air as long as my mom and dad, Michael, Ryan, and Lisa Iacucci were in my thoughts and in my heart.

As a suddenly savvy veteran of the post-Emmy press gauntlet, I led *The Practice* gang through the circus tents. "Okay, Dylan, go over there. David, they'll need you in that tent. Kelli, I'm sure everyone will want to take your picture." I was so happy that the show had won because now I could enjoy my award openly without feeling guilty. Finally it was time to eat.

It had been six hours since those turkey sandwiches. Annie and Kim led me to the Governor's Ball so I could meet up with Michael and my parents for dinner. It took me twenty-five minutes to advance ten tables, but if you ever hear me complaining about too many congratulations, slap me. When I finally got to our table, it was impossible to take a bite with everyone descending on me with kudos. Michael put his arm around me protectively and told me to eat as he whispered in my ear to make it look as if I were too occupied to be interrupted. Left to my own devices I would have received everybody at the party, but Michael knows me as well as anyone and he knew I had to eat or I'd turn into the Wicked Witch of the West. Once sated, I could have schmoozed all night, but there were other parties to attend. And since I'd never been invited to these parties before, I wanted to make sure I went to every single one of them.

As we made our way to the limousine, I had perhaps my favorite moment of the night when Jerry the limo driver jumped out of the car and began shouting "Oh my God, you won! That's so great!" We piled in for the twenty-minute drive to Morton's, where the Twentieth Century–Fox after-party was. We asked Jerry if he had helped himself to a sandwich and he said that he had and thanked us, adding sheepishly that he had also had a cookie though he wasn't sure if he should have since Michael hadn't said specifically that he could have a cookie. God, we loved Jerry. The perfect limo driver for the perfect night. As we pulled up to Morton's, Jerry called back, "Don't let them open the door for you. I want to do it!" So as the Morton's valet approached the door, I locked it and waited until Jerry came around. And as he reached for the door handle, I quickly unlocked it and took his hand as I stepped out. I never imagined that someone could get a thrill out of opening a door for me. But the thrill was mine.

The party was wonderful and I loved showing off my proud parents to everyone. But L.A. does shut down at midnight, and carriages were turning into pumpkins all over the city, so it appeared that even this precious night had to end.

We dropped my parents at their hotel and exchanged our final, exhausted hugs for the evening. Michael and I went back to my place, leaving the rest of the sandwiches with Jerry the limo driver. Don't worry, we tipped him too.

When I came home, I had ninety-two messages. Now, there is no way ninety-two messages would fit on one tape, unless, of course, your sweet brother came into the guest house he lets you live in for free, flipped the tape over, and then put in a new one when that side was filled so you wouldn't miss any of it.

Michael and I sat on my bed, listening to all the messages, from all our friends in New York calling up and screaming their congratulations across the country. It took almost two hours to listen to them all. I felt so blessed to have so many amazing friends.

As I got ready for bed, I found the slip of paper Andre Braugher had given me to write my number on. I looked at the writing on it and realized it was his acceptance speech. I know that when he collects his third Academy Award that little scrap of paper that he so glibly passed my way will be worth something. I tucked it in my box of treasures.

*   *   *

There are three things I remember about the Monday after the Emmys. The first was that my picture was on the front page of USA *Today* and my parents walked down Rodeo Drive, pointing to it and telling anyone and everyone "This is our daughter!"

The second was that I had a dentist appointment. And when he filled that cavity, it didn't matter that I had just won an Emmy, it still hurt. That was one reality check I could have done without.

And the third was this breathtaking letter:

> *Way to go, baby! You had me in tears for so many compli-*
> *cated reasons I can't even begin—but also just because you*
> *looked so beautiful, because you were so utterly out there, so*
> *open, so shining and happy and through every word you*
> *spoke, your love and happiness poured. You nailed it. You*
> *were and are fucking glorious!! Here's to the fat girls and the*
> *dwarfs of the world!*
>
> *I love you and am so proud—x x x Linda Hunt*

That Emmy Award carved in the likeness of an angel sits appropriately atop my television. (I don't have a mantel.) She's pretty . . . but she's a little thin.

Camryn Manheim

"It Ain't
Over 'Til . . ."

When I was approached about writing a book based on my one-woman show, I said, "Sure, sounds like fun. How hard can it be?" The answer: Really fucking hard. I imagine it's a lot like giving birth . . . only the labor lasts five months. After the first week, when I had painstakingly squeezed out three paragraphs, I thought there was no way I could fill the required 250 pages. But once you get me yapping, it's hard to shut me up. And now my editor has been forced to tell me to "wrap it up!" I still feel like I have countless stories to tell, like the one about winning an Academy Award. Or the one about how I changed the face of beauty by appearing on the cover of *Vogue*. Or how Ted the Canadian Marlboro man returned to the States to marry me. Oh, shoot, those haven't happened yet, but if they do, I promise I'll write a sequel: *Wake Up, I'm **Still** Fat!*

If I did it right, this book has been about self-acceptance. We all have our demons and our flaws, and unfortunately we let them define us. For most of my life I hated myself because I was fat. I let a single characteristic, which I perceived as highly negative, overshadow everything else about me. Sadly, I'll bet that sounds familiar to a lot of you. Hating ourselves just seems to come too easily. For me, it didn't matter that I was a loyal friend, an advocate for justice, kind to animals, a team player in volleyball, a good neighbor. It didn't matter that I always remembered birthdays. It didn't even matter that I was a nice person. All of that was obliterated by a blinding self-hate.

It wasn't just my good qualities that my fat-triggered self-loathing was obscuring. Since I blamed everything on my fat, I never bothered to address my other shortcomings. I never hated myself for being bossy, or too competitive, or self-centered, or overly demanding, or bitter, or too impatient. And, believe me, those are some damn good reasons to hate yourself. No, I hated myself solely because I hated my body. My mind and soul never entered into this equation: Fat = Hate.

But somewhere along the line, you destroy your spirit, make the necessary changes to love yourself, *or* accept yourself the way you are. Try as I might, I couldn't destroy my spirit. And try as I might, I couldn't change who I was. I was left with what to me seemed to be the most difficult option: loving myself just the way I am. It didn't happen overnight. It was a long haul, so I would never presume to suggest that it's simply a matter of waking up one morning and declaring "From now on, I love myself."

In fact, during this arduous odyssey, there was nothing I hated more than people patting me on the back as they condescendingly advised, "You just need to love yourself, and then you'll be happy." Okay, thanks for the tip, now where are the instructions?

*   *   *

Self-Love Might Start with This Simple Quiz

1. Are you a kind person?
2. Are you fair?
3. Do you tell yourself the truth?
4. Do you listen?
5. Do you give friends a ride to the airport without complaint?
6. Do you lend books even when you know you might not get them back?
7. When you stop and watch a street performer, do you put a little something in the hat?
8. Do you pick up an extra sandwich because you think your roommate might be hungry?
9. Can you keep a secret?
10. Do you put money in a stranger's meter if it's about to expire?
11. Even if it seems impossible, do you fight for what you believe in?
12. Do you stay up late doing the laundry so your kid's hockey uniform will be clean for the next day's game?

13. Do you cry at weddings because you're happy for your friend, not because you're jealous?
14. Do you rewind your videos (only half credit)?
15. Do you recycle?
16. Do you downplay good news so your friends won't be jealous?
17. Do you stick up for yourself?
18. Would you refuse to go out with someone because you know your best friend likes him?
19. If a wrong number leaves a message on your machine, do you call them to let them know that their message never reached its destination?
20. Do you teach your children to do all of the above (worth 5 points)?

Scoring (based on number of "yes" answers):

0: Let the self-hating begin!

1–5: Hey, it's a start, but don't get too self-congratulatory.

6–10: You're on your way, baby. I think someone deserves a hug.

11–15: You are on top of your game, kick the self-hate to the curb.

16–20: The elite. You should totally love yourself. In fact, you should make love to yourself right now. (But if you lied on the quiz, deduct 5 points for each lie and hate yourself just a little.)

If you didn't like the questions on this quiz, come up with your own. Think about what you value in other people and ask yourself if you share those traits. I bet you'll find you do.

*   *   *

I still don't have all the answers. Hell, I still have really bad days. I constantly catch myself sliding back into old habits, allowing other people to determine my self-worth.

Several months ago I was driving my friend Diane to the airport. We had the top down, the sun was shining, and we were singing along with Keb' Mo'. (Buy a CD, it will change your life.) Now, there is only one situation in which I actually feel cool. And that's driving with the top down, listening to Keb' Mo'. Most other times I just feel like a big dork. I could tell we looked cool because these two guys next to us in a BMW were checking us out. We rolled to a stop side by side at a red light. And sure enough, the passenger power window began its slow descent.

BOY: Hey.
CAM: Hey. (pretty cool, right?)
BOY: How ya doin'?
CAM: Couldn't be better.
BOY: We were just wondering . . . is your friend single?

Ouch. I can't lie, that hurt. All my hard work was unraveling on account of some jackass in a BMW (is that redundant?) whom I didn't even know and would never see again. Why would they be interested in the fat girl when they could be checking out sun-kissed, sexy Diane? Why would anybody be interested in the fat girl? Ever?

Wait, wait, wait. Time out! *You* don't get to make me feel like shit. That used to be my job, and I quit a long time ago. And that position has been dissolved.

After I dropped Diane off at the airport and began the solo drive home, I couldn't help but think about the cute boys in the BMW. I mean, the fact that I'm writing about it now means it left a mark. But a few miles up the 405 Freeway, I realized the top was still down, the sun was still shining, and you can't help but feel cool when you're groovin' to Keb' Mo'.

I hadn't completely dodged the bullet, it had definitely grazed me, but I didn't let it take me down. Of course, society seems to have a full metal jacket and keeps firing away.

Last month I was about to board a flight from New York to Los Angeles and I was carrying my beloved Gibson LG-1 guitar. Now, you know there was no way in hell I was going to check it in to baggage. I've seen *Dateline*. I know how checked bags get tossed around. The problem was I already had two carry-ons and was worried that I was going to have to get into a long explanation with the guy at the gate about how my brother gave me the guitar when I was sixteen and I've traveled all over the world with it . . . , etc., etc. So I looked around the line for someone with fewer than two carry-ons.

I saw this handsome, curly-haired guy with just a knapsack and asked him if he'd carry my guitar on board for me. He looked at me like I was handing him a bomb, so I comforted him by telling him "Look, I'm standing right next to you. It's not going to go off." He looked at the stickered case and figured most terrorists probably aren't into Crosby, Stills, Nash and Young.

After we were safely aboard, curly-haired Ethan returned my guitar to me and the flight attendants offered to put it in the garment closet. We'd been in the air about half an hour when Ethan stopped by my seat for a visit. Much to my surprise and elation, he was a big Keb' Mo' fan. I don't know if it was because he was adorable or because he had awesome taste in music, but I started to develop a little crush on this guy. And wouldn't you know it, Keb' Mo' was playing at the House of Blues in L.A. the following week and I had an extra ticket. Ethan was so psyched. This is how it starts, right? A guy carries your most precious possession onto a plane, you repay him by inviting him to an amazing concert, and then you get married. Right? When will I ever learn?

My crush grew when I realized that Ethan wasn't even aware that I was an actor on a television show. That meant that he had agreed to go on "a date" with me just because we had hit it off at 30,000 feet and not because he thought that I was famous. At the end of the flight, we exchanged numbers and later that week I called him with the concert info. During the phone conversation, I told him that some friends would be joining us for dinner and the concert. He seemed really excited.

At dinner, Ethan couldn't take his eyes off my friend Jane. Still, I was caught off guard when he leaned over and asked me, "Does Jane have a boyfriend?" Ugh. This time I couldn't hit the gas and race away, listening to Keb' Mo'. I was going to have to sit next to him, listening to Keb' Mo'.

When Ethan called to thank me for the concert, he asked if I would introduce him to my coworker, Lara Flynn Boyle. And once again I was at that familiar juncture. Do I take the time and spiritual energy to educate him and tell him how much that hurt my feelings, or do I just say "Gosh, I think I left her number in my dressing room, but I'll get back to you" as I toss *his* number in the trash? Some days I do have the time and energy to educate the handyman of my building about not hurting my feelings, or the wardrobe designers on a movie, or the props people who put candy on my desk. And I always feel an obligation to inform instead of dismiss, but on this day, it was better for me to just say good-bye.

Those are two of a thousand stories in which I've been passed over, dismissed, or ignored. And I know my experience is not unique. Every big woman I've ever met has a thousand stories of her own. And many of the "jolly" fat people that you meet live on a foundation of sorrow. I guess in order to really appreciate the blues, you've got to feel 'em deep down inside, which is probably why I've never met a fat girl who wasn't all too familiar with the deep-down-in-your-soul blues. But, you know what? There will always be jackasses in BMWs and insensitive guys on airplanes . . . and cruel teachers . . . and mean caterers . . . and nasty handymen. . . . There's one around every corner. And if you let them dictate your happiness, then you will spend your life singing the blues. As much as I love the way they sound, I'm not crazy about the way they feel.

Not too long ago, I was walking down Santa Monica Boulevard in West Hollywood when a woman of size recognized me. I could see <u>her</u> thousand stories in her eyes. And she could see mine. As she walked toward me with her arms outstretched, there was that silent moment in which everything was said. Two thousand stories colliding in a compassionate embrace. Our shared understanding negated all need for words.

I have lived my life in a culture that hates fat people. From magazine covers to late-night talk-show hosts. From would-be employers to would-be lovers. I have felt the judgmental scorn of society's contempt for people like me. It is against all odds that I've managed to arrive in my mid-thirties with any self-respect and self-worth. It's a miracle that I laugh every day and walk through my life with pride and confidence, because our culture is unrelenting when it comes to large people. I don't understand it and I doubt I ever will. We hurt nobody. We're just fat.

When I look back on the people and institutions that have hurt me along the way, I now know that I was stronger than they were and I have used that strength to forgive. My parents and I are closer than ever. I have a great relationship with and much affinity for New York University. I remain friends with former lovers. But most important, I have forgiven myself for buying into the beauty myth and perpetuating my own self-hatred. And as my self-acceptance has grown, I have also been blessed by having loved and been loved by men who have adored me and every inch of my body. No names—you know who you are.

Instead of lamenting the past, I have chosen to spend all of my positive energy on changing the world's perception of fat people. I am proud to carry a torch in the battle for fat acceptance. But it's just one of a million torches that need to be lit and held high.

My job is clear. I refuse to be portrayed on television and in movies as the pathetic, put-upon fat girl, so as not to promote the disparaging stereotypes of fat people. But you have a job too. When the torch gets passed to you, you have to take it, carry it high, whether at the office, in school, or in social circles, and refuse to play the fool. And for all you "unfat" people, there are plenty of other torches to go around.

Conversations with My Fat: Part Four

The first steps are a little wobbly. You don't just wake up confident and in love with yourself. You don't just cast aside a crutch you've been leaning on for however many years. No, at first you sort of pretend that you don't need it anymore. You "act" confident and brassy even though inside you're quivering. It's about the way you carry yourself, the way you walk into a room. The way you say "It's nice to meet you." The way you deal with the cable guy.

And then somebody—a casting director, a cute boy—says, "Hey, this girl is confident. She must have something going on." And it breeds real confidence and actual self-love, which just builds on itself. Self-acceptance begets acceptance from others, which begets even deeper, more genuine self-acceptance. It can be done. But no one is going to bestow it on you. It is a gift only you can give yourself.

Once I made this leap my relationship with my fat changed forever. We still talk, but on my terms. I don't blame him for anything and have absolved him of all responsibility regarding the outcome of my life. We still live together and he follows me wherever I go, but he addresses me with the respect I demand.

CAM: *Are you ready?*

FAT: *What? Where are we going?*

CAM: *You've known about this for weeks.*

FAT: *Aw, c'mon, blow it off. Let's stay home.*

CAM: *Nope. I'm going.*

FAT: *Don't you want to stay in, get pizza, and watch the movie of the week?*

CAM: *No, get your ass off the couch and get ready.*

FAT: *Maybe we could get some cookie dough . . .*

CAM: *Look, this isn't a negotiation! I'm speaking to the National Association to Advance Fat Acceptance, and you're coming with me.*

FAT: *Yes, ma'am. Wow, you look beautiful in that dress!*
CAM: *Thank you, you look beautiful in this dress too.*

We've reached a peaceful harmony, me and my fat. I can't say that on some days I don't get a little twinge of self-loathing, but, for the most part, me and my fat are getting along fine. I'm still a misfit. Only now I'm proud not to fit in.

They say "It ain't over 'til the fat lady sings." Well, this fat lady is singing . . . and the celebration has just begun.

Photo Captions and Credits

Page 1: Little Debi, age eight, before I changed my name and all hell broke loose. **Page 5:** Sweet sixteen and just been kissed as Chloe Blue at the Renaissance Faire. **Page 32:** Dear friend Kelley Kyle on the day we moved to Santa Cruz. **Page 38:** My sister and I (and some little kid) in Jerusalem. Lisa was my witness as I heard voices in the Holy Land. **Page 44:** It's an art to play a fifty-year-old when you're only twenty-five. Here I am as Mrs. Luckerniddle in Brecht's *Saint Joan of the Stockyards*. **Page 72:** My mom and dad all gussied up. **Page 85:** Bridget Fonda and I during filming of *The Road to Wellville*. **Page 95:** Riding my Honda CB650 on Mulberry Street on the Lower East Side. **Page 119:** *Radiance*, the first magazine to make me a cover girl. *Photo by Deborah Feingold.* **Page 134:** See how easy it is to look like you're having fun at the beach? **Page 138:** Some programs you keep forever. **Page 145:** The women of *The Women. Clockwise from top left:* Felicity Huffman, Sandy Duncan and Dorothy Louden, Mary McCormack, me, Celeste Holm and Sigourney Weaver and Kate Burton. **Page 155:** One woman, one show, one calorie. Opening night of *Wake Up, I'm Fat!* at the Public Theater. *Photo by Michael Daniels.* **Page 176:** *Mode* magazine fashion shoot, trying to look cool. *Photo © 1999 by Gerhard Yurkovic.* **Page 182:** Hanging out with Ryan Dunn in Greenwich Village. **Page 193:** Steve Harris and I flank David Kelley as he forks over his gambling debt. **Page 206:** My brother Karl and I proudly joined the Reverend Jesse Jackson in the fight against Prop 209. **Page 223:** Lisa and Camryn and Ben and Jerry in NYC. **Page 232:** Nance Williamson and I backstage during *Two Gentlemen of Verona* at the Delacorte Theater. **Page 241:** *Mode* magazine puts me through the rigors of being a fashion model. Gee, tough job. *Photo © 1999 by Gerhard Yurkovic.* **Page 249:** Donnell and Associates. *From left to right:* Lisa Gay Hamilton, Kelli Williams, Dylan McDermott, me, Michael Badalucco, and Steve Harris. **Page 262:** Working the red carpet in my Payless shoes. *Photo by Greg DeGuire.* **Page 279:** Relaxing on the set of *The Practice* in front of the fake Boston skyline.

Camryn Manheim is an actor, activist, writer, and playwright who rides a Honda CB-650, and whose current role as the smart, passionate, combative attorney Ellenor Frutt on ABC's *The Practice* earned her an Emmy Award and a Golden Globe Award for best supporting actress in a drama. Her film credits include *Happiness, Romy and Michelle's High School Reunion, The Road to Wellville, Eraser, Mercury Rising,* and *Wide Awake.* She is proud to have performed in most of New York's off-Broadway theaters, winning an Obie Award and an Encore Award for her performance in Craig Lucas's *Missing Persons.* In 1994 she brought her acclaimed one-woman show, *Wake Up, I'm Fat,* to the Joseph Papp Public Theater. She holds a master's degree in acting from NYU, and divides her time between New York and Los Angeles, but she is registered to vote in New York.